UPDIKE
and the
Patriarchal
Dilemma

*Masculinity in
the Rabbit Novels*

Mary O'Connell

SOUTHERN ILLINOIS UNIVERSITY PRESS
Carbondale and Edwardsville

Copyright © 1996 by the Board of Trustees,
Southern Illinois University
All rights reserved
Printed in the United States of America
Edited by Rebecca Spears Schwartz
Designed by New Leaf Studio

99 98 97 96   4 3 2 1

From *Rabbit, Run* by John Updike. Copyright © 1960 and renewed 1988 by John Updike. From *Rabbit Redux* by John Updike. Copyright © 1971 by John Updike. From *Rabbit Is Rich* by John Updike. Copyright © 1981 by John Updike. From *Rabbit at Rest* by John Updike. Copyright © 1990 by John Updike. From *Picked-Up Pieces* by John Updike. Copyright © 1975 by John Updike. From *Hugging the Shore: Essays and Criticism* by John Updike. Copyright © 1983 by John Updike. From *Assorted Prose* by John Updike. Copyright © 1965 by John Updike. From *Self-Consciousness: Memoirs* by John Updike. Copyright © 1989 by John Updike. Reprinted by permission of Alfred A. Knopf, Inc.

Rabbit, Run © 1964, *Rabbit Redux* © 1972, *Rabbit Is Rich* © 1982, *Rabbit at Rest* © 1991, *Picked-Up Pieces* © 1975, *Hugging the Shore: Essays and Criticism* © 1985, *Assorted Prose* © 1968, and *Self-Consciousness: Memoirs* © 1990 by John Updike, reproduced by permission of Penguin Books, Ltd., Harmondsworth, U.K.

Library of Congress Cataloging-in-Publication Data

O'Connell, Mary, 1944–
   Updike and the patriarchal dilemma : masculinity in the Rabbit novels / Mary O'Connell.
      p. cm.
   Includes bibliographical references and index.
   1. Updike, John—Characters—Harry Angstrom. 2. Masculinity (Psychology) in literature. 3. Angstrom, Harry (Fictitious character) 4. Updike, John—Characters—Men. 5. Patriarchy in literature. 6. Men in literature. 7. Updike, John. I. Title.
PS3571.P4Z8   1996
813'.54—dc20   94-39038
ISBN 0-8093-1949-7   CIP

The paper used in this publication meets the minimum requirements of American National Standard for Information Sciences—Permanence of Paper for Printed Library Materials, ANSI Z39.48-1984. ∞

For Frank, Chris, Luke, and Brian

Contents

Preface   ix
Abbreviations for Updike's Works   xv

1. Introduction   1
2. *Rabbit, Run*: The Mail from Tunis Probably   13
3. Gender Formation:
   But What's Wrong with That Man?   37
4. The Power of Naming:
   "Well That Explains Your Oratorical Gifts"   69
5. *Rabbit Redux*   95
6. Life in Furnace Township   125
7. Revolution and Chaos   137
8. Is Rabbit Rich?   164
9. Laius and Oedipus   186
10. *Rabbit at Rest*: More Mail from Tunis   209

Notes   241
Bibliography   250
Index   259

Preface

THIS "RE-VISION" grew out of a sense that something disturbing was occurring both in the texts of the first three Rabbit novels and in the critical community. Although at that time, I was unaware of Judith Fetterley's excellent work in *The Resisting Reader* (1978), I nevertheless felt that a woman reader was being asked to identify with a protagonist whose behavior toward women was sometimes clearly abusive. Such an identification, as Fetterley demonstrates, involves a self-negation that women readers need to defend themselves against, especially when the victims of abuse are portrayed as deserving the treatment they receive. Six women (Ruth, Janice, Rebecca, Jill, Mary, and Peggy), all of them characters that Rabbit has loved, die literally or metaphorically in the first three novels. Rebecca and Jill die as a result of Rabbit's carelessness; Janice and Ruth are depersonalized, reduced to silence, and left as if dead; Mary dies naturally but in mysterious fulfillment of her son's wish; and Peggy dies of breast cancer, in seeming retribution for her outspokenness. As I discovered that most critics fail either to notice the mounting death toll or to explore its implications and that critics generally characterize Updike as a nonviolent writer, I realized that something within the text or within the culture, or both, prevented us from seeing those bodies and therefore prevented us from identifying the homicidal pattern that emerged.[1]

From a critical perspective, I wanted to reopen and review the texts. From a political perspective, I was also interested in the popularity of the character of Rabbit and wanted to explore the attitudes motivating his behavior, as well as both the author's intent concerning these attitudes and the surprising level of acceptance among most of the critics. When I examined the texts closely, I found a great deal of evidence demonstrating patterns of psychological and physical abuse. But, unexpectedly, I also accumulated evidence, including structural evidence, suggesting that Updike was not just portraying Rabbit as a stereotypical male; he was scrutinizing masculine gender identity.

I began looking for ways to reapproach the novels with this new possibility in mind, and I came, fortunately, to Bruce Woodcock's book, *Male Mythologies: John Fowles and Masculinity* (1984). British novelist John Fowles has been deeply engaged in the conscious exploration of masculinity, and the critical purpose of Woodcock's work is to illuminate the relationship between the process of reevaluation and the various elements in Fowles's novels. Woodcock not only ably makes connections with theme, character, plot, and so on, establishing the central importance of Fowles's attitude toward masculinity in his art, but he also discovers that the unconscious habits of masculinity cause Fowles to contradict or subvert his conscious intention. One example he cites is that Fowles uses a romance novel form involving the pursuit and capture of a woman (22–23). As this form is a power fantasy that allows the male writer to control the course of the hunt and the fate of the idealized woman, the underlying form of a Fowles novel may be at odds with its intention (Frye 104). Woodcock claims that the male writer who questions masculinity will almost inevitably become involved in such contradictions because the socially constructed masculine identity is so pervasive as to render total objectivity, complete escape, or full resolution extremely difficult (7–25). Woodcock's approach struck me as a critical tool with enormous potential, and I imagined that a similar approach could be applied to past as well as contemporary writers and to unconscious as well as conscious explorers.

Of course, John Fowles is an avowed feminist who has been forthcoming regarding his views, intentions, and methods. He has discussed the psychology of his characters, and he has shared insight into the experiences that have shaped his personal attitudes toward masculinity. I anticipated that Woodcock's approach would have to be modified and that additional strategies would be needed to unlock the hidden text in Updike's tetralogy. Unsure of what those strategies might be, however, I could only enter the novels armed with the basic question, What is the role of masculinity in this work? Since then, in spite of the title of this book, I have come to believe that the broader and more useful question is, What is the role of gender in this work? as masculinity and femininity evolve in relation to one another.

Approaching the texts with the question of masculinity in mind had an illuminating effect; obscure, problematic issues became clear while new possibilities emerged. Furthermore, by pure good fortune I discovered that the resisting reader's stance was exactly the relationship that Updike sought in his audience; it was the stance that made the novels work. More than just straightforward chronicles, the Rabbit novels create meaning by challenging, undermining, and qualifying their own explicit content. Because Rabbit gains the reader's sympathy by controlling perspective, especially in the first novel, the resisting reader, active and skeptical, is the one most likely to discover what Rabbit conceals and to register the nuances of a layered discourse. Updike says that his novels are "moral debates with the reader" (*PUP* 483), but he does not develop the debates in the Rabbit series as a classic realist might, by leading the reader into the questions, weighing the sides, and reaffirming the status quo. Instead, his interrogative texts invite the reader to reexamine cultural assumptions by bringing "points of view into unresolved collision."[2]

In addition to Woodcock's work, my re-vision owes a debt to a number of feminist critics and theorists who have also furnished critical approaches and provided models of intellectual courage. Also, although none of the existing Updike criticism focuses on the exploration of masculinity as a central issue in the tetralogy, I have built this interpretation on foundations established by other Updike scholars whose works are cited throughout.[3] Nonliterary sources include male commentators on masculinity who have described their own experiences or have reported insights gleaned from men's groups and clinics. I have used these witnesses to validate that at least some men experience masculinity as I perceive it to be represented in the novels, *not* to establish any definitive view of masculinity. In other words, I included male commentators in an effort to be both accurate and respectful of male experience. I verified perceptions of female experience with female commentators, especially female critics, for the same reason. Finally, the cultural ramifications of the gender issues raised in the novels are so broad that they often demanded an interdisciplinary approach involving the works of anthropologists, historians, sociologists, psychologists, psychiatrists, linguistic scholars, philosophers, and theologians. Because I found the interdisciplinary approach so valuable, I have provided background material in order to make my own work accessible to readers in other fields.

The insights and reactions of friends and colleagues have also shaped this investigation significantly. A number of women readers, for example, found the Rabbit novels uniquely oppressive apart from any specific instances of abuse. One remarked that she wanted to rewrite *Rabbit, Run* from Janice's point of view, and her comment reminded me of the impulse among feminist writers to revise controlling myths in order to liberate and reclaim reality. This reader response led me to reinvestigate the "politics of the imagination" in the novels (Newman 115), and I discovered that conflicting impulses to repress and to recover feminine perspective influence character, perspective, language use, theme, plot, symbolism, and structure throughout the tetralogy.

Another valuable response came from readers who felt that my focus on Rabbit's destructive attitudes and behaviors distorted the novels, overbalancing the author's obvious "liking" for his character. Edward P. Vargo observed early on that "in any discussion of *Rabbit, Run*, the questions of style, plot, structure and total significance inevitably returns to the elemental question 'Do you like or dislike Harry Angstrom?' " (51). Vargo concluded that efforts to categorize Rabbit are futile, but the fact that readers and critics continue to respond so diversely suggests that something worth investigating is occurring with respect to our identification with this protagonist.

On one level, acknowledging that Rabbit is as likable and as good as Everyman is essential to the interpretation offered here. Critics note Rabbit's boyish charm; Updike admires his "great willingness to learn" (Kakutani, "Turning" 15); and most readers sympathize with his aspiration and confusion. Updike encourages our liking for Rabbit even while he explores the negative aspects of his masculinity. By doing so, he confronts us with the disturbing possibility that Henry James raises in *Washington Square* and *The Bostonians*, which is that likable "good" men behave appallingly as they pursue in their private lives the cultural and political imperatives inscribed in their gender identity. But whereas James leaves us at the door, Updike carries us through it, and across the years, and unfolds the ramifications of Rabbit's gender-based attitudes and behaviors in painful detail. We resist this vision because all of us, as children, parents, spouses, or lovers, need to believe that our intimate relationships are sheltered from the abuses of the society at large.

The question of Updike's "liking" Rabbit raises other issues. Ordinarily, the author's position as inscribed in the text guides reader response. In an interrogative text, however, this guide is missing, and no "unified and knowing" position is constructed for the reader

(Belsey 90). The absence of such a guide in the tetralogy has led some critics to accuse Updike of failing to take a moral stand, of having nothing to say, or of being merely a chronicler. Others fill the void by identifying Updike almost unconditionally with his protagonist and by using that identification as a basis for interpretation. Finally, as Bernard Schopen observes, critics sometimes attribute values and ideas to Updike, project them into the texts, and then use them to construct a privileged discourse (195). Catherine Belsey, however, points out that such "attempts to attribute a coherent and unified position to the author" of an interrogative text may be "a way of evading confrontation with the social and ideological contradictions" he raises (93). The interpretation offered here highlights those contradictions again.

Furthermore, the notion that Updike's intended reader likes Rabbit unreservedly underestimates the author's accomplishment. Where the author's position is questioning, where the protagonist's behavior is conflicted and controversial, and where the tastes and mores of the audience are in flux, diverse reader response is inevitable. But Updike provides what Sven Birkerts calls "a bond that runs deeper than our moment-to-moment response to Rabbit's not always likable personality" (4). As the years go by, we become accustomed to Rabbit's perspective; we learn the habits and limitations of his mind; we know his emotional range; we understand his sensitivities and anticipate his reactions. We recognize his modes of expression, his reticence, his mannerisms. We know his worst fears and his sweetest dreams. When we reach *Rabbit at Rest*, we even share the physical experience of his decline. In the end, we know Rabbit Angstrom better than any protagonist in American fiction. This profound knowledge, and the acceptance it fosters, is the real basis of our identification. To know all is to forgive all—only this level of attachment could sustain the unflinching scrutiny or withstand the searing honesty of Updike's portrait. The perspective offered here is not intended to undermine that attachment, but to counterbalance the weight of critical denial.

Finally, some clarifications are needed at the outset. "Patriarchy" is used here in the broadest sense to refer to the cultural practice of centralizing the male and of marginalizing the female in all areas of human life (French 91). "Patriarchal ideology" here refers to the assumptions, values, ideas, patterns of thought, and so on that support or perpetuate this arrangement. The ideological aspects of patriarchy are important to this discussion, which focuses heavily on the limitations inherent in Rabbit's habitual ways of seeing and responding to the world. Patriarchal ideology is understood as being written, more often than not as a hidden text, into every aspect of culture, principally into language itself (in consequence of which it shapes thought) and then into all other signifying systems. As a child enters the signifying systems of a culture, he/she absorbs the ideology they convey and assumes his/her gender identity by conforming to their implicit and explicit expectations. Thus, Woodcock and others maintain that the "problem" of patriarchy is not only "male power and control," or "the power of men over women," but also "the control of patriarchal social forms over the identities of both" (8).

Throughout this discussion, I refer to Rabbit as stereotypically masculine or as representing the dominant version of masculinity. Actually, perceptions of masculinity are subject to modification, and part of Rabbit's problem is that he lives through a period of transition. Nevertheless, Updike presents Rabbit as conforming in outlook, attitudes, values, traits, and behaviors to the model of masculinity encoded within the culture. I recall hearing Updike say, during a publicity tour for *Rabbit at Rest*, that Rabbit was the kind of boy one admired in high school. I will explore in detail what that model encompasses.

Linguistic scholars have shown us how difficult it is to generate ideas uncontaminated by ideology. Like other feminist critics, I have been frustrated that my efforts to clarify the gender issues in these novels have immersed me in the same language that generates and perpetuates them. It is clear to me that this study must rely on a courageous and inquiring spirit on the part of the reader, and my hope is that such a spirit will continue to shape a new community of understanding for the future.

I would like to thank Rosalind Trotter and Ann Romines for their substantial contributions to this book and Robert Ganz, Robert Combs, James Maddox, and Christian O'Connell for their careful readings and suggestions. I am grateful to Frank O'Connell for his patient support and to the many friends and relatives who encouraged my effort and buoyed my spirit. Finally, I thank George Washington University to which I submitted an earlier version of this study.

Abbreviations for Updike's Works

AP   *Assorted Prose*
HTS *Hugging the Shore: Essays and Criticism*
PUP *Picked-Up Pieces*
SC   *Self-Consciousness: Memoirs*

Updike and the Patriarchal Dilemma

ONE

Introduction

ONE OF the most promising effects of feminism has been a growing movement among men to examine their own cultural inheritance. As critic Bruce Woodcock puts it, men "themselves have begun to challenge their own power, values and behavior from within the experience of masculinity"; they "have begun to explore what they are, how they behave, how they are constructed as men, and the ways in which they inherit, uphold and propagate the legacy of patriarchy, their own power" (7–8).

The extent of popular interest in masculinity was strikingly demonstrated when the American poet Robert Bly appeared in a 1990 PBS television special entitled *Moyers: A Gathering of Men*. The program drew an "unprecedented number of calls and letters from both men and women attesting to the pain and confusion experienced by men," and Bly's book *Iron John*, an outgrowth of the special, soared to the top of the best-seller list (jacket). Bly has focused attention on an idea whose time has come, and serendipitously it seems, psychiatrists, psychologists, and marriage counselors have begun publishing anecdotal and clinical reports of the personal and social problems arising from a "conflicted internal sense of masculinity" (Osherson 22).

At the same time, on the academic front, Elaine Showalter observes significant changes in the humanities. Gender study has become widely influential, "marking a shift from the woman-centered investigations of the 1970's, such as women's history, gynocriticism, and psychology of women, to the study of gender relations involving both women and men" (Showalter, "Introduction" 2). Feminist criticism of male-authored texts has progressed beyond considerations of "problematic or misogynistic representations of women" to explorations of the role of masculinity in male-authored texts ("Introduction" 7).

The underlying premise of this study is that long before these currents rose to the surface of American popular culture, John Updike had begun work on the longest and most comprehensive representation of masculinity in American literature. *Rabbit, Run, Rabbit Redux, Rabbit Is Rich*, and *Rabbit at Rest* were published at roughly ten-year intervals beginning in 1960. Many critics hailed Updike as an astute social commentator, but they overlooked gender as an essential aspect of his cultural portrait. They dubbed Rabbit Angstrom an American "Everyman," yet they failed to recognize the importance of the hidden term, *man* (Falke 62). A few critics even complained that the early novels lacked substance, missing the substance that was too radical to be easily seen.

Speculating on the sources of this communal blindness, observing its operation, and learning or developing strategies to overcome it have proven as enlightening as the close review of the tetralogy itself. We know that culture perpetuates itself by teaching its members how and what to see, and it is particularly difficult, particularly threatening, for us to see anything that radically challenges the status quo.

Updike himself is also responsible for some of our difficulty; his preferences for indirection and interrogative raise questions regarding his conscious intent. Despite ample opportunity, he has not spoken directly of an interest in examining masculinity or answered charges of antifeminism by referring to the Rabbit novels. Also, though the weight of evidence here, especially the elaborate correspondence between form and substance in the novels, suggests a significant level of conscious intent even in *Rabbit, Run*, the level varies, for as male analysts now acknowledge, blind spots arising from unconscious anxiety, bias, ambiguity, and self-interest are a recurring challenge.

Finally, the depth, breadth, and seriousness of Updike's explorations have discouraged close scrutiny. If he had uncovered flaws susceptible to cosmetic revision, if he had not involved the whole culture in Rabbit's hopeless and pathological enterprise, or if he had shown some optimism regarding female ascendancy or the advent of a new man, his representation of masculinity might have borne looking into earlier. As it is, he probes the relationship between assumptions and values at the heart of Western culture and the shape of socially constructed masculinity. More painful still, he witnesses the destructive flowering of gender-based attitudes, values, and behaviors across generations and in the most intimate aspects of Rabbit's life.

Now, however, the contemporary interest in masculinity has provided the encouragement to confront these difficult issues, while the insights and approaches developed in the field of gender study have provided the necessary tools. This study will explore these issues by examining how Rabbit experiences masculinity and how his gender identity affects his personal and spiritual development, his relationships, and, ultimately, his society. As the evidence unfolds, it will become apparent that for many years John Updike has been analyzing and challenging socially constructed masculinity and that he has been revealing its limitations and proscriptions as the source of a great deal of unhappiness for both men and women. In addition to supporting findings in these areas, this discussion substantiates a relationship that links gender to form, structure, perspective, and language use in the novels and, whenever possible, alerts the reader to ambivalence that may have arisen from the difficulties inherent in the male author's examination of masculinity.

Terms and Context

The following outline of gender theories is intended to orient the reader and highlight issues that reappear throughout this study.[1] Until fairly recently, no distinction was drawn between the terms *sex* and *gender*. Now, however, theorists differentiate *sex*, or biological sexual identity, from *gender*, which refers to "the social, cultural and psychological meanings imposed upon biological identity" (Showalter, "Introduction" 1). Even granting this distinction, however, controversy surrounds the question of the extent of the influence biological factors have on gender identity. Sexual roles may be less relevant than formerly, but the impact of the chemistry and selection associated with those functions is still disputed. Conservative anthropologist Lionel Tiger, for example, hypothesizes that the behavior of men in groups (which Tiger relates to male dominance then and now) "reflects an underlying biological 'propensity' with roots in human evolutionary history" (xi). Naomi Weisstein maintains, in contrast, that the conservative bias underlying studies like Tiger's influences their methods and invalidates their findings (207–24). Still others, like Nancy Chodorow, have used cross-cultural studies to support the position that dorow, have used cross-cultural studies to support the position that "there are no absolute personality differences between men and women" (260).

The influence of sex on gender identity relates to the discussion at hand as Updike has said that he intended *Rabbit, Run* to portray a man compounded of "physical urgencies and spiritual illusions" (Kakutani, "Turning" 15). Rabbit's physical nature is manifested in his obsessive pursuit of women, his reckless reproduction, and his aggression toward rivals (including his son Nelson), all aspects of behavior which seem to have a biological, as well as cultural, basis. Each of the novels mentions the fact that Rabbit is uncircumcised, and in *Rabbit at Rest*, Rabbit himself wonders whether his life would have been different had he been circumcised.[2] Ritual circumcision bound the Israelites in submission to Yahweh, but more important here, circumcision bound the individual male and his sexuality in submission to the community and its laws. As an instinctual man, Rabbit feels oppressed by limitations of his freedom following from the responsibilities and obligations imposed by society on a husband and father (see Updike *HTS* 850).

In addition, consistent with Freud's theory that "the body forms the material basis for constitution of the subject" (Moi 166), Rabbit conceives of himself in terms of the phallus—"his image is of himself going right down the middle, right into the broad soft belly of the land" (*Run* 30). Throughout *Rabbit, Run*, he searches for straight lines that will lead him through holes in the confining social net, and he plays sports that allow him to enact symbolically the male sexual role. At end of his life, in *Rabbit at Rest*, he dreads the unnatural penetration and feminization of his own body by intrusive catheters. Furthermore, throughout the tetralogy, Rabbit perceives an opposition between self and other based primarily upon, and weighted in favor of, his own sexual identity. He pursues women, but he also feels threatened and repulsed by their differences.

Despite the importance of Rabbit's biological identity, however, this study focuses primarily on culturally and socially constructed gender identity. Feminist Hélène Cixous illustrates the concept of gender-based "binary thought" with the following list:

Activity/Passivity
Sun/Moon
Culture/Nature
Day/Night

Father/Mother
Head/Heart
Intelligible/Palpable
Logos/Pathos   (Cixous and Clément 63)

Cixous poses the question "Where is she?" to demonstrate that although most of the words on the list have nothing to do with sex, we can easily distinguish the masculine from the feminine column because we respond according to a cultural paradigm that values the masculine and devalues the feminine (63). Western thought, she says, is organized through dual, irreconcilable, hierarchical oppositions (64). Toril Moi explains that each set of terms reflects a "positive/negative evaluation" in which "the 'feminine' side can be seen as the negative, powerless instance" (105). Even if one doubts the list's accuracy or disapproves of attributing characteristics on the basis of gender, one still knows perfectly well which column is which. And even during periods when society is shifting terms from one column to another, as is presently the case, our ability to distinguish is nearly infallible.

For the purpose of this discussion, we can assume that the columns on a vastly extended list stand for the stereotypical or "dominant versions" of masculinity and femininity in our culture. Gender theory seems to center around a few pertinent questions, which, stated simplistically, are: How do we get on the list? What (and whose) purpose does it serve? Can we get rid of the list?

How do we get on the list? poses the question of gender formation. Personally affected by the story of Oedipus, Freud adopted a paradigm in which the male child desires his mother, directs "murderous wishes" toward his father, and anticipates "paternal retaliation" in the form of castration (Garner, Kahane, and Sprengnether 16). The process of negotiating his fears of attachment to the mother and his guilt and fear of retaliation from the father leads the boy into "increased compensatory masculinity" or male gender identity (Chodorow 285). Constructing a gendered subjectivity differs for the girl, who also initially desires the mother but who discovers that she is "ill equipped, her clitoris an inferior penis" (Garner, Kahane, and Sprengnether 18). In response, she rejects the mother and embraces the feminine position, which is characterized by "a desire for the penis, and thus for a series of substitute phallic objects, ultimately a baby, preferably a boy" (18). So, according to Freud's theory, both male and female psychic development occur in relation to the phallus.

While Freud's theory of male gender formation is grounded in personal experience, his speculation on the formation of female gender identity lacks that authority. Feminists have pointed to a number of weaknesses in his hypotheses, the essential one being that he works from within a phallocentric system to validate its assumptions (Garner, Kahane, and Sprengnether 15–18). Nevertheless, Juliet Mitchell and other feminists find Freud useful because his work clarifies the underpinnings of patriarchy (Garner, Kahane, and Sprengnether 16). These theorists differ from Freud only in their belief that "the patriarchal structure of relations" he describes is susceptible to change (16).

Jacques Lacan adapted Freud's paradigm by placing greater emphasis on the child's repressed desire for its mother. He posited Imaginary and Symbolic Orders, the former corresponding to the preoedipal period of undifferentiated union with the mother during which the child "perceives no separation between itself and the world" and the latter corresponding to culture and society as dominated by "the Law of the Father" (Moi 99–100). Moi explains that

> the Oedipal crisis represents the entry into the Symbolic Order. This entry is also linked to the acquisition of language. In the Oedipal crisis the father splits up the dyadic unity between the mother and child and forbids the child further access to the mother and the mother's body. The phallus, representing the Law of the Father (or threat of castration), thus comes to signify separation and loss to the child. The loss or lack suffered is the loss of the maternal body, and from now on the desire for the mother or the imaginary unity with her must be repressed. This first repression . . . opens up the unconsciousness. (99)

According to Lacan's theory, as the child acquires language, it assumes a place in the Symbolic Order, because to accept the distinction between "I am," "you are," and "she is" means surrendering "the claim to imaginary identity with all other possible positions" (Moi 99). The Law of the Father pushes the infant out of the unitary nest, forcing it to take up a position in the Symbolic Order and "to line up according to an opposition, man/woman, to assume its place as 'he' or 'she' in a pre-existing order of language and culture" (Garner, Kahane, and Sprengnether 21).

Some theorists criticize Lacan's "totalizing equivalence of the Symbolic [Order] and the law of the Father and his privileging of the phallus." Others argue that "psychoanalysis is phallocentric because the human order into which the subject is born is phallocentric"

(Garner, Kahane, and Sprengnether 22). In other words, the subject is pushed into a preexisting "list" that is suffused with cultural bias.

Preoedipal theorist Dorothy Dinnerstein, whose work will be discussed later, focuses on the fact that "for virtually every human, the central infant-parent relationship, in which we form our earliest . . . feelings toward existence, is a relation with a woman" (33). According to her paradigm, the infant's traumatic discovery of the mother's autonomy, that she is "imperfectly subject to its desires," explains the predisposition to consent to the "prevailing male-female arrangements" (60, 35). The experience triggers two reactions, need and fear, and throughout its life, the child tries to re-create the initial experience of owning the mother while now limiting her dangerous power. According to Dinnerstein, both sexes play their necessary part in the *cooperative* project of controlling woman (161).

These analysts speculate on the process of gender formation, yet each of their theories depends upon a preexisting cultural context. The *father*, or *phallus*, is already the controlling term; the individual conforms to a preexisting order of language; the female monopoly over child rearing is already institutionalized. Thus, it seems that even our earliest experiences are culturally determined. As might be expected, another area of study has arisen to explore gender identity as culturally induced through the process of socialization. For example, work like Nancy Chodorow's cross-cultural study "Being and Doing" disputes the presumption of "universal and necessary differentiation" and explains how gender differences arise from child rearing and socialization practices (259).

Cultural studies look for connections between the gender qualities encouraged and the overall operation of society. In other words, if the purpose of socialization is the formation of individuals who fit into and contribute to the overall pattern, then the overall pattern is a determining factor. Thus, cultural theorists may focus on the purposes of the list. Three such purposes are political, economic, and psychological.

As noted, the columns on Cixous's list do not merely reflect difference but are so infused with the patriarchal value system that "it doesn't much matter which 'couple' one chooses to highlight: the hidden male/female opposition with its inevitable positive/negative evaluation can always be traced as the underlying paradigm" (Moi 104–5). Many theorists emphasize the political purpose of this arrangement. In *Sexual Politics*, Kate Millett finds "sexual dominion . . . the most pervasive ideology in our culture" (25). Bruce Woodcock, integrating the perspectives of several theorists, believes that the purpose of the arrangement is "the power of men over women and the power of patriarchal social forms over the identities of both" (8). Marilyn French agrees that although "patriarchy began with a desire to assert 'masculine' power and to gain cultural centrality for males, and was originally a campaign to gain control over women, it needed to control men in order to accomplish this" (112). Thus, even though Rabbit enjoys privileges that he is unwilling to surrender, he is nevertheless described by Updike as being, in many ways, more confined than the women by gender identity.

Woodcock also stresses the notion that "there is no fixed, homogeneous or transhistorical form of masculinity" but rather "versions" of masculinity adopted in response to historical and situational needs (9). This flexibility not only explains the endurance of patriarchy but also explains why different generations can shift items from one column to the other without effecting real change; that is, the purpose of the list is not to accurately identify innate gender characteristics but to appropriate the terms of power and privilege to the male column.[3] As gender study develops, theorists are more likely to stress patriarchy as a hierarchical system, which, although it confers power and privilege on males, nonetheless exploits and harms both men and women. Still another group of theorists identifies the political purpose of the entire list, rather than its asymmetrical columns, as a means of imposing the patriarchal, and therefore exclusively heterosexual, view of human sexuality and marriage.

Another area of speculation involves the relationship between gender and economy. Materialists emphasize that gender identities are learned within an ideological framework and perceive gender conflict in terms of the workers' relation to capital (Showalter, "Introduction" 3). Andrew Tolson writes on the systematic cultivation in boys of the traits desirable in workers. Toril Moi discusses Simone de Beauvoir, the most famous of the socialist theorists, who interprets gender identities in terms of Sartre's paradigm of self and other, with woman constructed as the other and identified with the workers (Moi 91–92). An additional number of theorists, not necessarily materialists, have written on the influence of media advertising in perpetuating gender stereotypes in order to create a demand for consumer goods.

Chodorow's influential work considers the interaction of economic, psychological, and political influences (259–91). In "Being and Doing," she explores the effects of the initially biologically determined division of labor and demonstrates that gender roles are learned and related to adult values and work. Like Dinnerstein, she focuses on the female monopoly on child rearing but emphasizes that the initial painful experience of separation is compounded for the male. The girl has the advantage of being able to identify with mother, learn woman's work at home, and assume her sexual identity so that her socialization is less conflicted, at least until the point that she discovers that her gender is devalued (Chodorow 271–87).

The boy, in contrast, who also initially identifies with the mother and who remains in her care during socialization, must prove or earn his gender identity in opposition to hers. In other words, "the earliest identity for any child is 'feminine,'" but "this identification is more threatening to the boy, because more basic, than the elements of masculine identification that a little girl acquires" (Chodorow 276). Furthermore as "maleness . . . is not absolutely defined, it has to be kept and re-earned everyday" (Mead 303). The boy's task is further complicated by the division of labor that deprives him of an adult male model at home and of the opportunity to learn about men's work. As mentioned earlier, recent studies stress the critical role of the father whose absence has a detrimental effect on the boy's gender formation.

According to Chodorow and others, socialization by women produces a dread of women in males who then externalize the mother's threatening power and deal with it by either idealizing or devaluing the feminine. So, "culturally, this means that it is important for men to gain power and insure that the attributes of power and prestige are masculine, or more precisely, that whatever cultural role accrues to the male is then accorded power and prestige" (Chodorow 275). The cycle returns to the economy again where women's work is devalued, where work that confers status is restricted to men, and where the division of labor is perpetuated (275).

Cora Kaplan maintains that additional forces are at work. She says that gender identities do not develop as "pure binary forms" but are "ordered and broken up through . . . other categories of difference" like race and class (148). Updike says that he writes with a particularly American accent, and that accent may be partially reflected in the fact that Rabbit's masculinity is noticeably shaped by American ideology, which fosters extreme individualism, competition, and racism.

As we shall see, Updike considers all of these aspects of gender identity—the biological influence, the powerful mother, the process of socialization, the dread of women, the quest for power, the absent father, the influence of economics, and the systematic exploitation of both sexes—as he "constructs" Rabbit's masculinity and traces his progress from childhood to death. And, although he focuses primarily on Rabbit, he nevertheless looks closely and compassionately at the psychological development of women.

As the structural foundations of patriarchy continue to erode; as women, rejecting their position in society, continue to destabilize the list; as men become aware of the price of their power; and as men and women both begin to recognize the predictable, unsatisfactory outcomes produced by oppositional thinking in every aspect of life, we speculate on the possibilities for change. One possibility involves continued fudging with different aspects of the list. Some would like to validate the characteristics perceived as feminine by upgrading, for example, emotion in relation to logos, or by giving a higher valuation to women's nurturing work. Others would increase cross-sexual access to characteristics in both columns. This strategy, evolving from a Jungian perspective, sees the list as a sort of archetypal model that need not necessarily inhibit personal development. Individuals of both sexes are permitted, indeed encouraged, to cross over and develop capacities in the opposite column of the list, the idea being that these characteristics are complementary and will contribute to the development of the whole person. While both of these possibilities promise vast improvements over the current situation, neither involves fundamental systemic change, that is, change that abandons the list and its valuations entirely.

Gender theorists have identified formidable obstacles to systemic change (Can we get rid of the list?), suggesting that the list affects, if not determines, our way of seeing and representing the world and our way of valuing what we see. They maintain that the oppositional, hierarchical framework has become our habitual pattern for structuring thought, and unable to move beyond this mind-set, we produce more and more of the same. Mary Ellmann describes Western culture as permeated by the habit of "comprehend[ing] all phenomena, however shifting, in terms of our original simple sexual differences; and . . . classify[ing] almost all experience by means of sexual analogy" (6), while Jacques Derrida and Luce Irigaray maintain that value is ascribed in relation to "the transcendental signifiers of Western culture, the Phallus and the Logos"; "anything conceived of as analogous to the so-called 'positive' values of the Phallus counts as good, true, beautiful; anything *not* shaped on the pattern of the Phallus is defined as chaotic, fragmented, negative or non-existent" (Moi 66–67). The problem is not just that we approach the world in predictable ways, however, but that language itself, the invisible medium of thought, is imbricated with this ideology. Perhaps the most troubling insight comes from Cixous who sees in this pattern of binary thought "a universal battlefield" where "death is always at work" (Cixous and Clément 64), because "for one of the terms to acquire meaning, it must destroy the other" (Moi 105).

The reader will sense having been led from a review of the progress of gender theory to a consideration of the problem of Western dualism. In fact, this crucial intersection is an excellent place to begin the following examination of the Rabbit novels, because Updike uses gender to explore the tension Rabbit experiences between spirit and matter, self and other, life and death, the individual and society. Indeed, one reason why a gendered approach to the Rabbit series has proven fruitful is that it keys into and unlocks the symbiotic relationship between the cultural preoccupation with gender division and the philosophical and religious paradigms that shape our society. While the relationship is clearly symbiotic, the question of whether phallocentrism precedes or follows our religious and philosophical systems is disputed. Cixous, for example, asks the dangerous question of what would happen if it came out "that the logocentric plan had always . . . been to create a foundation (to found and fund) phallocentrism, to guarantee the masculine order a rationale equal to history itself" (Cixous and Clément 65).

Briefly, dualism posits a fundamental rift between matter and spirit, although Saint Paul expresses the division as between body and soul. Matter and spirit can also be imagined as the column headings on another (or perhaps the same) vast list. Besides shaping our way of seeing the world, dualism also fosters two models of relationship. The first model is oppositional and is embodied in its extreme form in the theory of an ultimate conflict between good (God, the soul) and evil (Satan, the body). The second model is superior/inferior and partially derives from (or is reflected in) the patriarchal conception of God as wholly other.[4] Feminist theorist Madonna Kolbenschlag says that "this image of God as a 'transcendent male mind,' who creates an objectified world subject to his sovereignty, provided the model for the way subsequent patriarchal power structures related to women, children, servants, workers, animal life, property and environment" (169). Kolbenschlag adds that the "dualism of the biblical tradition was compounded for Christianity by the duality of the Greco-Roman heritage" because

> the Greek view of reality habitually separated mind from body, thus dividing human rational and carnal capacities. . . . Carnality acquired increasingly negative connotations; hence it was assumed that the mind (rational powers) had a "natural" superiority over the

body (carnal faculties). This hierarchical duality became the paradigm for all sorts of "natural" superior-inferior relationships (so-called differences between subject and object, self and other, man and woman, master and slave, white and non-white, reason and emotion ad infinitum). (169)

The following chapter lays the interpretive groundwork for this study by demonstrating that Rabbit patterns his unhappy relationships on these two models, the oppositional model and the superior/inferior model, even though he is chronically frustrated by the irreconcilability of the oppositional framework or frightened by the prospect of being placed in the inferior position. At the same time that Rabbit follows these hopeless patterns, he is tantalized by the possibility of union. Updike sees Rabbit's desire for union, revealed in his spiritual yearnings, his love of nature, his attraction to women, and his fascination with blacks and Jews as his saving grace. The paradox of dualism is that while it perpetuates discord, it inevitably generates an impulse toward union, its own opposing force.

The material in this study is presented chronologically, tracking Rabbit's progress through the tetralogy, with some cross-referencing among the novels. This design allows for the substantive digressions necessary to adequately present the complexity of the material. The study is heavily weighted toward *Rabbit, Run*, because it is in this first novel that Updike constructs Rabbit's masculinity. Rabbit meets new challenges throughout the tetralogy—as he matures, as his marriage evolves, as his son advances, and as society increasingly undermines his status; but he begins each struggle grounded in paradigms established in *Rabbit, Run*.

TWO

Rabbit, Run
The Mail from Tunis Probably

As *Rabbit, Run* opens, Rabbit Angstrom, a twenty-six-year-old former high school basketball star, who feels overwhelmed by the "second rate" quality of his domestic life (101), abandons his pregnant, alcoholic wife, Janice, and his two-year-old son, Nelson. He spends the spring living with a young prostitute named Ruth Leonard but returns to his family when Janice delivers their daughter, Rebecca. After a brief idyll, Rabbit becomes frustrated and leaves again. In his absence, while Janice is drunk, the infant drowns.

Toward the end of the novel, Rabbit runs from his daughter's funeral into the pine forest above the cemetery. Fleeing from one grave, he discovers another "precipitate hollow," the "cellarhole" of a forgotten house. Aware that the "place was once self-conscious," he has an epiphany in which "he obscurely feels lit by a great spark, the spark whereby the blind tumble of matter recognized itself, a spark struck in the collision of two opposed realms, an encounter a terrible God willed" (274–75). The two realms here are matter and spirit, and it is by the spark of consciousness struck in their collision that humankind understands the peril inherent in its condition and has foreknowledge of death. Overwhelmed by his vulnerability, Rabbit scrambles away, as he will many times in his life, leaving unresolved the problem of his dual nature.

Updike says that "perhaps there are two kinds of people: those for whom nothingness is no problem, and those for whom it is an insuperable problem, an outrageous cancellation rendering every other concern . . . negligible" (*SC* 228). Rabbit Angstrom, initially created during a period when Updike himself suffered from intense anxiety about death, is the second kind of person. His obsession not only leads him into a love-hate relationship with the material world, the source of his danger, but also propels him in his quest for "something" spiritual that can affirm his importance and secure his immortality (*Run* 120).[1]

Rabbit desperately wants to transcend the limits of the material realm. He wants his physical life, especially his sexual life, to have spiritual significance. He wants to overcome the isolation that physical existence imposes on the individual self; he wants to connect with others—with God, with nature, with women, with children, with humankind. He wants, by faith and union, to be saved from the death that threatens him and his family. Yet over and over again, Rabbit behaves in ways that obstruct the realization of these goals.

Death for Rabbit is only the last violation. What Updike shows us in *Rabbit, Run*, and throughout the tetralogy, is that in all of Rabbit's relationships, in all of his encounters with the other in the world, Rabbit also fears the psychological death of self-loss or diminishment. In his relationship with his mother and with each of his sexual partners, he dreads what Gilbert Rose calls the "nullity of fusion" (qtd. in Woodcock 21). He feels crowded and displaced by his own children, especially Nelson. He fears nature, which seems to use him for its own purposes and then toss him aside like "junk," without regard for his specialness. And although he quests after something spiritual and transcendent, he lacks "the *going through* quality of it [Christianity], the passage *into* death and suffering that redeems" (*Run* 171).

Whether the spark that gives foreknowledge casts a pall over other aspects of his experience, or whether Rabbit's enculturation into a dualistic culture shades his perception of everything, including death, is one of the interesting questions the novels raise.[2] But what Updike clearly insists upon is that all of the areas of Rabbit's life are interrelated. Rabbit fears any loss or diminishment of the self; and because he perceives relationships as potentially threatening, he responds to others (including nature and God) defensively, even when his own intuition, the example of nature, and "the motions of Grace," mentioned in the novel's epigraph, suggest that this course is fatal. Thus, Rabbit represents the universal experience of the self as obstacle or trap, because it is he who subverts the very transcendence and union he desires. At the same time, however, the attitudes and behaviors that consistently produce this unhappy result are also associated with a specific cultural phenomenon—socially constructed masculine gender identity. Updike uses Rabbit's masculinity as a vehicle to convey the experience of self as limitation. The following material draws on a variety of sources to establish a framework for demonstrating Updike's use of masculinity by exploring the contrast between the novel's symbolic level, which provides models of the union Rabbit desires, and the narrative level, which describes his self-defeating behavior pattern.

Two Opposing Realms

Rabbit, Run inundates its protagonist and reader with "mail from twoness." Critics like Henry Petter have observed the symmetrical arrangement of many of the novel's structural, symbolic, and thematic elements (see "John Updike's Metaphoric Novels"). For example, the Springer and Angstrom families represent conflicting values, and each is dominated by a powerful but unhappy woman. Rabbit and Janice, the central couple, represent opposing forces. Rabbit loves two women, both of whom conceive infants; both infants are then endangered by his behavior. Rabbit abandons each woman twice; and each reveals her perspective in an interior monologue. Two ministers, representing different religious viewpoints, comment on the Angstroms' marital problems. Eccles visits the Angstrom and Springer homes twice; so do Rabbit and Nelson. Rabbit has two interviews with Mrs. Smith. The list goes on, and in addition, many of the novel's important symbols appear in pairs. Paired circles, including the basketball and hoop, the golf ball and cup, the baby's head and mother's breast, and the rose window and the light, recur throughout the novel.

Rabbit lives in a confusing world of repetitions and oppositions—of complements, doubles, and dichotomies. Rabbit, who is a cultural representative and who controls perspective in this novel, habitually reads conflicts. Thus, the questions he faces at this point in his life, and which the reader faces in trying to understand Rabbit's behavior, are posed not as choices between equivalent options or as opportunities for compromise but as choices between mutually exclusive alternatives. Yet as soon as Rabbit does choose Ruth over Janice, for example, the prostitute begins to represent the same burdensome limitations the wife did. Not only does Rabbit feel threatened by any diminishment of self, but he also feels trapped because, in an oppositional framework, no choice is satisfactory; choice, moreover, perpetuates rather than resolves dichotomies.

Updike admits he relishes this kind of dilemma.

> My books feed, I suppose, on some kind of perverse relish in the fact that there are insolvable problems. There is no reconciliation between the inner, intimate appetites and the external consolations of life.... There is no way to reconcile these individual wants to the very real need of any society to set strict limits and to confine its members. *Rabbit, Run*... I wrote just to say there is no solution. It is a novel about the bouncing, the oscillating back and forth between these two kinds of urgencies until, eventually, one just gets tired and wears out and dies, and that's the end of the problem. (Gado 92)

Despite what he says about irreconcilability, however, Updike maintains the haunting possibility of reconciliation. Even as the plot line of *Rabbit, Run* tells the story of Rabbit's failure, the symbolism affirms the possibility of resolution in the context of nature, in the context of an intuitive symbol-making capacity (the realm of dreams and art), and in the context of redemption. Updike conveys the most important "mail from twoness," or about twoness, in the metaphor of earth's revolution, in Rabbit's dream of a converging sun and moon, and in the Smiths' Easter garden. Each of these symbols affirms the possibility of resolution through union and balance and, in the case of the garden, through agape as well. And each, providing a model that Rabbit radically violates, also clarifies and measures his failure.

In his analysis of Updike's short story "Leaves," George Hunt notes that development occurs "*through* an imaginative exploration of the potential implications" of the "plurisignificant" central metaphor ("Reality" 215). The Rabbit novels incorporate this method of development, and similarly, the metaphors of union, with all of their associated references, provide a way of "grappling with the mysterious relationship between natural reality and man's imaginative consciousness" (215).

Three Models of Union Violated: Equinox and Solstice

Rabbit, Run opens on the evening preceding the vernal equinox, when Rabbit runs away from his wife Janice for the first time. Following Rebecca's birth and arrival home, he runs away again, "on the day before the summer solstice," and his desertion precipitates his daughter's death (217).[3] By bringing this correspondence to our attention, Updike, who acknowledges using puzzles in his novels (*PUP*

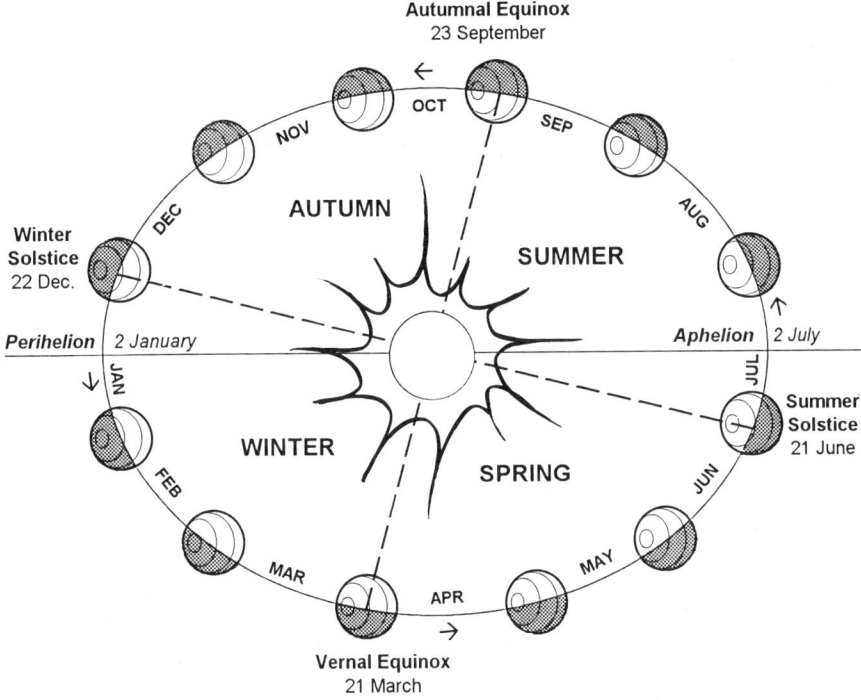

Fig. 1. Diagram of the earth's orbit.

481), not only juxtaposes the season of renewal with the Angstroms' separation and loss but also invites the reader to explore the analogy between the earth's revolution and the progress of Rabbit's life. Granting that Updike's symbolism is intentionally open to multiple, even contradictory, interpretations, it seems clear that the earth's progress is a paradigm of Rabbit's relations with others.

Because earth's axis is tilted, its annual revolution around the sun produces variations in the proportions of light and darkness and the seasonal changes associated with the vegetative cycle. Figure 1 is illuminating for our purposes, especially since Updike is a visually oriented artist, and it is possible that he had some such image in mind that he elaborated over the years. The figure of the earth looks strikingly like a basketball rimming a hoop, and the whole diagram with the sun at its center is reminiscent of the church window suffused with light. The visual image is, in fact, consistent with the complex of paired circles mentioned earlier and shares a common element, in its shifting proportions, with the metaphor of the converging sun and moon in Rabbit's dream sequence.

At the time of the vernal equinox, the opening of the novel, the sun is directly above the earth's equator, and night and day are equally long. As the earth progresses on its elliptical course, the proportion of light to darkness increases so that by 21 June, the longest day of the year, light dominates the earth.

On 21 March the two dichotomous elements are precariously balanced in a harmonious relationship. Light and darkness are now symmetrical components of a unified whole, and as a consequence, life is generated on earth and renewal ensues. However, as soon as this equilibrium is established, it begins to disintegrate, and light and darkness revert to their former relationship as separate, apparently competitive, entities. By 21 June, earth reaches the extreme point in its ellipse, and light dominates over darkness.

At the opening of the novel, a union, a marriage precariously balanced, is about to disintegrate. Rabbit Angstrom, raised to be special, feels diminished by his marriage to Janice, which seems hopelessly limiting and dreary. He begins to resist the union by asserting his self-interest. Like the earth "tilting" in the direction of light and pursuing the limit of its ellipse, Rabbit pursues the course of self-interest to its furthest extreme until on 21 June, he runs from his family again and his daughter subsequently dies. While self-assertion or the resistance to union seems to be a natural, even inevitable, aspect of a larger cycle in this novel, clearly, unlimited resistance leads to death rather than renewal.

In the seasonal metaphor, as light dominates the Earth, the darkness diminishes; similarly, Rabbit's self-interest diminishes the life of others. There is so much "tilting" in the middle of in the novel that, as critic Elizabeth Tallent observes, its "physical universe seems precariously out-of-balance" (79). For example, when Rabbit impulsively decides to leave Janice the first time, he tries to reassure himself by thinking of basketball, "but he feels he's on a cliff" and "there's an abyss he will fall into" (*Run* 28). Later, when he bolts from Rebecca's funeral, he "crouches and runs raggedly" up the steep slope of Mt. Judge (272). And during his last flight, an "illusion trips him" (284).

As in the seasonal metaphor, the dominance of Rabbit's self-interest affects the equilibrium of his dependents. Rabbit thinks little Nelson "walks like a trooper, with choppy stubborn steps" at the opening, but toward the end of the novel, when Rabbit is gone, the youngster "runs with a lopsided almost crippled set of steps" (19, 238). And at the moment of fatal imbalance, drunken Janice drops to her knees, and "the pink baby sinks down like a stone" (243).

The equinox-solstice metaphor not only illuminates the pattern of Rabbit's behavior but also emphasizes a central truth of *Rabbit, Run*—that the resolution of essential dichotomies, in this metaphor expressed as balance, is critical to life. Conversely, unyielding resistance, especially a failure to accept the limitations imposed by relationships, leads to death. Rabbit becomes "Mr. Death" because he resists the impulse toward return and resolution.

Updike uses the solstice-equinox metaphor again in *Rabbit Redux*. When Janice pursues her self-interest in an affair with Charlie Stavros, the Angstroms' marriage is again destabilized, and Rabbit dreams that he is riding the "parabolic curve" once more (26). In *Rabbit Is Rich*, where Rabbit is displaced by his son "at the heart of the world's business, making babies," the solstice-equinox metaphor is used in reference to Nelson's marriage (101). Images of imbalance and falling also recur in subsequent novels, especially in *Rabbit at Rest*, where Rabbit falls during a massive heart attack.[4]

Converging Circles

Following Rebecca's death, Rabbit dreams about a converging sun and moon and recognizes that his vision reconciles the dichotomous relationship between life and death. Unfortunately, when he awakens, he finds that "he has nothing to tell the world" and is unable to incorporate the dream's message into his waking life (*Run* 260). In his dream,

> he is alone on a large sporting field, or vacant lot, littered with small pebbles. In the sky two perfect disks, identical in size but the one a dense white and the other slightly transparent, move toward each other slowly; the pale one is directly above the dense one. At the very moment they touch he feels frightened and a voice like over a loudspeaker at a track meet announces, "*The cowslip swallows up the elder.*" The downward gliding of the top one continues steadily until the other, though the stronger, is totally eclipsed, and just one circle is before his eyes, pale and pure. He understands: "the cowslip" is the moon, and "the elder" the sun, and that what he has witnessed is the explanation of death: lovely life eclipsed by lovely death. Intensely relieved and excited, he realizes he must go forth from this field and found a new religion.

> There is a feeling of the disks, and the echo of the voice, bending over him importunately, and he opens his eyes. Janice stands by the bed in a brown skirt and a pink sleeveless blouse. (260)

In *Rainstorms and Fire*, Edward P. Vargo interprets this dream as a cosmic rite offering a "vision of death as the absorption and continuation of earthly life in a new and beautiful form" (74). The dream metaphor is sufficiently important that Updike chose its converging circles for the dust jacket of *Rabbit Redux*. The jacket of *Rabbit at Rest* features a modified version—a half circle descending into darkness—which also forms the shape of a gravestone. Some variant or memory of the metaphor recurs in each of the novels.

The details of the dream are significant: the disks are initially complete and separate, Rabbit becomes frightened at the moment of contact, and the merger involves a surrender of individual identity. The dream, in fact, offers a model of creative surrender, of a willing sacrifice of individual identity, that results in transcendence through union. Prompted by Rebecca's tragic drowning, the dream provides Rabbit with a resolution to the problem of life and death; however, it also provides him with the key to resolving all of the problematic dichotomies of self and other that are present in the novel in terms of symbolic circles, particularly the parent-child and the man-woman relationships. As noted earlier, Rabbit has always sensed the "rightness" in the convergence of the basketball and hoop, the golf ball and cup, the baby's head and mother's breast, the rose window and the light. These recurring images are the waking complements of the dream metaphor that clarifies their meaning.

Not only do individual circles converge, but various pairs converge to emphasize the connection between the different areas of Rabbit's life (Markle 42–47). For example, the rose window in the church across the street from Ruth's apartment becomes an important symbol. Rabbit notices it prior to his first sexual encounter with Ruth. The rose window, widely interpreted as a symbol of Rabbit's desire to connect physical existence (the stone facade) with spiritual significance (the light), has the additional value of a vaginal symbol in the context of the sexual moment (Uphaus 24; Strandberg 179). Rabbit pretends that Ruth is a beloved, virginal bride on their wedding night partly because he wants to realize the spiritual ideal of the rose window in his sexual life. Thus, the window becomes a double image connecting Rabbit's relations with women to his quest for spiritual significance. Joyce Markle further associates the church window with the light-filled basketball hoop and the complex of sport-sex images (43). In addition, when, during intercourse, Rabbit experiences Ruth as "the bell of a big blue lily slipped down on his slow head," the suggestions of flower, circle, and convergence connect this encounter and its cluster of images with the dream metaphor to come (*Run* 83–84). And as if this fabric were not dense enough, when the rose window appears again at the end of the novel, it is interwoven with both the problem of paternity and with the converging circles of the dream metaphor by means of Rabbit's conception of fatherhood as a "thin tube upright in time," that is, as a series of connected circles (282). The field of pebbles from the dream metaphor is now a "huge vacant field of cinders" that makes Rabbit's heart go "hollow"; he turns to the church window for reassurance but finds it "unlit, a dark circle in the stone facade" (283). Rabbit's inability to integrate spiritual values into the different areas of his life parallels his failure to incorporate the "new religion" of his dream into his waking life.

Technically, each pair of converging circles has a range of suggestive possibilities. The dominant association of a pair of circles shifts when juxtaposed with other pairs. Eventually, all of the suggestive possibilities are integrated. Rabbit's intuitive capacity provides him, in the dream of the converging sun and moon, with a key or Rosetta stone to unlock and resolve all of the relationships signified by other converging circles. The dream tells Rabbit that transcendence over the physical world, over death and other, is possible only through union, and union requires surrender.

In both parent-child and man-woman relationships, Rabbit fails to achieve the union he desires because he uses the oppositional framework rather than the proffered model of resolution. As Kathleen Verduin demonstrates in "Fatherly Presences," fatherhood is a recurrent theme in Updike's work. In *Rabbit, Run*, as in the next three novels, Rabbit is a poor father measured both in terms of the metaphors of union and in terms of his children's suffering. Updike does not furnish an exemplary father for contrast (and the lack of such a model is, of course, part of Rabbit's problem). However, *The Centaur*, originally envisioned as a companion novel to *Rabbit, Run*, does contain a model of fatherhood that is consistent with the dream metaphor; this is George Caldwell, a character created to make a record of Updike's own father, Wesley (*HTS* 849; *PUP* 500).[5]

The same freedom and self-interest that Rabbit pursues, George Caldwell sacrifices to the welfare of his family, and his sacrifice is specifically understood as an acceptance of death: "His will a perfect diamond under the pressure of absolute fear, uttered the final word. *Now....* Chiron accepted death" (*Centaur* 222). As Victor Strandberg suggests, Caldwell's sacrifice is a creative, redemptive act of agape that bestows, secures, and affirms his child's life, and perhaps more important, gives the child hope because such "love implies that the physical universe has a spiritual counterpart, that metaphysical dimension of reality whose existence has been so much in question and whose power is the only final recourse against death and entropy" (187).

Peter Caldwell, in his turn, extends and affirms his father's life. From the father's sacrifice, he learns the mystery of surrender: "I must go to Nature disarmed of perspective and stretch myself like a large canvas upon her in the hope that, my submission being perfect, the imprint of a beautiful and useful truth would be taken" (*Centaur* 218).

In *Rabbit, Run*, Rabbit conceives of the "vertical order of parenthood, [as] a kind of thin tube upright in time in which our solitude is somewhat diluted" (282). As a line consists in an infinite number of points, a tube involves an infinite number of connected circles. Thus, Updike reinforces the phallic, vaginal, and copulative associations of the converging circle metaphor and introduces the association of parenthood, especially of fatherhood. The infant descends through that tube as a product and participant in the whole design of convergence. The "good" father surrenders his physical and spiritual essence to a child who incorporates that life into his own. Parent and child share, affirm, and extend each other's lives. Understood in terms of the dream's unifying metaphor and the linear tube, shared life is the convergence of parent, child, and humanity and of past, present, and future.

Unfortunately, Rabbit interprets his children's lives not as a transcendence of his own but as a signal of his approaching death, and he is therefore unwilling or unable to commit himself to their welfare. Aside from the brief idyll with Nelson while Janice is in the hospital and aside from his first sight of Rebecca, Rabbit generally has an antagonistic attitude toward the young. He resents the young basketball players who seem to displace him, and they, in turn, are suspicious of his intentions. The novel justifies their perception of something "sinister" about Rabbit (*Run* 9). Janice's pregnancy "infuriates him with its look of stubborn lumpiness" (15). And his response to the approach of middle age is to reassure himself of his sexual and generative powers by becoming, like his namesake, reproductively promiscuous. Ruth's unborn child, the product of this reckless self-assertion, is endangered because in the absence of any commitment from Rabbit, Ruth considers abortion.

Although Rabbit enjoys his time with Nelson, he identifies his son with his loss: "The fullness ends when we give Nature her ransom, when we make children for her. Then she is through with us, and we become, first inside, and then outside, junk. Flower stalks" (208). Similarly, on the day of Rebecca's death, he experiences the infant's crying as well as the mother's discomfort primarily as obstacles to his own will. When Janice asks, "Why can't you try to imagine how I *feel*?" Rabbit responds, "I can. I can but I don't want to, it's not the thing, the thing is how *I* feel" (230). Rabbit consistently sees his children in an oppositional framework. The life he generates is a threat to his own; therefore, he will not support it despite the fact that his own intuition, particularly in the dream metaphor, tells him that surrender and sharing are the means to transcendence. Without his commitment, Rebecca dies, Ruth's unborn child is threatened with abortion, and Nelson becomes emotionally crippled.

Significantly, at the opposite extreme, Rabbit experiences the same fear and conflict in his relationship with his own powerful mother. Awaiting Mary Angstrom's arrival at the funeral home, Rabbit thinks:

> With his mother there's no question of liking him they're not even in a way separate people he began in her stomach and if she gave him life she can take it away and if he feels that withdrawal it will be the grave itself. Of all the people in the world he wants to see her least. Sitting there by himself he comes to the conclusion that either he or his mother must die. It is a weird conclusion, but he keeps coming to it, again and again. (266)

Clearly, in Rabbit's framework the parent-child relationship is a life-and-death struggle. It is, therefore, psychologically and symbolically appropriate that Rebecca dies in this novel and that Mary Angstrom is dying in *Rabbit Redux*.

Rabbit's intense, ambivalent relationship with Mary Angstrom not only affects his attitude toward his children but colors his response to the younger women in the novel as well. The dream metaphor also applies to Rabbit's marriage to Janice and his relationship with Ruth. The convergence of sun and moon is a natural metaphor for marriage, which is traditionally conceived of as two becoming one. Although Rabbit longs for the kind of union his dream expresses, his marriage and his affair fail precisely because his relations with the younger women fundamentally contradict the model in his dream. The dream metaphor posits discrete identity as a precondition for union, but Rabbit fears that his scarcely distinguishable self may either be overwhelmed by the powerful mother or cease to exist without her approval. He generalizes this fear into a conception of all women as threatening, and he typically reacts with anger and even violence to any perceived rejection by them. Rabbit's defensive response to these dangerous women is to enter into relations with them only on the basis of domination and control. For example, he cultivates Janice's "dumbness" in order to secure his own position, and he eventually actualizes his need to see Ruth on her knees. From this stance (oppositional and superior-inferior), a union that depends on surrender is virtually impossible. The dream metaphor specifically eschews domination: "The other, though the stronger, is totally eclipsed and just one circle is before his eyes" (*Run* 260).

Rabbit's partners, for different reasons, also lack the separate identity necessary for union. Whether or not he selects partners for this trait, Rabbit certainly cultivates their feelings of inadequacy. Having left Janice, Rabbit has a guilty nightmare in which her face slips into his hands while he tries to fix it in place. In another scene, Rabbit scrubs Ruth's face, smudging, or distorting, her identity. As we shall see in subsequent chapters, lack of discrete identity is critical in Janice and Ruth as it not only limits their capacity for union but renders them vulnerable to Rabbit's depersonalizing projections.[6]

Rabbit's first encounter with Ruth is especially revealing. The dichotomies between body and soul, self and other, love and hate are evident in this episode; and as usual, it is the fear of self-loss that motivates the behavior that subverts Rabbit's desire for union. That desire is indicated by his "deep wish to give comfort" and by the fact that "it is not her body he wants, not the machine, but her, her" (*Run* 76, 77). Despite his desire, however, as soon as Ruth opens to the possibility of union, Rabbit becomes frightened as he did in the dream metaphor (82), and "at the moment of release, the root of love, he betrayed her by feeling despair" (83). At this moment, he feels exactly as he will later with his son Nelson: "Nature leads you up like a mother and as soon as she gets her little price leaves you with nothing" (83). Unable to sustain his faith in the possibility of transcendence, Rabbit despairs.

It is not only at the moment of contact that Rabbit becomes reticent, however. Throughout the episode, aspects of his behavior are inconsistent with his goal of union. His striving for control rather than surrender makes him inaccessible to Ruth, while his depersonalization of Ruth renders her inaccessible to him. To illustrate, on the walk to Ruth's apartment, Rabbit is frightened by her sexual vastness: "'It's in the trade,' she says, and this really stops him. He doesn't think of her this bluntly. It frightens him to think of her this way. It makes her seem, in terms of love, so vast" (73).

Like many of the clients Ruth has known, Rabbit responds to devaluation implicit in her sexual vastness by trying to distinguish himself as a good "lover" (74). Essentially without regard for Ruth, Rabbit sets about winning her love in order to reclaim his individual identity or specialness. He "captures" her (82), and he is delighted the next morning when her deferential manner confirms that "he has her. He knows he has her" (89). Self-assertion, gaining control of that threatening vastness, is the ulterior motive behind Rabbit's sexual consideration as it is, partly, the motive behind the wedding pretense he uses to claim and domesticate Ruth's sexuality. Tallent observes that Updike's heroes generally have this "knack of turning the women they sleep with into wives" (4). At the same time, Rabbit exploits Ruth in his quest for the spiritual. He discounts what is other in her and imposes an identity that is no more than a projection of his own aspirations and needs. When he transforms her into his idealized version of woman, he reduces her from a person to an abstraction (Nickens 58.)

Pretending Ruth is a virginal bride on her wedding night is neither innocent nor harmless; in this novel, it represents an incapacity in Rabbit that is an absolute impediment to union and violates the model of openness and acceptance implicit in the dream metaphor. Like other forms of depersonalization, idealization and projection also indicate an unwillingness or "inability to apprehend the presence of an actual person in a woman" (de Rougemont 315). Rabbit's projection is not only an initial obstacle to union but the origin of Rabbit's subsequent disappointment and resentment as well. It is only after passion subsides that Rabbit focuses on the individual woman, who inevitably fails to fulfill her idealized role and consequently becomes the object of contempt and hostility. Her inadequacy becomes the reason for desertion and new questing. It is this pattern of projection and rejection that makes Rabbit the unhappy *Schussel* or restless, careless person, which the character the Lutheran minister Kruppenback calls him (158).[7]

The first encounter with Ruth illustrates Rabbit's progress from idealization to contempt and dissatisfaction. The beautiful, virginal bride becomes a "best bedfriend" and a source of pleasure, but as soon as the euphoria passes, she becomes ugly, repellent, threatening, and disappointing:

> "Boy, you better let me up."
> He murmurs, "Don't scare me," and snuggles more securely against her side. His thigh slides over hers, weight on warmth. Wonderful, women, from such hungry wombs to such amiable fat; he wants the heat his groin gave given back in gentle ebb. Best bedfriend, fucked woman. Bowl bellies. Oh, how! when she got up on him like the bell of big a blue lily slipped down on his slow head. He could have hurt her shoving her jaw. He reawakens enough to feel his dry breath drag through sagged lips as she rolls from under his leg and arm. "Hey get me a glass of water," he says.
> She stands by the edge of the bed, baggy in nakedness, and goes off to the bathroom to do her duty. There's that in women repels him; handle themselves like an old envelope. Tubes into tubes, wash away men's dirt, insulting, really. Faucets cry. The more awake he gets the more depressed he is. From deep in the pillow he stares at the horizontal strip of stained-glass church window that shows under the window shade. Its childish brightness seems the one kind of comfort left to him. (*Run* 84)

This wide swing in Rabbit's feelings is, as we shall see, disturbingly like those of his basketball coach and mentor, Marty Tothero.

As noted, Rabbit has little interest in "the presence of an actual person in a woman" (de Rougemont 315). This attitude and the hostility that inevitably accompanies it is commonplace in our literature. What is interesting in this episode, especially in a novel written in 1959, is that it is Updike, the author, who saves Ruth from his protagonist's devaluation. First, Updike clearly provides Ruth with a personality so engaging that readers resist Rabbit's attempts to transform her. In fact, the reader uses Ruth's perspective to assess Rabbit's limitations. And second, at the end of this episode, Updike has Rabbit fall asleep, momentarily freeing the reader from his controlling perspective. Ruth leaves the bed and Rabbit, still unsatisfied, asks for water. Updike affirms that Ruth has beauty and value beyond Rabbit's estimation; and she has the capacity to quench Rabbit's thirst: "He is asleep when like a faun in the moonlight Ruth, washed, creeps back to his side, holding a glass of water" (*Run* 84). By the end of his life in *Rabbit at Rest,* Rabbit's symbolic thirst will have grown almost unquenchable.

To summarize, Rabbit fears all intimacy but especially intimacy with women, who seem, like his mother, to embody nature and death and to have the capacity to overwhelm his sense of himself. And as much as he fears their power to swallow him, he also fears their power to reject him and thus devalue or undermine his sense of himself. There is a direct connection between Rabbit's fear of Mary and his anger toward the young women that flares into intimidation and violence. Rabbit feels devalued by the Texas prostitute, who "faked her half" (48); by Janice, who, following Rebecca's birth, refuses his sexual advances; and by Ruth, who once slept with his rival Ronnie Harrison. Each incident sparks an aggressive physical response in Rabbit. Finally, Rabbit is angry at women because, having projected ultimate values and ideals onto them, they disillusion and dissatisfy him.

It is true, as Bernard Schopen notes, that on one level Janice and Ruth represent the alternatives of social responsibility and inner light or individual freedom (198). And yet, the affair with Ruth can be profitably read as an exploration of why Rabbit's marriage is failing. Despite the differences in circumstances and personalities, Rabbit treats Ruth much as he does Janice. Critic Markle, for example, observes that Rabbit's last cruel sexual encounter with Ruth "is parallel with the only sexual encounter we see with Janice in which she is similarly not a partner but an unwilling masturbatory object" (57). Far from approaching the acceptance and self-surrender of the dream model, Rabbit's relations with women are convoluted and unhealthy. Fear and rejection of the other, not acceptance, motivate Rabbit's defensive behaviors of projection, manipulation, and intimidation. Self-preservation, not self-surrender, is the goal of these behaviors. Consequently, Rabbit's encounters with women end with a deepening separation instead of union.

The Smiths' Garden

The third significant metaphor of resolution in *Rabbit, Run* is the rhododendron garden.[8] Gardens also recur in each of the subsequent novels. In *Rabbit Redux*, Rabbit neglects the yard work at home but nevertheless fears that blacks are taking over the garden of America; in *Rabbit Is Rich*, he abandons gardening himself but gathers Janice's "lettuce" (wealth). In *Rabbit at Rest*, Updike uses two gardens to represent the dichotomy conveyed here by the Smiths' Easter garden and the dark pine forest, that is, between nature with and nature without God.

While Rabbit lives with Ruth, he takes a part-time job as a gardener, and in this episode, Updike gives an exquisite account of the transformation of the garden in spring. The extraordinary passage, often cited by critics and well worth rereading in full, illustrates the beauty of the poetic prose as well as the unusual mood and tone of the garden section. Updike creates the impression of altered consciousness here that is similar to the dream state in which Rabbit receives his vision of the converging sun and moon. He shifts to a cosmic perspective, not controlled by Rabbit, and he introduces another mode of knowing. The dichotomies that seem so entrenched elsewhere in the novel, seem to dissolve.

> Sun and moon, sun and moon, time goes. In Mrs. Smith's acres, crocuses break the crust. Daffodils and narcissi unpack their trumpets. The reviving grass harbors violets, and the lawn is suddenly coarse with dandelions and broad-leaved weeds. Invisible rivulets running brokenly make the low land of the estate sing. The flowerbeds, bordered with bricks buried diagonally, are pierced by dull red spikes that will be peonies, and the earth itself, scumbled, stone-flecked, horny, raggedly patched with damp and dry, looks like the oldest and smells like the newest thing under Heaven.... And at last, prefaced by azaleas, the rhododendrons themselves, with a profusion increasing through the last week of May. Rabbit had waited all spring for this crowning.... When the first blooms came they were like the single big flower Oriental prostitutes wear on the side of their heads, on the covers of the paperback spy stories Ruth reads. But when the hemispheres of blossom appear in crowds they remind him of nothing so much as the hats worn by cheap girls to church on Easter. Harry has often wanted and never had a girl like that, a little Catholic from a shabby house, dressed in flashy bargain clothes; in the swarthy leaves under the pert soft cap of five-petaled flowers he can imagine her face; he can almost smell her perfume as she passes him on the concrete cathedral steps. Close, he can get so close to the petals. On inspection each flower wears on the roof of its mouth two fans of freckles where the anthers tap. (*Run* 127–29)

The very idea of a garden suggests a nonmaterial realm in that the physical reality of nature is brought into relation with a nonphysical (spiritual) ideal of order and beauty. Even so, there are different kinds of gardens and gardeners. A rigidly formal garden may reflect the gardener's mistrust of nature and his desire to subjugate it to his art and will. Flowerlike women, whose sexuality (fertility) makes them agents of the physical world, have often been confined to this kind of literary garden, usually walled. In Horace Smith's garden, however, nature is not threatening, nor is it conceived simply as a medium for the artist-gardener. Nature and the gardener interact creatively, and the gardener's role involves devotion rather than domination. The gardener cooperates with the physical world to enhance its beauty, and that beauty in turn reflects and enhances his spiritual life. In this context, nature is beneficent, and consequently, female sexuality also has a spiritual as well as a physical dimension. Updike's garden is based on the premise of nature with God. More specifically, it is based on the reconciliation of matter and spirit symbolized by Easter. In "Seven Stanzas at Easter," Updike insists on the essential involvement of the physical world in the spiritual mystery of the Resurrection:

> Make no mistake; if He rose at all
> it was His body;
> if the cells' dissolution did not reverse, the molecules reknit, the
>   amino acids rekindle,
> the Church will fall.
>
> (*Verse* 164)

The Resurrection not only reconciles matter and spirit but holds out the possibility of reconciliation between man and the other; thus, Horace's Easter garden symbolizes the union, or reunion, that Rabbit desires.[9]

In his excellent work, *Pastoral and Anti-Pastoral Patterns in John Updike's Fiction*, critic Larry Taylor maintains that the mock-pastoral and antipastoral modes can be used either to expose the pastoral life as an unattainable or false ideal or to provide a standard for evaluating and ironically devaluing a more sophisticated way of life (19). However, in his specific consideration of *Rabbit, Run*, Taylor only discusses Updike's use of mock pastoral for the first purpose, that is, to satirize Rabbit's adolescent escape "to the pastoral American Dream of eternal youth and transcendental harmony with nature" (75). I differ with Taylor in my perception that Updike uses the antipastoral mode in *Rabbit, Run* for both purposes. While Taylor sees only a satire of Rabbit's desire to return to lost innocence, I also see Updike's very serious contrast between Rabbit's way of life and the ideals embodied in the garden. The difference hinges on one's perception of what kind of garden Updike has created. If the Smiths' garden is intended as a type of prelapsarian Eden, then return is impossible, and pursuing this illusion, according to Taylor, is both ridiculous and destructive. If the Smiths' garden is an Easter garden, then in the context of orthodox Christianity, although one cannot return to Eden, reconciliation through redemption is possible.

> For though that seat of bliss be failed
> A fairer Paradise is founded now
> For Adam and his chosen sons, whom thou
> A Savior art come down to reinstall....
> (Milton, *Paradise Regained* 4.612–15)

In *Rabbit, Run*, as in the other three novels, Updike uses myth to expand and enrich meaning. He has, for example, acknowledged a connection between Rabbit's story and that of Beatrix Potter's Peter, who also discovered death while pursuing freedom (*PUP* 48). Horace Smith's rhododendron garden, however, has far more in common with Eden than with Farmer McGregor's lettuce patch.

Updike deliberately draws attention to the garden. Structurally, the episode appears at the center of the novel, literally and figuratively balancing the two halves. As noted, stylistically, the striking shift into poetic prose indicates a return to the symbolic realm as well as a shift into a cosmic context. Furthermore, the garden episode taps into the richness of the other metaphors with its allusions to the sun and moon and the vegetative cycle of the seasons as well as with its use of flower imagery and its theme of blending colors and meanings.

Narrative details also indicate the significance of this garden. The Reverend Mr. Eccles tells Rabbit that a gardener is needed near Appleboro. Mrs. Smith, wife of the garden's deceased founder, Horace Smith, has kept it as a "religious duty" and complains that there are no real gardeners left (*Run* 121). Eccles tells Rabbit that the job will suit him perfectly, and although the minister makes this remark sarcastically, Mrs. Smith recognizes that Rabbit has the capacity to be a good gardener. Unlike the Lancaster florist who was unable to grow a cutting from the "Bianchi" rhododendron, Rabbit has the "strange gift" of "life" (132, 207).

Mrs. Smith's husband is a mysterious figure. Piecing together information about him, we learn that Horace Smith, "an incredible rhododendron enthusiast," planted the garden and nurtured it with remarkable devotion over the years (121). In an interesting detail, when Rabbit visits Mrs. Smith's parlor with Nelson, he notices two paintings (205). One is of Mrs. Smith as a young woman wearing a black dress (perhaps reflecting her materialism). The other, which Rabbit notices but does not recognize, is of Leda and the swan whose myth symbolizes a union of polarities: human and divine, natural and supernatural, material and spiritual, male and female. This blending involves a divine intervention or participation in human affairs. If not a type of Zeus, Horace Smith at least shares the divine capacity to blend dichotomies in his garden. Mrs. Smith, however, expresses her own emphatic dislike for blended colors. Like Rabbit, of whom she says "We think alike," Mrs. Smith is limited to dualities (133). She says, "Harry loved those salmon colors so; I'd say to him, 'If I want red, give me red; a fat red rose. And if I want white, give me white, a tall white lily; and don't bother me with all these in-betweens and would-be-pinks and almost-purples that don't know what their mind is'" (129). Horace, on the other hand, had the capacity not only to blend colors but to unite the physical reality, the beauty of the rhododendron garden, with a spiritual vision or value worthy of commitment and faithful service.

Horace also bears a resemblance to the biblical Creator-Father, who made a garden and entrusted it to humans and who combined creative vision and vitality with unfailing devotion. Also like that father, Horace apparently lost his only son. And, of course, the rebirth and flowering of Horace's garden is associated with the Resurrection; the rhododendron blossoms remind Rabbit of flowered Easter hats, and later, when Rabbit attends Eccles's service, he identifies flowered hats as emblems of faith:

> Correspondingly, he loves the ones dressed for church: the pressed business suits of portly men give substance and respectability to his furtive sensations of the invisible; the flowers in the hats of their wives seem to begin to make it visible; and their daughters are themselves whole flowers, their bodies each a single flower, petaled in gauze and frills, a bloom of faith, so that even the plainest walk in Rabbit's eyes glowing with beauty, the beauty of belief. He could kiss their feet in gratitude; they release him from fear. (217)

Horace, also called "Harry" by his wife, is the spiritual father that Harry Angstrom is lacking, an alternative to the spiritually impoverished coach Tothero and the rejected natural father, Earl Angstrom. Harry Smith provides his namesake with an appropriate legacy as well as, if Rabbit could only see it, a model for constructive relationship. That is, it is not only the garden that is passed along but also the role that Horace himself adopted of caretaker, preserver, nurturer. In

Horace's garden, in the role of gardener, Rabbit is given the opportunity to live out the possibilities of resolution in his waking life. The garden at Eastertide is a paradise regained in which Adam-Rabbit is restored to harmonious relations with God, nature, woman, and child. By participating in all of the aspects of gardening (pruning, burning, sowing, waiting, and witnessing), Rabbit is able to participate in and accept the cycle of life and death. In planting the seeds, he comes closest to understanding and accepting fatherhood as a spiritual-physical bestowal.

If Horace does symbolize the God that Rabbit seeks, then the garden episode allows Rabbit to enter a more positive relation with God than he does elsewhere in the novel. Although Rabbit's belief in God sets him apart from the other characters, scenes like the golf match with Eccles suggest that Rabbit aggressively pursues God and, as with the young women, projects the identity that he wishes to find. This religious attitude, as Updike points out, is one of "aggrandizement" (*Run* 126). In the garden episode, consistent with Updike's understanding of Barth's theology, God is the mysterious and unknowable other who intervenes creatively in the world, reconciling the essential dichotomies. Fatherlike, he provides Rabbit with a legacy, and most important, instead of a code of law to govern behavior, he provides an ideal embodiment of principles that Rabbit might apply to his life. Significantly, in the garden, in this relation, Rabbit believes "it was sort of like Heaven" (206).

Several critics have noted that Updike's women are aligned with nature as opposed to spirit. They are feared as the agents of the physical world and, therefore, of death. Because of the reconciliation in Horace's garden, however, Rabbit's perception changes. Initially, he associates the rhododendron blossoms with the physical beauty of prostitutes: "They were like the single big flower Oriental prostitutes wear," but they later remind him of "the flowered hats worn by cheap girls to church on Easter" (128). In Updike's work, empty sex, here prostitution, signifies spiritual death. On the other hand, the Easter hat, as noted earlier, is an emblem of faith in the Resurrection. This transition indicates a change of perception in which women (and especially their physical beauty) are no longer perceived as cooperating with nature without God, which casts men aside like "flower stalks," but instead are perceived as participating in nature with God as emblems, if not agents, of physical-spiritual resurrection (208).

In the garden then, Rabbit briefly lives the reconciliation of spirit and matter, life and death, and self and other. He realizes the goal that eludes him elsewhere because he follows Horace's model of a nurturing caretaker. The idea of devoted service, or stewardship, expands the notion of self-surrender. In this novel, without stewardship, spiritual gardens decay like the one beside the Sunshine Athletic Association. The element of society that Tothero represents neglects spiritual life, and consequently, its garden is "a junkheap of brown stalks" (21). Later, when Rabbit quits his job in the Smiths' garden, he is in effect abandoning his spiritual life. The betrayal is all the more pointed as his new job as a used car salesman represents both materialism and dishonesty.

In the episode following Rabbit's walk in the garden with Mrs. Smith, he and Ruth spend Memorial Day at a public swimming pool in West Brewer (133–40). Updike juxtaposes the garden scene, which affirms life through the reunion of matter and spirit, with the pool scene, which memorializes death and, therefore, the triumph of materialism. The contrast again reveals the extent to which Rabbit's life violates the model of union.

Rabbit has returned to his oppositional framework. The scene opens with Rabbit contemplating Ruth as an object; he sees her as a "statue" and feels the "chill clench of ownership" (133). He enjoys their separation ("her in the water, him in the grass and air" [134]) and thinks: "Clean, clean: it came to him what clean was. It was nothing touching you that is not yourself" (134).

Rabbit is angered by the touch of Ruth's skin, and later, Ruth thinks that Rabbit "just lived in his skin and didn't give a thought to the consequences of anything" (139). Rabbit is again limited by an oppositional framework, the boundaries of his egotism, and by the confines of the material realm.. He can neither get out of his own skin nor see past Ruth's exterior to the unhappiness (or the child) within. His stubborn separateness once again stands in contrast to Ruth's willingness to surrender. She remembers:

> When they're good together she feels like next to nothing with him and that must be it, that must be what she was looking for. To feel like next to nothing with a man. Boy that first night when he said that so sort of proudly "Hey" she didn't mind so much going under in fact it felt like she should. She forgave them all then, his face all their faces gathered into a scared blur and it felt like she was falling under to something better than she was. But then after all it turns out he's not so different. (138–39)

In view of Rabbit's definition of *clean*, it is ironically accurate that, in her interior monologue, Ruth relates her pregnancy to Rabbit's demand for a "nice clean piece" (139). Ruth's pregnancy is the by-product of a fearful and self-assertive sexuality that bears no resemblance to the thoughtful, willing attitude of Rabbit as gardener. And, as Ruth suspects, Rabbit's self-absorption inversely reflects his commitment to care for his offspring. Early in the episode, she reminds him that he is not supporting his wife (136), and at the end, she is afraid to tell him she is pregnant because "he'll probably get scared and off he'll go" (139). The last brief paragraph of the pool episode juxtaposes Ruth's tears and Rabbit's "idle remote smugness" to express the distance between Rabbit and the other: "'I'll tell you,' he says. 'When I ran from Janice I made an interesting discovery.' The tears bubble over her lids and the salty taste of the pool-water is sealed into her mouth. 'If you have the guts to be yourself,' he says, 'other people'll pay your price'" (140). Again, Rabbit fails to translate vision into reality. His spiritual life in the garden is unconnected to his life in the world.

Finally, Rabbit's relationship with God is distinctly different from what it was in the garden where he followed Horace's example. Ruth now observes his unwillingness to nurture and provide. Furthermore, although he now claims "I'm a mystic. I give people faith" (135), Ruth thinks that "he's got the idea he's Jesus Christ out to save the world just by doing whatever comes into his head" (139).

There are several other gardens in *Rabbit, Run*. Rabbit passes a neglected one on his way to find Marty Tothero and stumbles across a long-forgotten one in the forest. With Ruth, he walks through a litter-strewn park that suggests the spiritual impoverishment of modern society. When Eccles visits Kruppenbach, the Lutheran minister is tending his garden: "The sloping lawn, graded in fussy terraces, has the unnatural chartreuse evenness that comes with much fertilizing, much weed-killing, and much mowing" (156). Critic George Hunt suggests that Kruppenbach is a careful gardener because as a Barthian, he knows "the inroads the shadow side of Creation can make" (*Updike* 43). Kruppenbach, like the formal gardener mentioned earlier, distrusts and controls nature. His spiritual perspective is rigid, and interestingly, his wife has a "dimpled, obedient look" that Eccles thinks his own wife, Lucy, will never achieve (*Run* 156). Eccles, who tells Rabbit there are no gardeners left, brings Rabbit to a public golf course. Critics have observed that Eccles's Christianity has become too public and too much like social work, and clearly, his neglected wife and children have grown wild.

Sometimes the same garden means different things to different people. Mrs. Smith complains of a neighbor's foolish remark that "this must be what Heaven is like" (132). When Rabbit tells Mrs. Smith that "maybe what looks like rhododendrons to her [Mrs. Foster] will look like alfalfa to you," he is expressing the notion that there is an individual as well as a universal component to spiritual life (133). Similarly, in both *The Centaur* and *Of the Farm*, characters differ radically in their perception of the land (Taylor 102–11). The differences are less critical than the issue of whether or not a character is committed to his or her own vision and willing to tolerate other visions.

Updike invites the reader to speculate on the nature of Rabbit's garden. It clearly involves his spiritual life and reflects his relationship to the flower and the seed, that is, to the woman and the child. However, critics and characters alike are divided on whether Rabbit should settle down to gardening with Janice and Nelson or with Ruth and her unborn child. Rabbit's parents, Mary and Earl Angstrom, argue the question, and Rabbit himself will wonder about Ruth until the end of his life. Nevertheless, at this point, by demonstrating Rabbit's willingness to betray both of these women and to abandon his children, Updike is revealing Rabbit's unwillingness to commit himself at all.

There is a chicken-and-egg dilemma in Rabbit's condition. Is he unable to generate or recognize a vision worthy of commitment, or does his inability to commit himself prevent him from developing a worthwhile vision? These two capacities, commitment and vision, are critically interdependent in the mysterious gardener Horace Smith. Furthermore, they are critically interdependent in Updike's view, as his essay "Whitman's Egotheism" suggests:

> But Whitman never ceased willing a Oneness with his fellow-man, and it redeems his solipsism from selfishness and smallness. "And nothing, not God, is greater to one than one's-self is"—but incessant creative recourse to one's self ends, as youthful illusions of infinite capacity fade, in an arid emptiness and a desperate lunge over the frontier of sanity. Such a doom, so frequent among poets after Whitman, was avoided by him, who in the next line warned, "And whoever walks a furlong without sympathy walks to his own funeral, dressed in a shroud." (*HTS* 116)

Empathy, the basis of commitment, is creative, and without it, Rabbit is snared in the net of solipsism, his behavior becoming increasingly circular, futile, and desperate. Clinton S. Burhans discusses this viewpoint in his essay "Things Falling Apart."

In 1960, the year that *Rabbit, Run* was published, Updike said, "I believe that all problems are basically insoluble and that faith is a leap out of total despair" (Howard 80). Many years later, he added this corollary: "The self's responsibility . . . is to achieve rapport if not rapture with the giant, cosmic other" (*SC* 257). These two conditions, the call to union and the impossibility of answering without some fundamental leap beyond the self in faith, delineate Rabbit Angstrom's predicament as revealed in the tension between the symbolic and narrative levels of the novel. As critic John Neary suggests, Rabbit receives the same call many times throughout the novels (68–84). The question addressed in the following chapters is, Why is it so difficult for Rabbit Angstrom to respond to the "motions of Grace"?[10]

Critics who interpret Harry's behavior negatively cite his dread, cowardice, self-centeredness, sinfulness, or instinctuality; or they blame society for its failure to provide options, values, role models, or support. Burhans blames Rabbit's solipsism on "family, school, church":

> All three, then, disintegrating and distorted, combine to fail in their central function: to civilize Rabbit, to give his centrifugal impulses meaning and purpose, the "motions of Grace" and thus keep his centripetal ones from "hardness of the heart." Instead these basic institutions of his "external circumstances" warp and blunt and waste Rabbit's outward seeking and accelerate his inward turning, a movement which Updike outlines structurally as solipsism and details thematically as decay in the novel's almost clinical sexuality. (160)

The interpretation offered here emphasizes the following modification: society warps and blunts and wastes Rabbit's outward seeking not because it fails to civilize him but because it succeeds. The social institutions that have shaped Rabbit's gender identity have exacerbated and manipulated his fear and encouraged in every way his desire for control and the establishment of hierarchies. Rabbit is stereotypically masculine, and as we have discovered along with Updike over the past thirty years, such a man is likely to be unhappy and even dangerous.

THREE

Gender Formation
But What's Wrong with That Man?

RABBIT IS not just a stereotypically masculine character who fails to resolve the dichotomies in his life, but rather he fails to meet and resolve those dichotomies in part because he is stereotypically masculine. His masculinity is at the heart of his difficulties. There are several explanations for why Updike focused on masculinity at this point in his career. Hunt, who sees a natural division in Updike's first twenty productive years, says that "his first decades' work . . . records the strife, observation, and feeling of that pre-twenty-year-old wherein nostalgic recollections of boyhood are transmuted into art" ("Reality" 207). And Updike himself notes that "the difference between Olinger and Tarbox is much more the difference between childhood and adulthood than the difference between two geographical locations" ("Reality" 208). *Rabbit, Run* is among the last works reflecting on that early life, and surely one of the final, crucial tasks of adolescence is that of coming to terms with issues of gender.

Feminist critics have made us more aware of other authors who have spoken overtly and covertly about the difficulties of taking up or refusing culturally assigned roles. For example, in discussing Sherwood Anderson's "I Want to Know Why," Judith Fetterley examines the narrator's reluctance to assume his place among adult males who appear insensitive and exploitive. She notes that Melville, too, explores the consequences of excessive masculinity through older figures like Ahab and Claggart while younger men silently observe. She remarks: "In the image of Ahab, impaled on the bone which he has cut from the phallic whale and used as a surrogate limb, Melville makes an explicit statement of these consequences" (14). In *The Madwoman in the Attic*, Sandra M. Gilbert and Susan Gubar discuss a comparable phenomenon among nineteenth-century female novelists whose work reflects their resistance to established roles as they struggle to free themselves from social and literary confinement. The sympathetic and yet fiercely critical portrait of Rabbit Angstrom in *Rabbit, Run* may similarly reflect the young Updike's necessary personal appraisal of masculinity.

On the other hand, feminists now mark the fifties and early sixties as the dawning of conscious awareness that the patriarchal system was insupportable and destructive. Updike's early interest in the foundering of traditional masculinity may be another indication of his capacity for astute social observation. *Rabbit, Run* is both an early expression of the crisis of masculinity and an early example of a revaluation of masculinity by a male author.

To say that Updike explores the negative aspects of male power contradicts the assumption of a chauvinistic attitude made by critics like Mary Allen, who refuse to downplay the abuse of women in these novels. There is, however, an important distinction to be made between authors who create misogynistic male characters as heroes and authors, like Updike, who create misogynistic characters and expose and question and even satirize their behavior. Tallent, among others, warns that "Rabbit is Updike's creature rather than a variant of his self" (75).

The pornographic quality of some of Rabbit's encounters also seems to counter an interpretation of the novel as an exploration of the negative aspects of male power. As noted earlier, male authors who explore masculinity remain subject to their own ambivalence and unconscious habits. Woodcock notes that John Fowles's *The Collector* (1977), which is intended to expose and exorcise "the fantasy of the abductor-rapist," also excites and satisfies that fantasy sufficiently to reinforce the very perspective on women that Fowles ostensibly wishes to undermine (19). Furthermore, as author, it is Fowles himself who arranges the degradation and abuse of the character Miranda (Woodcock 27-43). *Rabbit, Run* offers a far less extreme case study of male behavior than *The Collector*.[1] In *Rabbit, Run*, except for Rebecca, the other females are only metaphorically killed, and many of the abuses that occur fall within what were until just recently considered "normal" limits. Nonetheless, a similar contradiction exists in the novel. When Rabbit degrades Ruth by demanding oral sex because he needs to see her on her knees (*Run* 174), Updike clearly means to expose Rabbit's outrageous male "crust," to use Fowles's word, and also to reveal his ignorance and insensitivity to Ruth as a person. Oral sex was more titillating in 1960, but even now, the scene resonates as a fantasy of male power over women. Updike exposes Rabbit's behavior, yet, at the same time, as author, he participates in that behavior by arranging Ruth's degradation; furthermore, he reinforces the fantasy by arranging it with skill. In fact, Updike gained a reputation for titillation early in his career. Gary Waller, for example, remarks that "Updike, whatever else one says about him, has no superior as a writer of high-level serious pornography, uninhibited yet tasteful, analytical yet emotionally evocative" (271). Many feminists consider pornography synonymous with exploitation; if this is so, the author's method and expertise may be at odds with his intention (Woodcock 39–41, 150–51). This contradiction is one of several that suggest that serious, possibly insoluble, conflicts hinder the male artist in examining masculinity. Even with the best of intentions, he may reframe and redistribute the same mythologies he hopes to explore or overthrow.

Another objection to the argument concerning Updike's intent may be that it conflicts with the author's own statements, made in *Self-Consciousness*, that he was similarly uncomfortable with the chic anti-Vietnam stance of his fellows and with the antimale attacks of feminists. He says:

> The fights for women's rights and gay rights emerged enmeshed with the Vietnam protest and have outlived it. Though not consciously resisting the androgyny ... I must have felt challenged. My earliest sociological thought about myself had been that I was fortunate to be a boy and an American. Now the world was being told that American males—especially white, Protestant males who had done well under "the system"—were the root of evil. (145)

Updike's discomfort with the popular movements arose in part from his "disposition to take contrary positions and to seek for nuances within the normal" (*SC* 146). When antiestablishment sentiments became so widespread as to constitute "orthodoxies of dissent," Updike's reaction was to shift slightly aside (*SC* 142).

No doubt, however, like many others, Updike did feel personally challenged by feminism, but his loyalty to masculinity primarily reflects his positive identification with his own father, Wesley. In speaking of the student protest movement and its attacks on authority, Updike recounts his emotional distance from the radicals, saying:

> To me authority was the Shillington High School faculty, my father and his kindly and friendly, rather wan and punctilious colleagues, with whose problems and perspective I had had every opportunity to empathize. I had overheard their mild-mannered conversations in the hall when the thundering hordes of unruly students had left; I was allowed to visit the boiler room, and see the male teachers at ease in their shirtsleeves, smoking and joking. . . . Authority to me was Woody Coldren, the superintendent of the Lutheran Sunday School and eventually town burgess, loudly leading us children in the singing of carols on Christmas morning in front of the blank screen of the movie theater. It was my grandfather and the town crew, tarring the tidy streets. It was the three town cops, in their comically different sizes. Such were the village elders whom I visualized tortured and executed by the Viet Cong, to show that the only possible social order was theirs. (SC 128)

The comment reflects Updike's affection for the amiable Shillington High School version of masculinity. However, the dissimilarity between those kindly men and the figures at the Sunshine Athletic Association in *Rabbit, Run* is made clear:

> Old men, mostly, but not very old, so their misshapen bodies have a nasty vigor—look up with interest at him.
> Their alert colorless eyes, little dark smears like their mouths, feed on the strange sight of him and send acid impressions down to be digested in their disgusting big beer-tough stomachs. (*Run* 53)

As these men are radically different, I conclude that Updike does not perceive masculinity monolithically but allows for different versions, not to mention nuances. In fact, even while confessing his loyalties in *Self-Consciousness*, he acknowledges another side saying: "The town authorities, and all the hard-working churchgoing burghers of Shillington, struck me really as stodgy and not to be emulated. At heart I scorned them. Who would want to be a Thirty-second-degree Mason, or the top Oddfellow? Who, by extension, would want to be President of the United States?" (128). Thus, Updike's loyalty is neither all-inclusive nor unqualified.

The final question to be addressed before returning to the text of *Rabbit, Run* is whether or not it is even reasonable to explore the misuse of power by a character so widely perceived as a victim. In fact, the powerful victim has a long, respectable history in literature. As critics have shown, Rabbit is a diminished modern protagonist whose stature is undermined through satire, irony, and the use of a narrator. Nevertheless, the small, helpless, rabbit-victim is also a powerful manipulator.

According to Judith Fetterley, the myth of male powerlessness not only insists that men are victims but also that women are the arbiters of male fates (171). And if women are not the arbiters, if they are not the Fates, they are likely to be the instruments, or Furies. Thus, Lear's happiness depends upon his daughters, and Oedipus's very self-concept depends upon his relationship to Jocasta.

The myth of male powerlessness is a strategy for gaining advantage, a strategy all the more effective if covertly or even unconsciously employed. In *The Resisting Reader*, Fetterley discusses representative examples of the myth's appearance in American literature. She demonstrates that the victim's position is an advantageous one for a variety of reasons, the most important of which is that the myth of male powerlessness in fact "serves to disguise and hence perpetuate the very reality it inverts" and "legitimizes the hatred of and aggression on women" (165, 188). To return to King Lear for a moment: while it is clear that from the myth's perspective his condition depends upon the goodwill of his daughters, it is also clear that he initially uses his psychological, emotional, social, and political power to manipulate his daughters for the enhancement of his own ego. Furthermore, Cordelia is idealized for remaining faithful in the face of this abuse.

Not only does the male victim profit from the myth's diversionary value, he also gains the advantage of center stage. It is *his* story that commands our attention and sympathy, especially if he is an "innocent" victim, in which case he also accrues moral stature (Fetterley 188). And even if he is not portrayed as entirely innocent, his sins are mitigated by his suffering: by the end of the play, Lear has our sympathy entirely. As Fetterley observes in reference to Hemingway's *A Farewell to Arms* (1929), although it is Catherine who dies, "All our tears are ultimately for men, because . . . male life is what counts" (71).

Male powerlessness has other advantages; helplessness makes demands, not only on the audience but on other characters within a work. Male helplessness asks service from women, whether it be in the form of rescuing, reforming, pitying, appeasing, mothering, or sacrificing. Where readers and characters might comfortably resist the demands of a powerful protagonist, the helpless and suffering victim is difficult to refuse. If female characters do refuse such service or if they are unsuccessful in rendering it, they may be assigned responsibility for the victim's condition and even be represented as oppressors themselves.

Feminist critics have established the literary precedent for the use and abuse of power by apparent male victims. *Rabbit, Run* is about a man who feels the net closing on him, but it is also about a man who defeats himself and devastates those about him through the misuse of his considerable power. Sometimes his power is that of a victim, while at other times it is that of an oppressor, but in both cases his power derives (as does the power of Oedipus and Lear) from his position as a male and is exercised primarily against women to secure advantage. Ruth, Updike's most perceptive observer, understands the relationship between gender and power. She says, "No mystery. That was the great thing she discovered, that it was no mystery, just a stuck-on-looking bit that made them king and if you went along with it could be good or not so good" (137).

Although *Rabbit, Run* has a tragic theme, its protagonist lacks the stature of tragic figures like Oedipus and Lear. Rabbit is an *angst* ream of human suffering, but he is also, as Taylor observes, an "angstrom" or "one ten-billionth of a meter" (70). Updike undermines his status with satire. He associates his protagonist not with power imagery but with a weak and ridiculous creature that suggests the themes of fear, flight, and promiscuity (Taylor 74–75). Instead of a warrior-king, Rabbit is an ex–high school basketball star; and his work, a factor that significantly affects male status, is as a MagiPeel Kitchen Peeler salesman.

Updike further undermines Rabbit's stature by presenting him as charming but, nevertheless, egotistical, insensitive, and self-deceptive. He is "boyish" rather than mature (Brenner 96–97). Finally, and most interestingly, Updike undermines Rabbit's stature structurally through the use of a narrator. Although the novel is dominated by Rabbit's perspective, the use of the third person denies him final authority over his own story and provides the fraction of distance that makes observation and objectification inevitable. The narrative technique also prevents Rabbit from achieving the degree of self-knowledge that a tragic hero requires. Thus, the narrator allows Updike to unfold a tragic situation while withholding the stature of full consciousness from his protagonist.

Although Rabbit is a contemporary protagonist in terms of his diminished stature, he shares important, revealing characteristics with heroes of the older myths. In common with figures like Lear and

Oedipus, Rabbit is a manipulator exercising what power he has to avoid self-compromise.

Friedrich von Schiller opens his essay "On the Sublime" with observations that apply to the classic hero:

> All nature proceeds rationally; man's prerogative is merely that he proceeds rationally with consciousness and intent. All other things "must"; man is the being that wills.
>
> For just this reason, nothing is so unworthy of man than to suffer violence, for violence undoes him. Whoever offers us violence calls into question nothing less than our humanity; whoever suffers this cravenly throws his humanity away. But this claim to absolute liberation from everything violent seems to presuppose a being possessing force enough to repel every other force from itself. If it is claimed by a being who does not occupy the highest rank in the realm of force, an unhappy contradiction arises thence between aspiration and capacity.
>
> This is the position in which man finds himself. Surrounded by countless forces, all of which are superior to his own and wield mastery over him, he lays claim by his nature to suffer violence from none of them. He is, indeed, enabled by his understanding artificially to enhance his natural powers, and up to a certain point he is actually successful in becoming the master of everything physical. (193–94)

Schiller has outlined the condition and response of the tragic hero who manipulates the elements in his environment in an effort to avoid that violence that threatens to overwhelm or annihilate his self-concept. Kingship provides a tragic hero with a position of stature from which to fall, but more important, kingship represents the maximum capacity of man to manipulate his world. As we shall see, however, Rabbit, who is a small, helpless victim from one perspective, is a powerful manipulator from another.

Mary Angstrom

Why and how Rabbit uses his power depends in large part on how he was formed as a male in the context of the Angstrom family. Updike provides Rabbit with a history that clarifies the impetus behind his behavior and suggests much about the process of gender enculturation in our society. Piecing information together, we learn that Rabbit's mother, Mary Angstrom, is a large, vigorous woman whom

Rabbit describes as having "force." She is also repressed and unhappy. Eccles "thinks of Mrs. Angstrom silent in the kitchen with her wet cheeks and red arms, a mad captive." She is a grim "humorist" taking on the whole world (*Run* 149–50). Her own life, her spiritual life, is represented by the unmowed strip of grass between the Angstrom home and a neighbor's, which becomes "her flowerbed" and which she bitterly defends against intrusion from the old Methodist next door. Mary Angstrom's meager garden, grown without sunlight or encouragement, becomes a source of anger and contention, just as her stifled capacities surface destructively in the family in her resentment of her husband, Earl, her rivalry with her daughter, Mim, and her obsession with her son, Rabbit. Denied an active, meaningful life of her own, Mary Angstrom covertly seeks access to power (that is, to self-realization, to excellence) through her son, and her access depends upon his cultivated allegiance.

Updike's sympathetic portrait of Mary as a "mad captive" is surprisingly like those drawn by female writers. Sandra Gilbert and Susan Gubar in *The Madwoman in the Attic* observe the distinction between the "monstrous" women drawn by male writers, reflecting their fear of what seems radically other, and the "monstrous" women created by female writers who utilize the "fair and foul" aspect of the male tradition to acknowledge a frightening inner reality (54–57). The price paid for repressed creativity is shown in the portrayal of the alter ego that has become powerful, unhappy, and destructive. Gilbert and Gubar note the recurrence in women's literature of paired figures like Snow White and her evil mother. Snow White is beautiful and passive unto death, while her alter ego is frantic, cruel, inventive, and universally despised for her efforts to survive (36–46). The relationship between these archetypes goes a long way toward explaining the dynamics among the women in *Rabbit, Run* as well as the desperate quality of the relationship between Mary and her agent-son. Janice, and to a certain extent Mim, play Snow White to Mary's Wicked Queen, while Rabbit's allegiance is the contested prize.

Updike's sympathetic portrayal of Mary Angstrom is unusual because it acknowledges that the "monstrous" woman is the consequence of cultural repression. The repression and passivity of the Snow White archetype are manifested in this novel in a variety of ways, including the death of the infant Rebecca, the prostitution of Ruth, and the evasion (alcoholism) and inadequacy of Janice. But the cultural inhibition of women carries a heavy price for men as well. Those women who are not unwilling to bear children into the future and those who do not physically or figuratively destroy the children they have may, like

Mary Angstrom, become the "monstrous" mothers who misuse their role as mediators of their sons' identities. Rabbit, at twenty-six with a wife, family, and mistress of his own, feels that Mary Angstrom is "still attached to the cord of his life" (*Run* 266). He thinks, "They're not even in a way separate people he began in her stomach and if she gave him life she can take it away" (266).

Throughout the novel, Rabbit is nostalgic for his childhood. He feels, for example, a "quick odd jealousy" when he sees through the Angstroms' kitchen window that his own son, has displaced him as the center of family attention (25). Later, when Rabbit visits his mother, he realizes that Nelson's very existence, which signifies both his adulthood and his relationship with Janice, "keeps them from having the kind of conversation they used to have, where his mother tells him something pretty funny that happened in the neighborhood and they go on to talk about him, the way he used to be as a kid, how he dribbled the basketball all afternoon until after dark and was always looking after Mim" (211). Mother and son want to live and relive what from Mary's point of view was the ideal moment in Rabbit's life, a moment when he still "belonged" to her as a boy without adult commitments and when he was on the brink of achievement.

Andrew Tolson, an early commentator on male cultural experience, notes that "masculinity is a kind of cultural bribe—a boy's social commitment is won at the price of his independence" (46). Male power and privilege are carrots that the culture uses to lead boys into the bondage of a certain kind of labor and domesticity. Mary Angstrom uses these carrots in a particularly crippling way with Rabbit. Rabbit's position in the Angstrom family (which Bessie Springer describes as having been "made too much of" [*Run* 143]) encompasses a variety of elements, including Mary's obsessive devotion, her preference for Rabbit over other family members, and his privileged impunity. His position is the lure she uses to motivate him in the direction of performance, what the character Tothero will later identify as "the will to achieve," and also to gain his exclusive, permanent loyalty.

Despite Rabbit's nostalgia, Updike suggests that the Angstrom home was a battleground where the boy himself was both prize and weapon (Burhans 156). Earl Angstrom recalls Rabbit's sensitivity to family arguments, saying, "Any rumpus in the family he'd take hard out of all reason" (*Run* 155). And Rabbit remembers how "he dreaded their quarrels: when their faces went angry and flat and words flew, it was as if a pane of glass were put in front of him, cutting off air; his strength drained away and he had to go to a far corner of the house" (24–25).

Clinton Burhans suggests that the strife in the neighboring Zim family mirrors the Angstroms' contention. Rabbit recalls that

> all day long Mrs. Zim, who was plain, with big thyroid eyes and bluish, slack skin, screamed at her daughter Carolyn, who was prettier than a five-year-old girl had a right to be.... All day long Mrs. Zim screamed to her and when Mr. Zim came home from work the two of them would shout for hours. It would begin with Mr. defending the little girl, and then as the neighbors listened old wounds opened like complicated flowers in the night. Sometimes Mom said that Mr. would murder Mrs., sometimes she said that the little girl would murder them both, as they lay asleep.... *How does that poor man endure? If Carolyn and her mother don't settle their differences they're going to wake up some fair morning without a protector.* (23)

Rabbit remembers that Carolyn, "who was prettier than a five-year-old girl had a right to be," responded to the haranguing by developing an impenetrable "cold-blooded" exterior (23). That exterior anticipates Rabbit's and, in the next novel, Mim's emotional detachment.

The Zims are living out their own complicated and horrible version of the Snow White story, and what is interesting here is that Mary Angstrom reveals her understanding of the conflict as one between mother and daughter over a protector. In the Angstrom family, Rabbit is the male who represents power to Mary and who is remembered as Mim's protector. Although Mim has a passive role in the conflict, like Faulkner's Caddy, her sexual maturity becomes threatening because it is the symbolic division between Rabbit's childhood (the condition of absolute loyalty to Mary) and his maturity (the possibility of commitment elsewhere). Mary rages against the daughter who seems to threaten her hold on Rabbit.

So Rabbit may be nostalgic for his childhood, but he is also haunted by its undercurrents. On his first night with Ruth, his disturbing nightmare encapsulates the Angstrom family dynamics.[2] The dream opens with the family gathered around the kitchen table, as they were earlier when Rabbit saw Nelson through the window. In that scene, nineteen-year-old Mim, wearing green eye shadow and dressed in black and gold, gives Nelson some food and "the reach of her slender white braceleted arm across the steaming table rings a barbaric chord into the scene" (25). This very sexual Mim, toward whom Rabbit displays powerful possessive feelings in a later scene, is clearly not the same one that he turns to in his imagination when he is overwhelmed by real life. His comforting childhood memories are either of baby Miriam or of a completely innocent and devoted, prepubescent young girl engaged in sledding and bike riding.

In his dream, the older Mim opens the door of the icebox, where Rabbit discovers a frightening secret. In other references ice and iceboxes are related to death and female sexuality. For example, Rabbit recalls that he once fell into the ominous runoff from the ice plant because he was showing off for some schoolgirls on the slippery gutter edge. Margaret Schoelkopf is memorable among those girls because "she had had so much life" that her nose bled spontaneously (*Run* 21). Later, in the Eccles's kitchen, Lucy asks from behind the refrigerator door, "How did you sleep?" and Rabbit answers, "Like death" (192). Also notable is that the color white, used frequently in this dream to convey a Melvillean horror, refers elsewhere to female sexuality (214). The references to bleeding suggest menses and, as with Margaret's nosebleeds, a transition to sexual maturity.

In Rabbit's dream, female sexuality, represented by Mim's braceleted arm, provides access to the "cave" containing the dark adult secret of physical death.

> A girl at the table reaches with a very long arm weighted with a bracelet and turns a handle of the wood icebox and cold air sweeps over Rabbit. She has opened the door of the square cave where the cake of ice sits; and there it is, inches from Harry's eyes, lopsided from melting but still big, holding within its metal-black bulk the white partition that the cakes have when they come bumping down the chute at the ice plant. He leans closer into the cold breath of the ice, a tin-smelling coldness he associates with the metal that makes up the walls of the cave and the ribs of its floor, delicate rhinoceros gray, mottled with the same disease the linoleum has. Having leaned closer he sees that under the watery skin are hundreds of clear white veins like the capillaries on a leaf, as if ice too were built up of living cells. And farther inside, so ghostly it comes to him last, hangs a jagged cloud, the star of an explosion, whose center is uncertain in refraction but whose arms fly from the core of pallor as straight as long eraser-marks diagonally into all planes of the cube. The rusted ribs the cake rests on wobble through to his eyes like the teeth of a grin. Fear probes him; the cold lump is alive.
>
> His mother speaks to him. "Close the door."
> "I didn't open it."
> "I know."
> "She did." (84–85)

Mary Angstrom wants that door shut because both the invitation of female sexuality and the knowledge of his destiny threaten her position. The first undermines his loyalty and the second signals the end of his childhood. To deflect his mother's anger, Rabbit sacrifices Mim. More important, however, than the overt betrayal is the betrayal involved in his failure to accept his own responsibility and claim the dark secrets as his own. Rabbit's sexual irresponsibility, his flight from death, and his betrayal of Janice and Ruth are rooted in this fear and failure.

> "She did [it]."
> "I know. My good boy wouldn't hurt anyone." The girl at the table fumbles a piece of food and with terrible weight Mother turns and scolds her. The scolding keeps on and on, senselessly, the same thing over and over again, a continuous pumping of words like a deep inner bleeding. It is himself bleeding; his grief for the girl distends his face until it feels like a huge white dish. "Tart can't eat decently as a baby," Mother says.
> "Hey, hey, hey," Rabbit cries, and stands up to defend his sister. Mother rears away, scoffing. They are in the narrow place between the two houses; only himself and the girl; it is Janice Springer. He tries to explain about his mother. . . . Janice has a pink dance dress on, and is crying. He repeats, numb at heart, about his mother, that she was just getting at him but the girl keeps crying, and to his horror her face begins to slide, the skin to slip slowly from the bone but there is no bone, just more melting stuff underneath; he cups his hands with the idea of catching it and patting it back; as it drips in loops into his palms the air turns white with what is his own scream. (85)

Mary turns her relentless wrath against Mim. And even while Rabbit deflects Mary's rage, he experiences a guilt and grief that threaten his identity, distorting his face. The sister, Mim, turns into the wife, Janice, but the situation remains much the same with Rabbit trying to explain that, although Mary's tirade is not directed at him, its purpose is to get at him, to punish his disloyalty, and to bring him back under Mary's control. Janice's identity, which also seems to depend on Rabbit's allegiance (and his assumption of adult responsibility), is threatened, and her face too begins to slide. If this dream accurately reflects the dynamics in Rabbit's relationships with women, his white scream is an understated response.

Mary Angstrom's need to secure Rabbit's primary loyalty is the source of her animosity toward Janice and the motivation behind her efforts to undermine her son's marriage. The scenario she invents describing to Eccles how Janice tricked Rabbit into marriage is untrue according to Rabbit's own account; however, Mary's version reflects her understanding that Janice's sexuality was the weapon that defeated her. In addition to her primary motivation, Mary undermines the marriage out of class resentment, a theme emphasized in *Rabbit Redux*. A proud woman, she remembers Janice's unwitting condescension ("Why the first thing that girl said to me was Why don't I get a washing machine?" [*Run* 149]) and she dislikes the Springers' wealth, indolence, superiority, and social climbing.

Updike has provided Rabbit with a plausible psychological history. By emphasizing Mary Angstrom's role as the controlling mother, he accomplishes two contradictory, or perhaps complementary, ends. First, Mary's portrait is sufficiently unusual and Rabbit's inability to separate is sufficiently abnormal that the reader is able to withhold complete identification. Not every man has such a powerful mother nor is every son as apron-bound as Rabbit. He may be pitied because he lacks a stronger role model in his father or contemned for his inability simply to "grow up," but either way, the seemingly exaggerated portrait protects the reader, and I suspect the author as well, from an unpleasant association. We are spared the overt suggestion that we share Rabbit's family feelings and the further implication that we also share the warped, destructive attitudes that are the inevitable outgrowth of those feelings. We feel safer because Mary Angstrom is not, after all, the usual sort of mother.

On the other hand, the special resonance of this relationship and its impact on the reader derives precisely from the fact that Mary Angstrom *is* an accurate reflection, not of how mothers are, but of how they are perceived in the negative aspects of their power by developing mother-reared infants. Mother is not only an abundant source of pleasure and affirmation but a supernaturally powerful figure who can also withhold whatever she can give, who seems to be responsible not only for what she does but for whatever occurs, and who is able to demand and secure compliance (Dinnerstein 92–159). Dinnerstein maintains that, as a result of the female monopoly on child rearing, "*the crucial psychological fact is that all of us, female as well as male, fear the will of woman.* Man's dominion over what we think of as the world rests on a terror that we all feel: the terror of sinking back wholly into the helplessness of infancy" (161). The fear of union or reunion is the very source and energy of male power and, furthermore, determines how male power will be exercised, because "it guarantees certain forms of antagonism" toward women:

> These antagonisms include fury at the sheer existence of her autonomous subjectivity; loathing of her fleshly mortality; a deeply ingrained conviction that she is intellectually and spiritually defective; fear that she is untrustworthy and malevolent. At the same time, they include an assumption that she exists as a natural resource, as an asset to be owned and harnessed, harvested and mined, with no fellow-feeling for her depletion and no responsibility for her conservation or replenishment. Finally, they include a sense of primitive outrage at meeting her in any position of worldly authority. (Dinnerstein 36–37)

In other words, helpless dependence and disappointment generate fear and antagonism, which translate into a need to control female will. The fulfillment of that need is realized primarily in destructive sexual arrangements, but as all subsequent phenomena (for Rabbit that includes nature and death) are perceived from within the shadow of that initial relationship, it affects many other aspects of life as well.

Updike includes two sexual encounters from Rabbit's young adulthood that echo aspects of his experience with Mary Angstrom, further reinforcing his need to control women. At the hospital, Rabbit nostalgically recalls his first love and the feeling of triumph he has since been unable to recapture. Rabbit and Mary Ann's high school romance was based on Rabbit's achievement; he came to her a "winner," and she was the prize that confirmed his worth. Later, when Mary Ann married elsewhere, Rabbit was devastated. This unpleasant lesson was reinforced with the Texas prostitute who devalued Rabbit by "faking" her half of a sexual moment. What Rabbit learned from these encounters is that while cooperative women can shore up self-esteem, uncooperative women can destroy it utterly. It therefore becomes desperately important to Rabbit to control the behavior of women. When Rabbit realizes he "has" Ruth, he thinks, "With women, you keep bumping against them. . . . they give, like a plant, or scrape like a stone. In all the green world nothing feels as good as a woman's good nature" (89).

Earl Angstrom

Rabbit's father, Earl Angstrom, is only a peripheral figure in the drama played out between mother and son. Critics like Judie Newman consider that Earl's weakness, his lack of authority in his home, signifies the contemporary decline of male authority, and, in Freudian terms, explains the young man's inability to escape his mother's sphere of influence. Newman, for example, says that "in the civilization of the Fifties the repressive father has been edged out, replaced by society itself which now acts directly on the individual" (39). It is true that Earl lacks vitality and what Tolson refers to as male "presence" (16). Rabbit cannot look at his father without recoiling from his defeated aspect. For example: "His weary hunch and filthy fingernails annoy his son; it's as if he's willfully aging them all. Why doesn't he get false teeth that fit? His mouth works like an old woman's" (*Run* 211). However, although he is a quieter, more tired, less fully developed character, Earl shares with *The Centaur*'s George Caldwell a long-suffering generosity and faithfulness that identify him with the alternative tradition of fathers discussed by Verduin in her essay "Fatherly Presences: John Updike's Place in the Protestant Tradition." Verduin observes that Updike's recurrent fathers are not types of Barthian forcefulness. They are likely to be "defeated, but highly compassionate and human individuals" representing manliness "defined not in terms of sexual adventure but of work and responsible paternity" (259). Furthermore, they stand, even if silently, against "adultery and divorce" (257).

When Earl takes Janice's part against Rabbit and Mary, he does so not out of the fear of public scandal that motivates the Springers but out of compassion for Janice's suffering and out of his understanding of the human cost involved in abandoning responsibilities. He tells Mary and Eccles, "He [Rabbit] is my enemy. . . . That night I spent walking the streets looking for him he became my enemy. You can't talk. You didn't see the girl's face. . . . Suppose I had acted the way Harry has" (*Run* 153).

Furthermore, Updike emphasizes Earl's compassion and faithfulness at the opening of *Rabbit Redux*, where the old man is shown caring for his dying wife and offering friendship to his still troubled son. He is clearly not the popular image of masculinity, but like George Caldwell of *The Centaur*, Earl is at least a decent, good man. Unlike Peter Caldwell, Rabbit, at least in *Rabbit, Run*, simply rejects his father as a model of manhood.

One explanation for why he does so is plainly oedipal; Mary Angstrom interferes with the development of a close father-son relationship.[3] Another is that Earl signifies values and certainties rejected by modern society. A third explanation, which will be discussed further in relation to *Rabbit Is Rich*, is consistent with recent studies in father-son relationships. Psychologist Samuel Osherson observes, for example, that sons of "all-suffering fathers" fear that suffering and entrapment are the male fate, and boys with "weak" fathers fear becoming weak themselves. These sons not only develop ambivalent feelings about their own masculinity but may, like Rabbit, have a special need to dominate women (27–33).

A fourth possibility, based on Lacanian theory but also supported by the text, is that the immediate father has a less-significant influence on the individual's gender identity than does the symbolic Law of the Father. Lacan offers a paradigm in which "both mother and child are themselves already located within the Symbolic Order of language and culture, in which the mother's desire [for what her child will become] is governed by the 'Law of the Father'" (Garner, Kahane, and Sprengnether 21). In other words, Rabbit wants to become the sort of man that his mother wants him to be, but his mother's desire is only the figure of masculinity projected in the language and culture of her patriarchal society: "The Father's law enjoins the subject to line up according to an opposition, man/woman, to assume its place as a 'he' or 'she' in a pre-existing order of language and culture" (Garner, Kahane, and Sprengnether 21). Under the influence of his mother, out of his need to please her, and out of his need to assert his own power, Rabbit rejects Earl and instead follows the model imposed by society.

As commentators on male experience attest, the cultural version of masculinity introduced in the family is systematically reinforced by social institutions, such as schools, athletic organizations, and the military. With the family, such institutions are "the primary context of masculine 'socialization'—in which a boy's emerging sense of himself is directed into socially acceptable behavior" (Tolson 22). In our society, these institutions tend to be "organized around the principle of struggle: they present their members with a regulated structure of status and achievement" (24). Interestingly, social historians note that the late Victorian period saw an intensification of the masculine ideal that included, among other things, a shift away from intellectual and spiritual strength toward "a new stress on physical characteristics" (I read *dominance*) and "on the demonstration of pure willpower"; public schools fostered this image; athletic clubs proliferated; and militarism increased (Weeks 40). Jeffrey Weeks, for one, relates this phenomenon to the rise of imperialism in England, and it is certainly a connection that Updike makes in *Rabbit Redux*, as he focuses on American expansionism. However, what is specifically important here is that by providing Rabbit with an athletic and military background,

Updike indicates that Rabbit is formed according to the culturally approved model of masculinity.

Marty Tothero

Marty Tothero, Rabbit's high school basketball coach, is the surrogate father who represents and teaches the patriarchal version of masculinity to his boys. Tothero deserves close study as a major influence in Rabbit's psychological history. Tothero's legacy is the flawed orientation toward other that precludes union. Tothero, however, is more than a specter from Rabbit's past. Just as the subplot with Ruth can be read as an exploration of why Rabbit's marriage is failing, Tothero can be read as a caricature revealing the kind of man Rabbit is and is becoming. Tothero's fears, pathologies, vices, and inadequacies are Rabbit's as well.

Taylor aptly notes that Updike satirizes this "tot hero," but Rabbit believes Tothero possesses the personal power and social and political influence Earl Angstrom lacks (70). On his way to pick up Nelson, Rabbit remembers that "his old basketball coach, Marty Tothero, who before scandal had ousted him from the high school had a certain grip on local affairs, lived in this building supposedly and still, they said, manipulated. Rabbit dislikes manipulation but he had liked Tothero. Next to his mother Tothero had had the most *force*" (*Run* 21). Updike makes it clear that Tothero speaks for adult society (Brenner 92). Not only does he mouth the conventional platitudes and admonitions, he even slips into the plural when giving advice or stating expectations. When Rabbit initially comes to him for help and promises to think things over in the morning, Tothero responds with: "Good boy. That's all we want" (*Run* 46). Tothero has a "disciplinarian's" manner, using the "trick of holding silent" to command attention (198). And, of course, he speaks to Rabbit patronizingly as to a child, in one instance requiring not only compliance but promptness and courtesy as well. When Rabbit wakens at the Athletic Association, Tothero says: "Now we'll just go down there and don't be too long in the toilet. And I haven't heard any thanks from you for all I've done for you, and all I *am* doing" (52–53).

More important than his manner is Tothero's key thematic position. In *Rabbit, Run*, basketball is a metaphor for a certain kind of aspiration and achievement on which male identity depends. It is also the metaphor for sexual intercourse and by extension for relations with women. Thus, as the teacher of basketball, Tothero teaches masculine self-concept and male perspective on women, that is, essential elements of gender identity. Again, it is Ruth who understands Tothero's function:

> "The coach," [Rabbit] says, "the coach is concerned with developing the three tools we are given in life: the head, the body and the heart."
> "And the crotch," Ruth says. (61)

Tothero's conversation is dominated by the nature of success and the nature of women; on the one hand, Tothero purports to know and to have taught his boys the secret of success, and on the other hand, he reveals pathological attitudes toward women.

It is more difficult to discuss Tothero's idea of a successful man than to discuss his ill-concealed misogyny. For one thing, in the novel, as in society under the strategy of silence, more is implied about masculinity than is ever overtly stated; for another, when the subject is discussed it tends to be euphemized. A good example of this phenomenon becomes evident in Tothero's speech, delivered before Rabbit and the two prostitutes at the Chinese restaurant:

> "Thirdly... the heart. And here the good coach, which I, young lady, certainly tried to be and some say *was*, has his most solemn opportunity. Give the boys the will to achieve. I've always liked that better than the will to win, for there can be achievement even in defeat. Make them feel the, yes, I think the word is good, the *sacredness* of achievement, in the form of giving our best." He dares a pause now, and wins through it, glancing at each of them in turn to freeze their tongues. "A boy who has had his heart enlarged by an inspiring coach," he concludes, "can never become, in the deepest sense, a failure in the greater game of life. And now may the peace of God, et cetera." (62)

Life is a game structured on opposition. Young men are expected to win (to dominate, to control, to assert their will) over opposing forces. They are judged as men, however, not only on their wins or losses but on the quality of their will, which connotes desire, aspiration, drive, devotion, determination, commitment, and willpower. According to Tothero, the strength of the desire is more important than its ultimate goal; it needs to be sufficiently intense that young men will produce their best and greatest effort. Ideally, the "will to achieve" is so intense and requires such commitment of the whole person that it takes on the aspect of spiritual striving, which is why

Tothero refers to the "sacredness of achievement" and closes with a benediction.

Even this rudimentary translation reveals that Tothero's perspective is incompatible with the metaphors of union discussed in the previous chapter. The problems in Rabbit's life, the resolutions he seeks, cannot be won, and union with the other cannot be realized in an oppositional framework. Thus, the patriarchal stance encouraged by Tothero is profoundly, tragically self-defeating. But Updike says more. He says Tothero's ideology is corrupt and, worse, is ultimately corrupting.

Despite his words, winning is indeed the most important aspect of the game to Tothero. As he listens to Rabbit recall an incident on the court, "his mouth is full of food and his hunger for revenge is ugly" (*Run* 63). Later we learn from Ronnie Harrison that Tothero sent enforcers in to strong-arm opponents. And the reputation for scandal and manipulation speaks of a man who circumvents or violates rules to get what he wants.

But why would Tothero (or society) promulgate a philosophy he disbelieves? Why conceal his real attitude? Again, Ruth gives the clue. Immediately following Tothero's speech, she turns to Rabbit and asks, "What do you do?" (62), intuitively observing the "interdependent relationship that exists between society's economy and its culture" (Harrison 23). She uncovers the real intention behind Tothero's teaching, which is not only to mold acceptable models of manhood but to produce good workers. Tothero's coaching prepares boys for life, not for the life of idealists, but for the life of worker-producer-providers in materialist, capitalist America. Newman's book, *John Updike*, which examines the central importance of work in the first three Rabbit novels, supports this interpretation of Tothero's role. And Newman reminds us of Updike's remark, in an interview with Jane Howard, that "my novels are all about the search for useful work. So many people these days have to sell things they don't believe in and have jobs that defy describing" (Newman 33).

Tothero himself, of course, is not economically productive. Only marginally employed, he seems to live off others, borrowing cars and leaving tabs unpaid. Ironically, from this perspective, Tothero's declaration of the "sacredness of achievement" has the false ring of the factory owner who fosters pride of workmanship in his employees and the banker who encourages honesty in the workplace (*Run* 62). Exploitation is at the heart of Tothero's philosophy.

The athletic coach is a male culture bearer who teaches boys to strive and sacrifice, to compete and dominate, preparing them for the larger game of life in which society replaces hoops and championships with other counters. And as Judith Fetterley and many others have observed, in our society, the counters for male dominance are money and women (73). Even though Tothero's "will to achieve" doesn't bring Rabbit money in high school (as, in fact, it might today), it brings him success in the form of self-esteem and "records" and reward for success in his first sexual liaison with Mary Ann. Rabbit remembers that "he came to her as a winner and that's the feeling he's missed since. In the same way she was the best of them all *because* she was the one he brought most to.... So that the two kinds of triumphs were united in his mind" (*Run* 184; emphasis added). On the one hand, Rabbit's sense of worth as a man depends on performing successfully in society's terms; on the other hand, women have no value of their own but derive their value from men, either as rewards or as representations of male self-esteem.

It is in the coach's bed that Rabbit remembers his first prostitute ("Sweet woman. *She* was money" [*Run* 48]), and it is Tothero who knows and introduces Rabbit to prostitutes, to Ruth, whose value Rabbit calculates at "a dime a pound" (70). The objectification and exploitation of women is the inherent other half of Tothero's ideology.

The concept of man as worker-producer-provider (money-maker) and of woman objectified as a symbol of success (money) are dual aspects of a system that Rabbit would like to escape. He rebels against his own spiritual and physical exploitation, but because he fails to surrender the "privilege" of exploiting women as symbols and as servants, his bid for emancipation fails. The truth that Updike portrays is that Rabbit is not only exploited but corrupted and, therefore, enslaved by Tothero's version of masculinity.

To understand the interrelation of Tothero's basketball ideology, male aspiration, gender identity, work, money, and women, it is helpful to return to the proximate source of confusion, "the penetration of sexuality by money" in the nineteenth century (Harrison 22). Remember Woodcock's observation that different versions of masculinity evolve in response to historical pressures (10). The exaggerated conception of man as worker-producer-provider, which prevails even today, is traceable to economic, social, political, and religious pressures of the Victorian era. Briefly stated, those circumstances include the need for more aggressive participation in the economy by the average man, the new availability of wealth to the middle class, and the need for a rigidly monogamous form of marriage to control the dispersal of private property. While marriage became an important economic phenomenon (both as a reward for and a conveyance of economic gains), it also, in response to a decline in faith, came to be idealized as the repository of cultural values (Weeks 24–25). Marriage "was preserved as the ideal way of life to which both sexes aspired— the summit of male ambition, and the target of female expectation" (Harrison 5). However, in order to enter this state, young men had to demonstrate their "worth": "'Manhood' indeed became synonymous with being able to maintain one's family, an important element in virility" (Weeks 68). Marriage, and of course the woman involved, was conceived as "a prize for those who had demonstrated their material eligibility" (Harrison 24). Put in the crassest terms, men were judged worthy or unworthy, manly or not, according to how much money they had or were able to produce, and women were objectified both as the prize awarded to men for succeeding in those terms and as the emblem of their success. Under conditions where access to wealth no longer depended exclusively on inheritance, the qualities consistent with producing money were valued in men. Those qualities include, to return to Tothero's speech, "the will to achieve" in all of its variant forms: ambition, competitiveness, drive, self-sacrifice, determination, and so on into the twentieth century.

Similarly, a young man's "perception of women and their sexuality was unavoidably influenced, if not completely determined by his estimation of their material value" (Harrison 12). But a woman was valuable as she represented the money she brought to the marriage, not as a provider. In fact, as manhood became synonymous with being a provider, "many working-class women retreated into the home," a move that increased the growing division of male and female roles (Weeks 68). Women came to represent money itself, either the money they brought to the marriage or the money men had to produce to win them. This symbolic role continued, following the marriage; a wife represented her husband's money (now his self-esteem) in many aspects of life-style.

According to Thorstein Veblen's leisure-class theory, when wealth and property are thought to confer honor, leisure acquires new significance, becoming the symbol of "triumphant accumulation" (Harrison 32). In middle-class households, where the husband was obligated to be an industrious provider, the "responsibility for vicarious leisure and conspicuous consumption devolves on the wife" (Harrison 33). To summarize, according to Fraser Harrison:

> The penetration of sexuality by money was the factor which determined the character of relationships between middle class men and women. The sexual appeal of women had become indistinguishably

associated with their material worth and, similarly, male virility was inseparably identified with monetary power. It is by this basic scale of bourgeois values that mid-Victorian marriage must be assessed, if it is to be understood. (22)

This Victorian legacy has been evolving, destructively, in our society for a hundred years, and its influence is naturally reflected in literature. It is, for example, enlightening to consider Updike's perspective in *Rabbit, Run* as a development of Fitzgerald's insight into the nature of success in *The Great Gatsby* (1925), with Marty Tothero playing Meyer Wolfsheim to Rabbit's Gatsby. However, one must bear in mind that, as Skeeter demonstrates in *Rabbit Redux*, the success envisioned in the American Dream refers to white male success. The similarities between Wolfsheim and Tothero and the identification of women with money are striking enough to invite the comparison, but it is the differences between the novels that illuminate Updike's interests.

Wolfsheim is another cultural representative who is said to have "made" the protagonist (Fitzgerald 172). He is physically and morally similar to Tothero. Nick Carraway's description of Wolfsheim is revealing: "A small, flat nosed Jew raised his large head and regarded me with two fine growths of hair which luxuriated in either nostril. After a moment I discovered his tiny eyes in half darkness" (Fitzgerald 69–70). Similarly, Marty Tothero "looks like a big tired dwarf. He seems tremendously foreshortened; a balding big head and a massively checkered sports coat and then stubby legs" (*Run* 44). These characters share an unpleasant barbaric quality. They eat ferociously. Tothero speaks of his wife as having skin like lizard hides clumsily sewn together, and Wolfsheim wears cuff links made of human molars. And although Wolfsheim isn't a coach, he is distinguished for having fixed the 1919 World Series, betraying the "faith of fifty million people" (Fitzgerald 74).

Wolfsheim and Tothero are both instrumental in harnessing and misdirecting the protagonist's youthful idealism. They take what the novelists suggest is authentic human longing and turn it toward the goal of winning, concretely expressed as making money—Wolfsheim by introducing Gatsby to racketeering, and Tothero by cultivating the qualities of a winner and worker.

The book that Gatsby kept as a boy, containing his schedule of wholesome activities and "general resolves" for self-improvement (Fitzgerald 174), reflects an innocence and commitment similar to that which the Angstroms describe of their son (*Run* 152). As a young man,

Gatsby is judged "unworthy" of Daisy Buchanan and subsequently devotes his life to proving his worth by amassing a fortune. Although Meyer Wolfsheim's role is small, he is the one who on a practical and concrete level directs Gatsby's energy and facilitates his obsession with making money. In Wolfsheim's underworld, one need not be a worker, only a producer, and winning, even illegally, is acceptable. Gatsby mistakes Daisy, but Meyer Wolfsheim represents an aspect of society that exploits youthful aspiration, and then, like Tothero, evades responsibility when the inevitable tragedy occurs. Never Gatsby's equal as a romantic hero, Rabbit is a private, rather than an officer, in the army when he is thrown over by Mary Ann. Nevertheless, the implicit judgment of unworthiness "launched" him into a career that his father describes as "chasing ass" (*Run* 184, 152). Gatsby is saved from disillusionment by death; Rabbit becomes a serial quester after self-esteem embodied in women.

Rabbit's case is more complicated, not only because *The Great Gatsby* is a more starkly symbolic novel but also because in the intervening years the corruption of the dream had continued to unfold. Updike's vision is intellectually more refined. First, what he sees in 1960 is that the corruption of getting money need not involve gangsterism. In a materialistic society, the daily work of the average man may compromise idealism. For example, part of what appalls Rabbit in his father is the extent to which Earl's work has sapped his spirit. And second, where Fitzgerald allows Gatsby to remain untainted by the corruption of his money and his method of achieving it, Updike acknowledges that a loss of innocence is inevitable. When Rabbit leaves the symbolic work of gardening to make his living as a used car salesman, he says the work is "easy enough, if it isn't any work for you to lie" (*Run* 217). At least since Arthur Miller's *Death of a Salesman* (1949), the salesman has embodied the spiritually and morally enervating effects of materialism.

Another similarity, which contains elements of the Victorian legacy, is evident in *Gatsby* and *Rabbit, Run*: the women in *Rabbit, Run* are forced into the same symbolic roles as Daisy Buchanan. Daisy is Gatsby's "grail"—the representation of his own dreams and illusions and the prize he must win to regain his self-esteem. Furthermore, "Daisy does not simply represent or incarnate that magical world Gatsby desires; she is herself the ultimate object in it. It is she for whom men compete, and possessing her is the clearest sign that one has made it into that world" (Fetterley 75). While Gatsby is idealizing Daisy, Fitzgerald wants us to see, through Nick Carraway, that the "real" Daisy is careless and destructive; she is the dream turned nightmare. Either way, Daisy has no existence outside of the Gatsby/Carraway conceptions of her (Fetterley 98). Fitzgerald's women are nonpersons, objects and images of male desire, or conversely, negatively, objects and images of male fear and hatred.

The women in *Rabbit, Run* receive, perhaps, worse treatment from the protagonist but better from the author and narrator. Gatsby says Daisy's "voice is full of money" (Fitzgerald 120), but Rabbit says his Texas prostitute "was money" (*Run* 48). Ruth, as noted, is priced by the pound, while dominance over Lucy Eccles feels to Rabbit like "an inherited lien on a distant piece of land" (222). Despite his contempt for the materialistic Springers, Rabbit chose a wife whose money, subsequent novels confirm, is important to him.

Fetterley observes that in *The Great Gatsby* the "male mind" is represented by Gatsby on the one hand and Carraway/Fitzgerald on the other; the protagonist reflects positive male projections onto women, while the narrator registers the hostility attendant upon finding women unequal to those expectations. Fetterley identifies this pattern as one of "investment/divestment" (79). In Updike's more honest version, however, the "male mind" is reintegrated, and the unhealthy patterns, the swings from positive to negative projections, are revealed in the same minds. Tothero, for example, vacillates between regarding his friend Margaret as "cunt" and "lady love," "princess" and "tramp." His praise for Margaret turns almost instantly into revulsion. Tothero tells Rabbit, "She is a remarkable girl, Harry, with seven strikes against her from birth, but she's done a remarkable thing. . . . It makes me happy, happy and humble, to have, as I do, this very tenuous association with her" (*Run* 54). Yet a moment later, Tothero says with disgust, "Do you realize, Harry, that a young woman has hair on every part of her body? . . . They are monkeys, Harry. Women are monkeys" (*Run* 54).

It is an important part of Updike's strategy to show that Rabbit shares his mentor's ambivalence and vacillation. In his first sexual encounter with Ruth, Rabbit transforms Ruth into a virginal bride and afterward observes that "there is something in women that repels him" (84). And Ruth has known enough men to be frightened that only a hair's breadth separates Rabbit's physical affection from violence. But perhaps the most telling similarity between Rabbit and Tothero is that each goes home one day, imposes the image of death on his wife, and abandons her. Tothero says: "It began with her skin. One day in the spring, in nineteen forty-three or four, it was during the war, without warning it was hideous. It was like the hides of a thousand lizards stitched together. Stitched together *clumsily*. Can you picture that?

That sense of it being *in pieces* horrified me, Harry" (54–55). Similarly, Rabbit returns home to Janice and makes a parallel discovery: "Just yesterday, it seems to him, she stopped being pretty. With the addition of two short wrinkles at the corners, her mouth has become greedy; and her hair has thinned, so he keeps thinking of her skull under it. These tiny advances into age have occurred imperceptibly, so it seems just possible that tomorrow they'll be gone and she'll be his girl again" (13).

Updike, then, reintegrates the "male mind," exposing its dualism. Furthermore, unlike Fitzgerald, who limits Daisy exclusively to the Gatsby/Carraway conception, Updike and his camera-eye narrator allow us to see the women as they are when Rabbit has left the scene or is sleeping and to gain a sense of their interior life and suffering. Focusing on the women, even briefly, as they exist apart from Rabbit's mind, reveals both his fallibility and the fact that the women are victimized by the projections he uses to justify his behavior.

Despite similarities between *The Great Gatsby* and *Rabbit, Run*, the novels are fundamentally different. The Tothero theme in *Rabbit, Run* is only part of a larger vision, and even within the limits of this comparison, the perspectives differ. Fitzgerald is concerned with the failure of the American Dream; Updike is as interested in the failure of the dreamer and the nature of the dreaming. Fitzgerald uses projection, seemingly unconsciously, as male authors have traditionally done, while Updike seems to deliberately explore the phenomenon. And unlike Fitzgerald, Updike observes the influence of economics, as well as other factors, on masculine self-concept and attitudes toward women.

With Tothero, Updike shows that the dominant model of masculinity in our culture, which the "tot hero" represents, is both monstrous and bankrupt. He provides a number of clues. Tothero lives in the filthy attic of the Sunshine Athletic Association, where a conglomeration of comic books, old *National Geographics*, tournament charts, and softball uniforms suggests both decay and arrested development. Also, Tothero is marginally employed to maintain this club for old men who smell to Rabbit like a "depressing kind of sin" (*Run* 21). The garden outside is overgrown, indicating a condition of spiritual ruin. Lacking the courage to face the problem of his own death, Tothero, like Rabbit, has essentially deserted his wife. He has no loyalty. He has no commitment to the "mature" behavior he recommends to Rabbit; he has no principles, seeking only the gratification of insatiable and desperate appetites. He tells Rabbit, "You can't understand an old man's hunger, you eat and eat and it's never the right food" (*Run*

50).[4] Tothero has no children, no future. His most intimate relationships are abusive and degrading. Despite his gospel of achievement, he has accomplished nothing, and in this, he is like Eccles who preaches faith but cannot believe. Even Rabbit sees that he is in "sad shape" (67).

As the novel progresses, Tothero grows increasingly repulsive physically (44, 67, 92, 258). At the hospital, he assumes the external symptoms of spiritual enervation, becoming paralyzed and inarticulate. He is ironically reduced to complete dependence on the wife he sought to escape. In his final appearance after Becky's death, Tothero is a caricature, a "smirking gnome" who, in a novel where balance is critical, is so lopsided he needs a cane to remain upright. He lies, denying his part in the Angstroms' tragedy and evading his responsibility. And he finally denies the existence of God, telling Rabbit that, "right and wrong aren't dropped from the sky. We. We make them" (257). Unlike the mysterious Horace, Tothero, the dominant model of masculinity, has absolutely nothing to offer Rabbit as he faces the ultimate problems of life, and the final interview leaves Rabbit feeling "depressed and dirtied" (258).

But Updike's most chilling observation is that as young men adopt this model, they themselves become corrupt. Not only Tothero but all of the men at the Athletic Association are hideous. In the passage cited earlier, Rabbit observes, "Their alert colorless eyes, little dark smears like their mouths, feed on the strange sight of him and send acid impressions down to be digested in their disgusting big beer-tough stomachs" (53). Updike, in fact, details Rabbit's progress toward becoming like Tothero. Tothero observes that "you and I are two of a kind" (50), and although he tells Rabbit, "I don't believe that my greatest boy would grow into such a monster," the word *monster* "clatters after them as they climb the stairs" (46). Rabbit gets into "the old man's hollow" (47) and wears his perfectly fitting shirt (later he wears Fred Springer's shirt). He wears Tothero's attitudes toward women, his habit of projection, and his vacillation between love and hate. He too becomes an accomplished manipulator.

Rabbit may even have some intuition of what is happening. At the hospital, he fears that his unborn child will be a monster. Significantly, he associates this possibility with both the quintessential male act of impregnation and his most stereotypically masculine behavior—the exploitation of Ruth to restore his threatened self-esteem. "His idea grows, that it will be a monster, a monster of his making. The thrust whereby it was conceived becomes confused in his mind with the perverted entry he forced, a few hours ago, into Ruth" (183). However, Rebecca is born, not a monster, but what in Rabbit's framework may be the alternative—an exquisitely feminine little victim. Interestingly, many years later, in *Rabbit Is Rich*, Rabbit's son, Nelson, who inherits his father's conflicted masculinity, also fears that his child will be born a monster, "a pink-eyed baby rhinoceros" (337).

Marty Tothero, teacher, coach, and surrogate father, acts on behalf of society to intensify, refine, and direct the dominant version of masculinity introduced in the family. At the same time, he embodies the corruption and weakness of the ideology behind that version and illustrates in his own life what Rabbit is becoming and why his relationships fail. In fact, with all three characters—Mary, Earl, and Marty—Updike not only provides a coherent psychological history but, more importantly, clarifies the forces and tensions at work in Rabbit's present situation. To repeat, in *Rabbit, Run*, the essential human condition is one of self-conscious dualism that manifests itself in many areas of Rabbit's life and generates such intense anxiety that it demands resolution. The novelist offers two paths of resolution; the first, conveyed through the metaphorical structure, depends on some measure of surrender to open the way for reconciliation through union or transcendence. However, Rabbit's difficult, incomplete separation from Mary Angstrom leaves him fearful of self-compromise. He not only dreads sinking back into an undifferentiated state but aggressively strives to enhance the self through control of the other.

So Rabbit is psychologically prepared for the second path, which is favored by his culture for individual males and male groups. Tothero teaches this path; it involves temporarily reducing the anxiety of dualism through conquest and the establishment of a hierarchy of power, of winners and losers, superiors and inferiors. Male theorists speak of the prison of hierarchy. For example, Emmanuel Reynaud's *Holy Virility: The Social Construction of Masculinity* seems to describe Rabbit's situation, including his attitude of watchful wariness and his dry-tinder reactions to perceived threats from the women and from Ronnie Harrison. Reynaud says:

> Relations between men center around the struggle for power; whether individually or in a group, they are permanent rivals in the appropriation of women, wealth and glory. Friendship itself, so often proclaimed a typically masculine sentiment, is more a pact of non-aggression, a brief respite from the fight, than a genuine

> pleasure in being together: it is no more than a delicate balance between competition and being on the watch. The slightest incident is enough to tip the scales. At the tiniest hope of victory, the fragile truce is, as often as not, cheerfully broken.
>   It does not generally occur to man that he can establish non-competitive relationships; he needs constantly to measure himself and place himself on a hierarchical ladder. Hierarchy is not only his principle of organization within patriarchy, but simultaneously the means and the end of his struggle for power—it is the framework for his relations and the ground on which he fulfills himself. And so he gets involved in endless conflicts in order to climb the rung, which he experiences on an individual level by a great variety of blows and knocks, and socially by total shambles—war, crisis, famine, pollution, plunder, murder, robbery. And yet, in spite of the damage caused by these battles, he still considers hierarchy necessary. (98)

Instability and anxiety are built into this hierarchical system as part of its self-sustaining syndrome (Reynaud 98–101). Conquest temporarily reassures and strengthens the self in relation to others, and the male privileges gained by moving up the ladder are great inducements to participation. On the other hand, one is forced to accept the self-negating domination of those higher up on the ladder, and of course, as contests are perpetual, one's own position is always precarious. Reynaud observes that "man . . . flounders between submission and domination. At no point is he in control of his own life; he manages only to accumulate more or less power over the lives of others" (100–101). External threats are disturbing enough, but there is internal danger as well. Tolson recalls this danger as "a fear of losing control, not of external forces but of personal power and indispensability" (87). No wonder that Rabbit cherishes as one of his happiest adolescent memories a moment of freedom from the pressure of hierarchy, a moment of pleasure and possibility without competitive purpose. He reminds Tothero of his "best night."

> The game isn't a league game so nothing matters much, and I get this funny feeling I can do anything, just drifting . . . I *know* I can do anything. The second half I take maybe just ten shots, and every one goes right in, not just bounces in, but doesn't touch the rim, like I'm dropping stones down a well. And these farmers running up and down getting up a sweat, they didn't have more than two substitutes, but we're not in their league either, so it doesn't matter much to them, and the one ref just leans over against the edge of the stage talking to their coach. Oriole High. Yeah, and then after-

wards their coach comes down to the locker room where both teams are changing and gets a jug of cider out of a locker and we all passed it around. Don't you remember? (*Run* 65)

The maintenance of self under the conditions of hierarchy can be a dangerous, all-consuming business. For Rabbit, certainly, it becomes the central drama of life with people, relationships, nature, and even God viewed and valued primarily as they play a part in the struggle for self-aggrandizement.

Rabbit resents and resists many aspects of the prison of masculine gender identity. He dreads his mother's expectations and disapproval and dislikes being manipulated. He mistrusts older men like Fred Springer and the gas station attendant who pressure him to conform. He resists dehumanizing, exploitive labor with sporadic unemployment, and he flees from narrow, unsatisfying domesticity. There remains, however, the crucial fact that for all that he wants his freedom from those above him on the ladder of force, Rabbit still wants to exercise power over those below; he specifically retains the privilege of controlling women.

Updike knows that freedom is impossible under these conditions, for he cites Sartre on this point in his epigraph to *Of the Farm* (1966): "Consequently, when, in all honesty, I've recognized that man ... is a free being who, in various circumstances, can want only his freedom, I have at the same time recognized that I can want only the freedom of others." Larry Taylor observes that Updike explores the connection between love and accepting the freedom of the beloved in both *The Centaur* (1963) and *Of the Farm* (1965), the novels immediately following *Rabbit, Run*. In the former, George Caldwell makes the sacrifice necessary to free his son Peter, and in the latter, Joey is paradoxically emancipated by allowing his mother the freedom of her own perspective (Taylor 102–11). *Rabbit, Run* is a negative reflection of the same phenomenon. Rabbit's failure to love is confirmed by his unwillingness to allow the freedom, the otherness, of others. Furthermore, his desire to control others prevents him from achieving his own freedom.

This chapter has been concerned with validating the premise that Updike is involved in a serious exploration of masculinity and with establishing that the defensive and destructive attitudes and behaviors that prevent Rabbit from achieving the union and transcendence he desires are rooted in his masculinity. Without diminishing the insights developed here, it is important to acknowledge the plurality of a novel that has generated such disparate interpretations. Even in regard to the theme of masculinity, the text allows for different possibilities. This circumstance is due partially to the fact that male authors exploring masculinity inevitably betray some ambivalence; and it is also due partially to the fact that *Rabbit, Run* is essentially what Louis Althusser calls an interrogative text, which, rather than offering a privileged perspective, invites the reader to answer questions directly or indirectly posed. Catherine Belsey discusses Althusser's observations:

> The world represented in the interrogative text includes what Althusser calls "an internal distance" from the ideology in which it is held, which permits the reader to construct from within the text a critique of this ideology.... In other words, the interrogative text refuses a single point of view, however complex and comprehensive, but brings points of view into unresolved collision or contradiction. It therefore refuses the hierarchy of discourses of classic realism, and no authorial or authoritative discourse points to a single position which is the place of coherence and meaning. (92)

Updike's preference for the interrogative form will be explored later. For now, I only want to acknowledge that the text contains alternative perspectives on masculinity. For example, Updike judges Rabbit's failure harshly; the unhappy young women left for dead on their beds and Rebecca and Nelson abandoned are terrible indictments against him. Yet in assessing the extent of Rabbit's personal responsibility, one encounters the ambivalence of the text and confronts questions regarding the intention and objectivity of a male author who examines masculinity. For although the judgment is harsh, the same psychological history that identifies and clarifies Rabbit's behavior can also be understood as mitigating his guilt—his inability to escape its perspective confirming the extent of his enculturation in a corrupt society. From this viewpoint, Rabbit and his creator can be seen as reflecting the dogged resistance of men and women who, while acknowledging the evils of patriarchy, appeal to arguments of social determinism and innate male weakness to avoid change and perpetuate the status quo.

The novel also allows the alternate possibility that Rabbit does not want to escape the prison of masculinity at all but wants, rather, to perfect it by freeing himself from the powers above while extending his control over those below. The text can be interpreted as indulging the ultimate male fantasy, and from this perspective, rather than constituting a negative assessment of stereotypical masculinity, the family tragedy can be seen as signaling the inevitable awakening from fantasy, reinforcing for the reader, if not for the protagonist, that one must accept not only the privileges of masculinity but the entire patriarchal package, responsibilities and limitations included. According to Northrop Frye, "Self-recognition, or attaining one's original identity, reverses all the Narcissus and twin and doppelganger themes that occur in the descent" (152); the ascent to reality reaffirms the cultural status quo and implicitly rejects the possibilities offered below. Thus, *Rabbit, Run,* which seems to offer a negative evaluation of masculinity, also contains the elements of a conservative text, reaffirming masculinity by accomplishing the triple goals of reinforcing the basic motivation of patriarchy (the desire for power), while at the same time providing a safety valve for subversive impulses, and, finally, justifying a more rigorous reimposition of the status quo.

Again, a similar conservative perspective can be deduced from the novel's form, which follows, in surprising detail, the pattern of descent observed in romances and described by Northrop Frye in *The Secular Scripture* (97–126). The movement of the novel conforms to seasonal changes (Frye 80). The descent is preceded by an incident of boasting. A loss or change of identity is accompanied by a metamorphosis in which the protagonist, Harry, is identified with an animal. Rabbit is provided with a mazelike map and a demonic companion (Tothero) as he descends into a watery dream world, an instinctual world characterized by sexual liberation. In this world, Rabbit combines a quest for God with the hunt and capture of Ruth. The novel includes the ritual sacrifice of an innocent, which precipitates the dreamer's return home. Frye observes that the protagonist often gains valuable knowledge in the lower world and that such stories usually culminate in an ascent involving the restoration of identity and a return to the everyday world.

Such archetypal patterns, once presumed to express a preexisting and universal human nature, are now likely to be reexamined as the repetitions by means of which a culture perpetuates itself.[5] Without becoming involved in the larger discussion of whether or not the romance and the novel are intrinsically masculine forms, it is possible at least to note the obvious—that such stories reinforce a model of male character and behavior, that by indulging male fantasies they simultaneously encourage them and facilitate their repression, and that by their final ascent, they encourage acceptance of the limitations placed on the individual male by society. To the extent that *Rabbit, Run* conforms to the pattern of descent and return, it can be interpreted as a conservative text.

A conflicting impulse, however, is revealed in the tentative nature of the ascent, that is, in the novel's uneasy closure. Rabbit's return to the everyday world does not effect an authentic resolution. The frightened protagonist flees one last time, and as the novel ends, "he runs. Ah: runs. Runs" (*Run* 284). Certainly, the opening of *Rabbit Redux* indicates that his subsequent return does not produce happiness either. Updike's comment in "On One's Own Oeuvre" that the title of *Rabbit, Run* "is a piece of advice, in the imperative mode" (*HTS* 851) reflects his sympathy for Rabbit's flight, based, I believe, on his intuition that this culture generates (or at least exacerbates) dilemmas that its dominant ideologies lack the richness and power to resolve. The multiple, contradictory possibilities of the text, the absence of comfortable closure, and the alternative choices implied in the metaphorical structure confirm that *Rabbit, Run* questions, rather than reinforces, the cultural assumptions upon which it is based.

FOUR

The Power of Naming
"Well That Explains Your Oratorical Gifts"

HAVING ESTABLISHED the source and motivation behind Rabbit's power, the task of examining specific examples of its use remains. This work could be approached by identifying the arenas where male power is typically exercised in our society (e.g., the political, social, economic, physical, sexual) and by exploring Rabbit's behavior in those arenas. Using this method, it would, for example, be easy enough to provide evidence that Rabbit claims an absolute right to determine the conditions of sexual intercourse and that his ability to enforce that claim depends on the implied threat of physical violence, the threat of emotional abandonment, and the threat of social ostracism. It is easy enough also to illustrate the negative effect of his behavior; imposing his claim devastates the women and prevents him from achieving the kind of intimacy he desires. Even Rabbit finds "something sad in the capture" (*Run* 82).

Although this straightforward approach has yielded feminist critics impressive results elsewhere, it tends to obscure several issues of importance here. First, as Woodcock has observed, schematizing masculinity in this manner diverts attention from the fact that it is an evolving phenomenon, adaptability to cultural and personal circumstances being one of its fundamental strengths (9–10). For example, social historians observe that as overt control over women as property (a power that depended heavily on physical dominance) declined, the loss was compensated for by an increased manipulation of cultural symbols during the Victorian period, with the result that women internalized patriarchal expectations. Leslie Fiedler observes that

> the imposition of the Clarissa-image on the young girl represents an insidious form of enslavement; all the idealizations of the female from the earliest days of courtly love had been in fact devices to deprive her of freedom and self determination, but this last represents the final attempt to imprison woman within the myth of Woman. (36)

Historically, the shift in emphasis from physical to psychological dominance created the illusion of progress without significantly effecting change in the real condition of women. Similarly, the genius of patriarchal adaptability allows that strategic concessions be made for the purpose of appeasement, that is, for the purpose of avoiding or postponing significant change. Woodcock acknowledges that when men espouse the "values and goals of feminism,"

> the same arguments, their political function changes quite simply because of the relationship between those arguments, whose aim is to challenge male power, and male power itself. One must inevitably suspect a conscious or unconscious attempt to contain their impact, or somehow subvert or appropriate the cutting edge of feminism by containing it within male-defined limits. (17–18)

The concept of masculinity as an evolving phenomenon is obviously relevant to a series that traces the development of a marriage over three decades. The Angstrom marriage is strained not only by the changing needs of maturing partners but also by the pressure of social trends. If *Rabbit, Run* describes the failure of stereotypical masculinity, then Rabbit's development in subsequent novels must be measured, in part, by his adherence to or departure from that model; but such an evaluation depends upon distinguishing changes in attitudes and behaviors that are merely adaptations and appeasements from changes that evidence real growth. Critic Mary Allen, for example, makes this kind of distinction in analyzing *Rabbit Redux*, where Rabbit faces the challenge of increased feminine freedom. She believes that despite any superficial accommodations, there is little or no development, because at the end of the novel, as Rabbit stands signaling to Janice from the motel lobby window, he thinks just what he has always thought: "God she's dumb" (*Redux* 401). Allen says, "The strength of *Rabbit Redux* is the natural way it links with the Angstroms of ten years earlier, not by illustrating sweeping developments of character but by showing how people continue in their habits" (89).

So, the first problem with schematization (providing a simple, single, definable model of masculinity [Woodcock 9]) is that it implies a clarity and inflexibility that does not exist, while obscuring the fluid adaptability that is essential to patriarchal resistance. The second problem is that schematization supports the illusion of detachment and impersonality. While ideology is not a "deliberate set of distortions" purveyed to the public by "groups of sinister men in shirt sleeves" (Belsey 58), nevertheless, the cultural phenomenon of male domination is inevitably established within the context of personal relations, in the daily lives of people like Rabbit, Janice, and Ruth. *Rabbit, Run* inverts the emphasis of the radical feminist slogan, "The personal is political," by illustrating that the political is intensely, painfully personal. It is Updike's substantial contribution to reveal just how intimate is the level on which male dominance is established.

For example, what Ruth and Janice want more than anything else is to be known and accepted. Janice thinks that "what made her panicky ever since she was little [was] this thing of nobody knowing how you felt and whether nobody could know or nobody cared" (*Run* 232). And what touches Ruth about Rabbit is that "you were *there* for him instead of being something pasted on the inside of their dirty heads" (136). Of course, the desire to be known and loved is universal, but the women's need is exaggerated because they have been made to feel unwelcome and unacceptable. Janice's mother is clearly hypercritical, and both Janice and Ruth have lacked their fathers' affirmation and support, a significant factor in a series that raises the Agamemnon theme of the destruction of female children due to paternal carelessness. Fred Springer says of Janice, "Her mother and I somehow never made her feel secure, never perhaps you might say made her welcome" (252). Similarly Ruth, who has "pretty poor parents," reveals her sad jealousy of confident girls, "snips" with the right sort of fathers (137). Both women have internalized parental rejection as self-loathing, and they come to adult life vulnerable and desperate. Janice comes to marriage, believing it to be a "refuge" (233), and Ruth becomes a prostitute because men "were a kind of wall she kept battering against because she knew there was something there" (136).

Rabbit, like Updike's later suburban Don Juans, knows how to take advantage of vulnerability. Janice and Ruth, and even Lucy Eccles, are less susceptible to Rabbit's charm and sexuality than to his unusual sensitivity to women. He observes women closely, testing the waters, gauging and interpreting their reactions and estimating his chances. In addition, Rabbit has surprisingly accurate intuitive knowledge as well. When he undresses Ruth, washes off her makeup, and prevents her from using a diaphragm, he demands complete vulnerability. Although sexually experienced, Ruth allows this violation because Rabbit seems to offer her what she cannot resist: the possibility of being utterly known and accepted, of becoming "transparent," or as Ruth herself says, "to feel like next to nothing with a man" (*Run* 138). Rabbit's understanding of women, however, is finally divorced from love because it is knowledge gained and used for manipulation.

To illustrate, on their first night together, Rabbit discovers Ruth's sensitivity about her weight.[1] He plays on it, first making her feel self-conscious and awkward and then reassuring her that her size appeals to him. On their last night together, he belittles Ruth for having been a prostitute in order to pressure her into performing fellatio. Updike also reveals the appalling cruelty involved in Rabbit's achieving dominance over his wife. Because he needs to feel superior to Janice, he cultivates her inadequacy by reminding her "every hour on the hour" of how dumb she is (*Redux* 75). Certainly, the most dramatic and destructive example of this manipulative behavior occurs when he comes home from church "clever and cold with lust" and coaxes his alcoholic wife to drink in order to loosen her up (*Run* 224).

Although Updike claims Rabbit's sexual life over thirty years is "almost chaste," the questing aspect of Rabbit's seduction of Ruth, along with his accomplished manipulation, place him in the Don Juan tradition (Trueheart F4). Don Juan's seductions are sometimes understood as transactions between men, that is between Don Juan and God, Don Juan and Satan, or even Don Juan and the cuckold. Kathleen Verduin, for example, shares Denis de Rougemont's perspective on Don Juan when she observes of one of Rabbit's progeny that "one indeed wonders if for Piet Hanema in *Couples*, death fearing and sensitive as he is to the decline of faith in modern culture, his compulsive adulteries are not a secret means to call God out of hiding" (260).

Whether such seductions are purely self-aggrandizing or whether they involve complicated transactions with other men, the victims of Don Juan's seductions are equally dehumanized. They are reduced to names on a list, and the longer the list, the less important the women become. Updike, however, is unusual in that he refuses to devalue any of Rabbit's partners. While by no means adequately describing the perspective of women, *Rabbit, Run* at least describes what Don Juan does *to* women before he can think, like Rabbit, "he has her" (*Run* 89).[2]

The use of intimate, secret, privileged knowledge to manipulate another was once considered the consummate evil in American literature. It was, however, also an evil confined to men, perhaps because an unconscious censorship discouraged openly expressing the notion that a man in the position of Chillingworth (*The Scarlet Letter*) or Holgrave (*The House of the Seven Gables*) might use his advantage to destroy women. Hawthorne is less circumspect in "The Birthmark," but it was Henry James who eventually openly raised the disturbing possibility that such manipulation might be a staple of the relations between men and women (Fetterley 22–23, 101–53). To return to a point of departure, schematizing masculinity creates the impression of detachment, of impersonal, even morally neutral, forces at work, whereas Updike as a novelist is intensely interested in the personal. Again, it is Updike's substantial contribution that he reveals how and on how intimate a level male dominance is established.

Finally, and most important for this discussion, schematization obscures a tyranny of the imagination, the real base of male power, that precedes its other manifestations. Patriarchy has imposed its perspective as the real or universal perspective by exercising control over the vehicles of thought and expression, "the system of representations (discourses, images, myths)" in our culture (Belsey 57). As mentioned earlier, critics have noted Updike's interest in the "politics of the imagination" elsewhere; Judie Newman, for example, says that Updike's *The Coup* (1978) is "a highly self-conscious deliberation upon the parallel activities of fiction-making and political exploitation" and that *The Witches of Eastwick* (1984) insists upon "the necessity of a harmonious relation between the imagination and the outer world" (116, 144). Reluctance to examine family life as a political arena has, however, prevented critics from identifying similar concerns in *Rabbit, Run*. The remainder of this chapter will be devoted to demonstrating that in *Rabbit, Run*, male power is primarily exercised through the control of perspective, specifically through the control of language. Rabbit not only taps into the power of the general perspective of the culture, his legacy by virtue of his gender, he also claims the prerogative of imposing and enforcing his individual perspective. To appreciate the enormity of such power requires at least a brief glimpse at developments in the field of linguistics.

Because of the inseparability of thought and sound, language seems to us transparent and neutral. But these qualities, and the many assumptions that have followed from them, are coming under increasing scrutiny (see Belsey 37–65). Linguistic theorist Ferdinand de Saussure demonstrates that language is not merely nomenclature but, far more important, a system of differentiations in which individual words "function not through their intrinsic value but through their relative positions" in a network (Saussure 118). Even though individual words may be arbitrary, the system of differentiation of which they are a part is not. That system of differentiation is suffused with the ideology of the culture that produces and uses it (Belsey 37–42). Furthermore, ideology is inscribed in *"the signifying practices*—in discourses, myths, presentations and representations of the way 'things' 'are'" (Belsey 62).

Combine this insight (that language and other signifying systems are inscribed with ideology) with the insights of Jacques Lacan, discussed earlier, who theorizes that individual subjectivity or consciousness of self is constructed through the acquisition of language. The child who learns language learns "to recognize itself in a series of subject positions from which discourse is intelligible" (Belsey 60), and only by assuming a place, or position, can the child enter and participate in the primary signifying system of culture. Also, language acquisition reinforces a distinction learned during an earlier stage of the child's development (between the perceived *I* and the perceiving *I*) by introducing the split between "the *I* of discourse . . . and the *I* who speaks" (Belsey 64). As a result,

> there is a contradiction between the conscious self, the self which appears in its own discourse, and the self which is only partly represented there, the self which speaks. The unconscious comes into being in the gap which is formed by this division. . . . The repository of repressed and pre-linguistic signifiers, the unconscious is a constant source of potential disruption of the symbolic order. (Belsey 64–65)

Lacanians say subjectivity and the unconscious are constructed through the acquisition of language, while Saussureans maintain that the terms of the discourse through which they are constructed are inscribed with ideology. If the dominant ideology, patriarchy, is inscribed into language, then it is inscribed into each subjectivity formed through the acquisition of language and to a great extent allows and disallows what the individual, and collectively the culture, perceives, thinks, feels, imagines, makes, and so on. Language theorists, feminists, critics, and others continue to explore the ramifications of this paradigm shift away from the notion that signifying systems reflect preexisting realities or that individual consciousness is the origin of meaning or knowledge. They express their insights in a variety of ways. Andrea Dworkin says that "the power of naming enables men to define experience, to articulate boundaries and values, to designate to each thing its realm and qualities, and to determine what can and cannot be expressed, to control perception itself" (*Pornography* 17). Mary Daly observes, "Women have had the power of *naming* stolen.... We have not been free to use our own power to name ourselves, the world, or God" (8). In Rabbit's world, Janice Angstrom, who reflects the profoundly debilitating effect of this loss in many ways, says, for example, "Makes you feel filthy *they* don't even have decent names for parts of you" (*Run* 231; emphasis added).

Written language has nearly as profound a formative influence (Belsey 66). In recent years, feminist critics have focused attention on the relative exclusion of women from the discourse of literature (see Gilbert and Gubar, *The Madwoman in the Attic*). Their exclusion has had at least two important effects. On the one hand, as writers, women have been unable to articulate, develop, and disseminate alternative visions of the world: "Lacking a pen/penis which would enable them ... to refute one fiction by another, women in patriarchal societies have historically been reduced to *mere* property, to characters and images in male texts because generated solely ... by male expectations and designs" (Gilbert and Gubar 12). And on the other hand, as readers, they have been subject to the coercive force of male texts. As Fetterley observes, "To be excluded from a literature that claims to define one's identity is to experience a peculiar form of powerlessness which ... results from the endless division of the self against self, the consequence of the invocation to identify as male while being reminded that to be male—to be universal, to be American—is to be not female" (xiii). Women readers, according to Fetterley, have participated in literature through a kind of self-negation, by identifying, if not always with male protagonists, still with male perceptions, values, and interests.

Scholars are now beginning to comprehend the extent of the formative, limiting, self-perpetuating power of patriarchal ideology as inscribed in language, and they are also beginning to understand the extent and effect of male control over signifying practices. One of the most interesting features of *Rabbit, Run* is that the novel incorporates the patriarchal tradition of language control as a structural element. Not only is the novel the work of a male author focusing on a male character, but men speak almost all of the words, and the words they speak convey male culture and perspective. Events are seen through a masculine perspective. While the male characters strive to define, project, induce, and enforce their version of reality by manipulating a repertoire of linguistic skills, the young women are mostly silent, repressed, as it were, into narrated interior monologues. Rabbit admits that he has no idea of what his wife thinks or why she behaves the way she does. In truth, he doesn't want to know because he can maintain his version of reality only at the expense of hers.

Language and Structure

The issue of who controls perspective and how and why remains crucial throughout the Rabbit series, but *Rabbit, Run* manifests this concern in a hierarchy (or perhaps a spectrum) of language users. Among the characters, Rabbit himself, whose perspective dominates the novel, is at the top of the ladder of verbal force. At the opposite extreme is the inarticulate, and finally, silent infant Rebecca June Angstrom, who represents repressed feminine perspective. Other characters are spread across this range; the verbal power of each of character is noted. Gender is the primary determinant. Not only is the protagonist male, so that the reader identifies with a masculine viewpoint, but the novel seems, at least at first glance, to focus only on masculine interests. Critics have noted that male characters speak almost all of the words in *Rabbit, Run*. And male characters seem to have cornered the verbal market in other ways—Earl sets type for the printed word, Rabbit and Fred use their verbal expertise in business, and the ministers sermonize.

Gender is not the sole determinant of verbal status, however. Other categories of difference affect a character's position. To illustrate, two characters are excluded from adult male power because of age or illness; they are two-year-old Nelson and stroke victim Marty Tothero, both of whom are characterized by speech difficulties. Tothero, the surrogate father who formerly enjoyed considerable influence and verbal force, declines in the course of the novel (*Run* 44, 21) to the point that, when Rabbit visits him in the hospital, the coach can only drag out a few vowels (198), and in their final meeting, Tothero has some difficulty vocalizing his self-serving lies. Nelson is portrayed as lacking the verbal resources to articulate his suffering, and the boy is reduced to tears and gestures. Individual differences also affect verbal status. Mary Angstrom is a formidable figure by any standard; and her personal strength is reflected, as Eccles notes, in her unusual verbal capacities.

Before reviewing the other characters, it will be useful to consider the positions of the author and narrator, especially since later discussion links Updike's interest in the problem of linguistic power with his personal experience as recorded in *Self-Consciousness*. The male author has traditionally been conceived of as a godlike creator who "fathers" a text. His imagination conceives, and his linguistic expertise represents, the world of the novel (Gilbert and Gubar 4). He not only controls the characters and events but also manipulates the perceptions of the reader. For this reason, Joan Didion describes writing as aggression, "an imposition . . . an invasion of someone else's most private space" (Braudy 109). Updike, however, wishes to represent the world as unmediated by his personality and judgments. Whether or not such a goal is achievable, Updike is in the position as author, of wanting to both maximize and negate his verbal power. In *Rabbit, Run*, he succeeds in at least creating the illusion of transparency.

Beneath, and distinct from the author, is an omniscient, omnipresent narrator that Updike himself likens to a cameraman or camera lens (*HTS* 850). This narrator represents Rabbit's thoughts, feelings, and speech, as well as the events that occur, in the third person and in the present tense. This type of discourse, even when presented from the character's point of view, generally contains two discernible voices—the narrator's and the character's. However, in *Rabbit, Run*, because the narration so fully assumes the distinctive qualities of Rabbit's mind and speech, the narration seems to be a speakerless "representation of one subjectivity or self" (see Prince's definition of "free indirect discourse"). The narrator has no obtrusive personality and, like the author, enjoys the illusion of transparency. Only when the narrator shifts to a different point of view (say to Ruth's or Janice's) is the reader momentarily cognizant of his existence. Updike shifts viewpoint, in order, indirectly, to undermine Rabbit's relentless control over perspective. Paradoxically, the author's will (his intention and verbal authority) and the narrator's mediating function are manifested only in these attempts to limit Rabbit's linguistic power.

Among the characters, Rabbit possesses the greatest verbal force. His perspective dominates the novel not only because the reader identifies with him and experiences events from his point of view but because he imposes his reality on other characters and forces them to conform. Rabbit has rejected his father's typesetting trade but, like the other male characters, still makes his living by manipulating language. He is a pitchman for the MagiPeel Kitchen Peeler, a job that Eccles says accounts for his considerable "oratorical gifts" (*Run* 102). When he returns home from work at the beginning of the novel and finds Janice watching *The Mickey Mouse Show*, Rabbit scrutinizes the host Jerry's verbal technique to pick up useful tips. Later, Rabbit claims to Janice to have had a professional interest in the show.

> Rabbit watches him [Jerry] attentively; he respects him. He expects to learn something from him helpful in his own line of work, which is demonstrating a kitchen gadget in several five-and-dime stores around Brewer.... That was good. Rabbit tries it, pinching the mouth together and then the wink, getting the audience out front with you against some enemy behind, Walt Disney or the MagiPeel Peeler Company, admitting it's all a fraud but, what the hell, making it likable. We're all in this together. Fraud makes the world go round. The base of our economy. (*Run* 14–15)

Rabbit tries in this novel to find something to support an alternative worldview to counter materialism. Without such a vision, his language, reflecting his values, becomes increasingly pragmatic and manipulative. In the end, even Rabbit is unnerved by the prospect of lying for a living at Fred Springer's used car lot. Economic exploitation is only one facet of Rabbit's language use, however. The opening apartment scene further reveals that Rabbit uses language in an aggressive, manipulative manner to control his wife.

Here again, the problem of the transparency of language arises. This use of language against women is so commonplace in our lives and literature as to be invisible. Freud himself admitted to exactly the same treatment of his own wife when he said, "I have been trying to smash her frankness so that she should reserve opinion until she is sure of mine" (qtd. in Jones 110). The almost universal dislike and blame of Janice among critics of both sexes demonstrates the general privileging of masculine perspective, even in the face of contradictory information.

As Joyce Markle accurately observes, the exchanges between Rabbit and Janice in the apartment reveal that he is "the appropriate husband to the setting" (55). His superiority, verbally constructed and defended (and openly challenged in later novels), is spurious at best. Rabbit smolders over Janic's inadequacy and lethargy. In fact, Janice also longs for renewal. He wants to quit smoking and reclaim his youthful, athletic body. Similarly, pregnant Janice has bought a bathing suit in anticipation of being slender again. She says, "It made it feel closer to when I could fit into it" (*Run* 16). Although Rabbit himself despises Janice's pregnancy, thinking it makes her lumpy and clumsy, he is so threatened by even this hint of rejection, that her explanation sparks a violent, repressive verbal attack: "What the hell ails you? Other women *like* being pregnant. What's so damn fancy about you? Just tell me. What *is* so frigging fancy?" (16).

Moments later, Rabbit is irritated again and thinks that Janice is dumb because she fails to get his joke: "You're supposed to look tired. You're a modern housewife" (17). According to Rabbit's view, Janice's intelligence depends on her ability to appreciate and approve of what he says, despite the fact that his humor denigrates her. The penalty for not getting his joke is to be labeled stupid and punished with more verbal abuse (Allen 83). Next, Rabbit demeans Janice for watching the Mouseketeers; but when she notes his interest, his "indignation rises" at her failure to appreciate his motives, and he punishes her by mouthing a verbal cliché, which encodes male violence and rejection as the penalty for disagreement: "Screw you. Just screw you" (*Run* 17).

The actual level of Janice's intelligence is less important than the fact that it is, once again, Rabbit's perspective, his reality, that determines what Janice is or may be. Her slightest deviation from that standard provokes him into language designed to silence her or make her conform. Rabbit later admits that he has no idea what his wife thinks or why she acts the way she does. The truth of the matter is that he doesn't want to know and that much of his behavior toward Janice is based on a need to maintain his perspective at the expense of hers.

Rabbit's perspective and verbal skills are pitted against those of the Episcopalian minister, Jack Eccles, who is sent by the Springers to bring Rabbit back in tow. Eccles not only lives by "selling his message," but he is also a "listener by trade," whose mouth seems to Rabbit like a "flirtatious cave" (*Run* 158, 102, 118). Eccles's pursuit of Rabbit is described in terms of a hunt or game, and the young minister initially believes that he can save Rabbit if he can just trounce him (103). Eccles's linguistic powers are so impressive that "Rabbit feels now the danger of talking; his words are coming back to him, little hooks and snares are being fashioned" (100); and he foresees being trapped in a net of "explanations, embarrassments, prayers, reconciliations" (97). However, Jack Eccles's verbal power is limited, finally, because it also relies on manipulation rather than conviction, and Rabbit, who is astute at spotting fraud in others, discovers this weakness and remains unconverted. Discouraged by his own lack of faith, Eccles at one point thinks that "with his white collar he forges God's name on every word he speaks. He steals belief. . . . He murders faith in those who listen to him babble. He commits fraud with every schooled cadence of the service" (144).

Several critics have commented on the decline in power of

orthodox religious figures in Updike's work.[3] Jack Eccles reports the troubling decrease in faith from grandfather to father to son in his own family, and this loss is reflected in his uninspired sermon. Although Eccles's sermon applies directly to Rabbit's situation, Rabbit remains unmoved, noting that the minister gives "an unpleasant and strained performance" (219). On the other hand, the Reverend Mr. Kruppenback, who has strong conviction, lacks the compassion that would make his message accessible to others. He drives Jack Eccles away. Neither compassion without faith (mere "busyness" [159]) nor faith without compassion (doctrinal rigidity) seems to work. These ministers, who use language to sell a religious perspective are unable to inspire their listeners. The loss of potency in modern institutional religions is also reflected in the suggestion of homosexuality among the ministers in the tetralogy. Even in this first novel, Rabbit fears that "Eccles is known as a fag and he has become the new boy" (122).

Rabbit's father, Earl, and his father-in-law, Fred, also live by their words. Earl Angstrom is a Linotypist at Verity Press. Updike admits to having good opinion of printers in *Self-Consciousness*, where he says that "The printer in my naive sense of the literary enterprise is a solid fellow, my only real partner, and everyone else a potentially troublesome intermediary between him and myself" (108). Although Earl makes his living with words, he conveys the stories and perspectives of others and has no compelling personal vision to empower him or to pass along to his son. Rabbit rejects his father as a model of masculinity because of this lack of force and thinks "[Earl's] mouth works like an old woman's" (*Run* 211). Fred Springer plays only the smallest part in *Rabbit, Run*, but subsequent novels indicate that Fred's pragmatic use of language in the service of materialism ultimately triumphs. Fred's verbal expertise, which includes lying, eventually makes him a wealthy man. In *Rabbit, Run*, Fred uses language to smooth things over at the coroner's office in order to avoid manslaughter charges and to ease Rabbit's return into the family. Following Rebecca's death, Fred negotiates a bargain with Rabbit, the terms of which are crucial to the subsequent novels.

Mary Angstrom and Rebecca (Bessie) Springer are transitional figures in the spectrum of language users. Both possess what Rabbit calls "force," although he says of Mrs. Springer, "Your wife's parents can't get to you like your own can" (209). Both women are verbally accomplished. During his pastoral visits, Eccles underestimates each woman and finds himself quickly outmaneuvered. He observes that Bessie's voice cuts like a file and that Mary confronts the world with grim satire. Both women use their linguistic skills within the family (rather than the community or market place) to dominate family members. Rabbit thinks of Fred Springer as a "slave" in relation to his wife, and we hear Bessie Springer's destructive tactics on the telephone with Janice. When Eccles visits the Angstroms, Mary humiliates and controls Earl by verbally painting him "into a tiny corner" (154).

Despite their expertise, Mary and Bessie fit into the verbal power structure here because, although they are women, they convey the patriarchal view. In fact, in *Rabbit Redux*, Rabbit recalls that his mother has "a mannish mouth too clever for her life" (12). Mary and Bessie teach the masculinity that Tolson describes as a combination of qualities, including "competitiveness, personal ambition, social responsibility and emotional restraint" (86). Mary Angstrom taught Rabbit competitiveness and personal ambition using the carrot of privilege. Her relation to the symbolic Law of the Father and her role in forming Rabbit's personality have been discussed previously. Bessie Springer, on the other hand, invokes the forces of church (Eccles) and state (threatened police intervention) to pressure Rabbit into accepting his social responsibility. Meanwhile, she teaches Nelson and his friend Billy the value of both emotional repression and bullying. She admonishes Nelson to quit being a "sissy" and handle his aggressive playmate by himself without crying. Finally, Mrs. Springer's materialism represents the ultimate end of Tothero's ideology.

Mary and Bessie have gained what power they have by manipulating the patriarchal system. Nevertheless, they are themselves the repressed, unhappy victims of that system. Bessie Springer is confined to her home with both legs wrapped in elastic and her life constricted by her dread of gossip. Mary's stifled development is seen in her neglected garden. As Mim says in *Rabbit Redux*, "She's a great woman with nowhere to put it" (309). Like Bessie, Mary is confined to her gloomy home and resentful life. Despite their verbal skills, when it comes to expressing their feelings, the older women are as inarticulate as the younger ones; Bessie's "dark eyes are lacquered with tears" (144), and Mary Angstrom is a silent "mad captive" "leaning against the sink with soaked cheeks gleaming under her glasses" (*Run* 154–55).

At the farthest end of the language spectrum are Janice, Ruth, and Rebecca, all of whom are silenced by Rabbit. In fact, Rabbit uses the word *dumb* so often to describe his wife that it becomes clear that she is not only made to feel stupid, she is also "struck dumb" when her perspective does not conform. The double meaning is intentional, for in *Rabbit Redux*, Updike has Janice clarify that she has "difficulty" when she tries to speak with Rabbit while her lover, Charlie Stavros, has given her a voice: "She went on with difficulty, for a blurring, a halting comes over her tongue, her head, whenever she tries to think, and one of the many beautiful things about Charlie Stavros is he lets her tumble it out anyway. He has given her not only her body but her voice" (53). In order to enforce his own perspective, Rabbit denies Janice a voice. Ironically, paradoxically, although Rabbit successfully represses Janice, much of what he dislikes about her is the by-product of that repression. He is, for example, frightened by her panic episodes and confusion, yet Janice reveals that these panic attacks are the manifestation of her well-founded fear that no one knows or cares who she is. He is repulsed by her alcoholism, yet she drinks because "the feeling of being alone would melt a little with a drink" (*Run* 232). Her lack of initiative, her dependency, her vacant withdrawal, her escapism, all of which make Rabbit feel trapped, are her responses to repression, invalidation, alienation, and powerlessness.

Once again Rabbit's relationship with Ruth provides insight into his marriage. Ruth is a character loved by readers precisely because she is mouthy and candid and has an astute, if sometimes cynical, perspective of her own that challenges Rabbit's. In the course of their relationship, however, Rabbit replaces, or rather suppresses, what appears to the reader to be Ruth's truth with his own version of reality. He begins by washing Ruth's face and identity away, imposing the image of a virginal bride, and seeing her as a "ghost in her silver slip" (*Run* 76). The next morning, he recognizes his triumph in the fact that Ruth will no longer verbalize her preference even in so small a thing as what she would like for lunch (89).

Like Janice, Ruth is won over, not by Rabbit's "erotic magnetism" (Detweiler 44), but by his capacity to know women, and is betrayed when she learns that he doesn't want to know. She becomes increasingly reticent about her internal life, including the secret of her pregnancy, because she anticipates Rabbit's rejection. Tears replace words in Ruth's mouth at the swimming pool, where Rabbit sees only her "surface," and again when he leaves her to go to Janice in the hospital. Just as Janice will be, Ruth is silenced—structurally, emotionally, and psychologically confined to an interior world.

> "Ruth. Hey. If you don't say anything I'm not coming back. Ruth."
> She lies there like some dead animal or somebody after a car accident when they put a tarpaulin over. He feels if he went over and lifted her she would come to life but he doesn't like being manipu-

lated and grows angry. He puts on his shirt and doesn't bother with a coat and necktie but it seems to take forever putting on his socks; the soles of his feet are tacky.

When the door closes the taste of seawater in her mouth is swallowed by the thick grief that mounts in her throat so fully she has to sit up to breathe. Tears slide from her blind eyes and salt the corners of the mouth as the empty walls of the room become real and then dense. (*Run* 178–79)

There is perhaps no more eloquent an acknowledgment of female repression in American literature than Ruth, silenced and left as if dead, with the taste of semen and tears in her mouth. She recalls another accident victim, Myrtle Wilson of *The Great Gatsby*. Rabbit is not entirely unaware of what he does either; looking at Ruth on the bed, he thinks: "I've killed her" (178). Yet he replays this devastating scene with Janice: "Even this late he might have stayed if she [Janice] hadn't accepted defeat by doing this. . . . But she asks for it, lying there in a muddle sobbing, and outside, down in the town, a motor guns and he thinks of the air and the trees and streets stretching bare under the street lamps and goes out the door" (230). Rabbit renders these women inarticulate, and when their incapacity becomes a silent reproach that angers him, he uses it as the rationale and justification for abandoning them.

These illustrations show Rabbit's tendency to impose his version of reality through his control of language. One final example that rewards attention, however, involves the plastic arts and demonstrates that other systems of representation are also inscribed with ideology and can be manipulated for control. Trained as an artist, Updike is fluent in nonverbal as well as verbal signifying systems. Although the painterly and sculptural images in *Rabbit, Run* are necessarily embodied in language, they still suggest how male control of nonverbal systems operates and, in this case, negatively affects women.

Of all the possible images of Janice that Rabbit might have selected from two years of shared daily life, his favorite is the following:

> But there were good things: Janice so shy about showing her body even in the first weeks of wedding yet one night coming into the bathroom expecting nothing he found the mirror clouded with steam and Janice just out of the shower standing there doped and pleased with a little blue towel lazily and unashamed her bottom bright pink with hot water the way a woman was of two halves bending over and turning and laughing at his expression whatever

it was and putting her arms up to kiss him, a blush of steam on her body and the back of her soft neck slippery. (43)

When he returns to the apartment to gather his clothing, the white triangle of the bathroom floor reminds him again of "the time after her shower, her bottom blushing with steam, lifting her arms gladly to kiss him, soaked licks of hair in her armpits. What gladness had seized her, and then him, unasked?" (94). Rabbit refers to this image nostalgically as the measure of what he has lost and the measure of how far Janice has fallen. The scent of soap on Ruth triggers a similar image:

> She has washed her hair. It pulls back from her forehead in darker straighter strands evenly harrowed by the comb. Clean, she is clean, a big clean woman; he puts his nose against her skull to drink in the demure sharp scent. He thinks of her naked in the shower, her hair hanging oozy with lather, her neck bowed to the whipping water. "I made you bloom," he says. (103–4)

The sculptural version of Ruth appears at the swimming pool: "When she came out of the bathhouse she looked great, her head made small by the bathing cap and her shoulders stately. Standing in the water she looked great, cut off at the thighs like a statue" (133).

Moments later, when Ruth joins Rabbit beside the pool, Updike gives the game away by having Rabbit pinch Ruth "hard," hurting her, because "something angered him at the touch of her skin. The sullen way it yielded" (135). As with Janice, Rabbit much prefers his cooperative, idealized version to the troublesome individual woman.

Similar images appear elsewhere in Updike's work. In fact, Mary Allen observes that "of all his images, the one that Updike paints most tenderly is the woman emerging from the tub or shower" (75). Allen also notes that in the short story "Museums and Women," Updike makes a connection between the future wife and "the truly disturbing image of the desired woman, simply a marble object in a sexual posture" (74).

Rabbit's selected images are familiar. They are all versions of Venus (Oates, "Updike's American Comedies" 60–61), motherless goddess of beauty and love, generated by the creative male mind and rising from the sea. While such images, fully inscribed with prejudice, are conveyed to Rabbit by the signifying systems of his culture, he, on his side, sifts through the material of his own life to find an appropriate match. Thus, Rabbit selects, affirms, and exploits the cultural ideal in his personal life. The compulsion to idealize women, however, is destructive, in fact homicidal, as Updike reveals in the mirror image of the pointedly feminine Rebecca Angstrom drowned in her bath.

Rabbit's images are the verbal equivalents of the genre paintings of nudes examined by John Berger, Fraser Harrison, Emmanuel Reynaud and others, who observe that, as with literature, "male dominated art can service the male imagination and . . . power" since the imagined female "can only surrender to the male gaze" (Harrison 31–32). Their observations are relevant to any discussion of projection as a means of silencing or molding the female perspective or to any discussion of "killing" women into art.

In such paintings, as in Rabbit's images, the male artist colludes with the presumed male viewer in "catching" the women unaware. Although the scenes typically give the illusion of being accidental, they are, on the contrary, carefully arranged for male "delectation" (Harrison 84). According to Berger, "the female nude as painted by men involves a deliberate selection of images of women at the point of potential submission, for the purpose of 'depriving the woman of her sexual autonomy'" (Harrison 31–32). The "subject" is "caught" exposed in a disadvantageous position that emphasizes both her sensuousness and her defenseless but willing condition. Berger notes that body parts are covered or revealed depending on whether they are perceived as threatening or reassuring (Harrison 82). The paintings often incorporate the subterfuge that the woman is preoccupied with admiring herself while, in fact, she is displayed for the male voyeur (Harrison 84). It is important that the woman be presented as willing, even colluding, with the male viewer. Harrison observes that:

> Female defenselessness is precious to the male's sexual vanity: his belief in his own potency is enhanced by the sight of a woman who has been denied the means of resistance. The artist who implies that there is an alliance between the woman's body and the desire of the male onlooker which the woman herself is powerless to restrain is furnishing a deeply reassuring image. (28)

Idealizations of women can serve male power in direct, political ways as Harrison illustrates from the work of the late-Victorian painter, Frederick Leighton. In a time when traditional roles were beginning to be challenged, Leighton's genre paintings dramatized female dependency on male strength and favor and reinforced and perpetuated traditional perceptions of women (Harrison 80–88).

Critics identify a number of masculine needs that may be satisfied by the idealization of women. The sense of nostalgia or unattainability associated with these idealizations suggests a quest for the lost mother. John Fowles writes that "the vanished young mother of infancy is quite as elusive as the Well-Beloved . . . indeed she is the Well-Beloved, although the adult writer transmogrifies her according to the pleasures and fancies which have in the older man superseded the nameless ones of the child" (33). Fowles's critic, Bruce Woodcock, adds, reminiscent of Dinnerstein:

> The self-perpetuating activity of novelistic fantasy, in which the pursuit of an ideal woman forms such a part, are for Fowles the male writer's compensation for the psychological trauma of the Oedipal split; and the male novelist is an addicted voyeur, continually re-enacting fantasies designed to reappropriate the lost mother and then deny that reunion. (22)

In reference to Denis de Rougemont's *Love in the Western World* (1939), Updike himself says in a similar vein that "love as we experience it *is* love for the Unattainable Lady. . . . A woman, loved, momentarily eases the pain of time by localizing nostalgia; the vague and irrecoverable objects of nostalgic longing are assimilated, under the pressure of libidinous desire, into the details of her person" (*AP* 286–87).

The work of Dworkin, Harrison, Berger, and others supports the notion that idealizations are also a means of gratifying male needs and desires both immediately in the enjoyment of the product at hand and, in the long term, by perpetuating the ideology they represent.

Still others observe that these idealizations are the by-product of male fear and hostility. Art affords an opportunity to control what is threatening. In this instance, the male artist obviously controls the "subject," making her be or do or feel exactly as he likes. He can manipulate or even eliminate, as Berger suggests, specifically threatening aspects of femininity or emphasize reassuring qualities. Joyce Carol Oates, who discusses the appearance of Venus as Vera in *The Centaur*, observes, "She is simple, vital, enchanting, and yet . . . no threat"; furthermore, she "may be projected into nearly anyone" ("Updike's American Comedies" 61).

Fetterley explores the hostility implicit in the compulsion to change women, observing that to improve them in order to make them more desirable implies that something is profoundly "wrong" with their natural or individualized state (24). Her analysis of "The Birthmark" is pertinent because Updike, like Hawthorne, deliberately gives the game away, revealing that no matter how innocently or attractively presented, the quest for perfection in others is destructive, even homicidal, especially if one equates perfection with one's own needs (22–33).

Because Rabbit selects reflections of the cultural images from his personal life, the images he chooses do have a basis in reality. As Allen observes, Janice *is* physically and emotionally "good-natured" (84), and Rabbit himself says as much of Ruth. The problem is that these selected images become the fixed standard by which Rabbit measures his partners. The steamy, pink Janice becomes for him the "right" Janice, while the living, changing Janice, the tired, overwhelmed, discouraged, sullen, lumpy Janice is both a failure and a betrayer. Rabbit sees her as incompetent and uncooperative because she fails to conform to his ideal. Most offensive of all to Rabbit is that Janice should be uninterested, unwilling, or even unavailable for sex. This fundamental contradiction of his idealization seems to Rabbit to justify his desertion prior to Rebecca's death. Later it galls Rabbit to acknowledge, even to himself, that his behavior has been "wrong and stupid" (*Run* 249). Rabbit comes perilously close to what Simone de Beauvoir describes as sexual autism, "the inability to modify one's sexual behavior based on the perception of another individual" (Dworkin, *Pornography* 25).

To reiterate, male control of perspective, whether through control of language or other signifying systems, is an efficient, many-edged weapon. The process of idealizing women into art, literary or plastic, involves, first, a negation or "killing into silence" of the original, actual, or even potential individual. For this reason, Fetterley observes of canonical American literature, "The only good woman is an idea in one's head; she doesn't exist" (19). This initial denial alone has a demoralizing effect on Janice and Ruth. The process then works both positively by assigning values, virtues, roles, and limitations and negatively by suppressing (keeping nonverbal or preverbal) other perspectives and possibilities. The idealization is thus established as a standard, on the one hand, generating a pressure to conform and, on the other, providing a measure of failure that will justify subsequent behavior including, in Rabbit's case, coercion, rejection, and further questing. And, of course, Ruth and Janice are measured according to other male-centered systems as well and are found, in addition to being aesthetically and sexually lacking, to be economically, domestically, socially, and spiritually deficient.

Rabbit wants Janice to be receptive, supportive, flattering, understanding, tidy, agile, efficient, bright, generous, sexy, domestic, maternal, eternally young, physically quick, and more. Negatively he sees her as ugly, stupid, drunken, clumsy, slovenly, lazy, rejecting, incompetent, irresponsible, obstructive, sexually difficult—and she's a rotten cook to boot. He also sees her as a symbol of death and as a trap set to limit his freedom and saddle him with social responsibility. That so many readers and critics have confirmed the absurd demands incorporated in Rabbit's idealizations and accepted his dehumanizing estimations, when the author provides evidence that his protagonist is a fallible and hostile witness, tells the depth of our prejudice.

Why do readers accept Rabbit's valuation? The question leads back to the problematic ambivalence of the male author who examines masculinity. There is no doubt, as Allen insists, that Updike offers up the old idealizations and kills off women who seem to be threatening. And although he also offers us the antidote to this poison in his ironic treatment of Rabbit and in his representation of interior lives that reveal the female characters as fully human individuals who deserve our attention and compassion, the reaction of readers and critics suggests that the familiar pleasures provided by the images of a pink Venus, a nursing madonna, a good-natured, abusable whore, and a dead bitch are not fully countered by the intended antidote. Why not? Is the author's intention entirely sincere and consistent? Does his art fail his intention? Is he, like Hawthorne, "as eager to be misread and to conceal as to be read and reveal" (Fetterley 31)? Or is the prejudice of his audience simply invincible?

Rebecca Angstrom and the Lost Feminine

To return to the hierarchy of language users, Rabbit's daughter, Rebecca June Angstrom (Becky), stands at the furthest extreme from the protagonist. Updike emphasizes three characteristics in this child; she is feminine, inarticulate, and doomed. Rabbit is struck by her femininity when he sees her for the first time at the hospital.

> The baby is held by the nurse so her profile is sharp red against the buttoned white bosom of the uniform. The folds around the nostril, worked out on such a small scale, seem miraculously precise; the tiny stitchless seam of the closed eyelid runs diagonally a great length, as if the eye, when it is opened, will be huge and see everything and know everything. In the suggestion of pressure behind the tranquil lid and in the tilt of the protruding upper lip he

reads a delightful hint of disdain. She knows she's good. What he never expected, he can feel she's feminine, feels something both delicate and enduring in the arc of the long pink cranium. (*Run* 201–2)

At almost the same moment that Rabbit recognizes her femininity, he registers her vulnerability, thinking that "rough looking will smash the fine machinery of this sudden life" (202). Later, when she is brought home, she is associated with images of death. She sleeps "in the coffinlike hollow of the plaited crib" (226), and her "presence fills the apartment like a little casket of incense" (215). Finally, like the other women, Rebecca is described as both needy and inarticulate: "The baby scrawks tirelessly. It lies in its crib all afternoon and makes an infuriating noise of strain, *hnnnnnah ah ah nnnnh*, a persistent feeble scratching at some interior door. What does it want? Why won't it sleep?" (224). Rabbit thinks of Rebecca, as he does of Janice, as a foreigner whom he cannot understand.

The scene in the Angstroms' apartment on that Sunday is one of Updike's best. The pressure of the ordinary events of domestic life is revealed, like the sun in Camus, to have unbearable, mind-shattering power. Rebecca cries inconsolably. Rabbit blames Janice for not having enough milk, and Janice claims that Rabbit's restless tension is affecting the infant. Even little Nelson is troubled. The narrator suggests that Rebecca's crying is a "a wild, feeble warning" against the approach of a threatening "shadow" (224). At the end of this day, one of the longest days of the year, Rebecca relaxes suddenly and is quiet (226). The child is silent, already metaphorically dead.

> But as, amid the stacked dishes on the sink, under the worn and humid furniture, and in the coffinlike hollow of the plaited crib, the shadows begin to strengthen, the grip of the one with which Becky had been struggling all afternoon relaxes, and suddenly she is quiet, leaving behind a solemn guilty peace. They had failed her. A foreigner speaking no English but pregnant with a great painful worry had been placed among them and they had failed her. At last, night itself had swept in and washed her away like a broken piece of rubbish. (226–27)

Rebecca is the manifestation and ultimate symbol of repressed female language and perspective.

While there is no question that the author kills Rebecca, several critics feel that Rabbit is blameless of her death, either because they perceive him as the victim of society or accept his interpretation of events. At Becky's funeral, Rabbit points to Janice and says, "I didn't kill her. . . . You all keep acting as if *I* did it. I wasn't anywhere near. *She's* the one" (271). Janice's guilt aside, interpretations that maintain Rabbit's innocence reflect a still prevailing double standard of parental responsibility, not necessarily shared by Updike. Were a woman to abandon her newborn, possibly ill, infant to the care of a known alcoholic whom she had plied with drink, and the infant died as a result, she would unquestionably be perceived as morally, possibly criminally, guilty of neglect, if not of negligent homicide. As responsible fatherhood is an important theme in Updike's work, it is a mistake to diminish the weight of responsibility he heaps upon Rabbit, especially as that responsibility compounds in *Rabbit Redux*, where Jill also dies as a result of Rabbit's carelessness.

Furthermore, in the "Special Message" to the Franklin Library edition of *Rabbit Redux*, Updike himself associates Rebecca and Jill with Agamemnon's sacrificial daughter: "The cost of the disruption of the social fabric was paid, as in the earlier novel, by a girl. Iphigenia is sacrificed and the fleet sails on, with its quarreling crew. If Harry seems hard-hearted, 'hardness of the heart' was what his original epigraph was about" (*HTS* 858–59). Northrop Frye observes that the theme of female children endangered by fathers is a recurrent one in romance literature (81). It seems more likely that Updike is exploring this theme rather than simply denying its validity.

The debate over Rabbit's guilt or innocence in the death aside, however, the fact is that Becky is metaphorically dead, swept away like rubbish, even before the accident occurs. Like other female characters, she is left in her bed as dead. Whether Rabbit is directly responsible or not, Updike means us to understand that Rabbit, the stereotypical male, is involved in killing the feminine. This point is supported not only by the symbolic deaths of Janice and Ruth but by events in subsequent novels. In *Rabbit Redux*, Mary Angstrom, who Rabbit has said "must die" (*Run* 266), is not only dying but losing her capacity for speech. And Jill, who, Allen notes, is threatening precisely because she is both intelligent and articulate, burns while Rabbit watches passively (Allen 89–95).

Updike's remark that "the fleet sails on, with its quarreling crew" is insightful. As long as feminine perspective is sacrificed, the masculine world proceeds unchanged with business as usual. Without the perspective of the other, without the advantage of "stereoscopic vision," the crew is trapped within its skewed construction of reality, and its dichotomous vision generates dissatisfaction and conflict. Perpetual questing and quarreling are the inevitable result, and change is impossible. To recall Updike's remarks on Walt Whitman, "Incessant creative recourse to one's self ends . . . in an arid emptiness and a desperate lunge over the frontier of sanity" (*HTS* 116).

Rabbit pays dearly for killing the feminine perspective. Obviously, destroying the other precludes satisfactory human relations; but just as important, in Jungian terms, by silencing the feminine voice, Rabbit represses aspects of his own nature, represses perspectives and capacities vital to resolving the problems in his life. For example, at the opening of the novel, Rabbit thinks that his solution lies in the straight lines on his map, the roads to escape, but the straight lines begin to crisscross and become a confining net. Straight lines are illusions or partial realities; lines arc into circles; the linear resolves into the organic. In *Rabbit, Run*, many of the circles are associated with women, and as noted earlier, Rabbit is intuitively attracted to the hoop, the cup, the breast, the rose window, the flower, and so on. Rabbit's dream of converging circles suggests that on some level, he possesses the knowledge and capacity necessary for union. It is partly because he suppresses this knowledge that he consistently violates the model of union. Similarly, in the metaphor of the solstice, Updike implies that Rabbit's natural instinct for separation and self-enhancement, the quest for unlimited freedom, is ultimately destructive unless it is balanced with a willingness to return and a capacity for surrender and sacrifice, for, as Updike quotes Whitman, "Whoever walks a furlong without sympathy walks to his own funeral, dressed in a shroud" (qtd. in *HTS* 116). The women in the novel, despite many imperfections, possess the necessary capacity for surrender. It is Rabbit who recoils at the critical moment, betraying them with his despair.

In order to achieve the union, transcendence, and resolution offered in the metaphors, Rabbit will need to find and reclaim the lost feminine symbolized by Rebecca. This need is incorporated into the narrative structure of the next two novels (*HTS* 871). When Rabbit does find the daughter again in *Rabbit Is Rich*, Nelson's child is described in the same language as Rebecca.

> Teresa [Nelson's wife] comes softly the one step into his den and deposits into his lap what he has been waiting for. Oblong cocooned little visitor, the baby shows her profile blindly in the shuddering flashes of color jerking from the Sony, the tiny stitchless seam of the closed eyelid aslant, lips bubbled forward beneath the whorled

nose as if in delicate disdain, she knows she's good. You can feel in the curve of the cranium she's feminine, that shows from the first day. Through all this she has pushed to be here, in his lap, his hands, a real presence hardly weighing anything but alive. Fortune's hostage, heart's desire, a granddaughter. His. Another nail in his coffin. His. (437)

The problem of authorial ambivalence arises here again. In *Male Mythologies*, Woodcock observes that, although Fowles has the intention of revealing that the stereotypical male needs to learn feminine perspective and capacities, by presenting woman as the source and bestower of such knowledge, he only repackages the pernicious myth of woman as male savior (19). By suggesting that Rabbit needs to rediscover his own neglected capacities, Updike can be interpreted as avoiding this dilemma. However, by framing Rabbit's task in terms of a search for Rebecca, Updike revives the never-ending quest for the lost "well-beloved," which is not only related to the myth of the woman savior but which, as we have seen, tends to have fatal consequences for "real" women like Jill in *Rabbit Redux*.

Theory and Form

In the essay "Getting the Words Out," Updike talks about his own stuttering, and the feelings of insecurity, inadequacy, and panic he describes parallel those experienced by Janice. He says that stuttering is a paralysis "that stems from the dead center of one's being, a deep doubt there" (*SC* 87). He recalls an intense fear of not being known or accepted as himself: "I was afraid . . . of being misunderstood, of being mistaken for somebody else. I doubted my worthiness to mar the air with my voice" (102). And he describes a panic, like Janice's, that makes him use "the machete of my face, to hack my way through a jungle of their minds' thrusting vines and tendrils" (85). Most interestingly, he says:

I stutter, then, when I am "in the wrong" as, for example, with:

(1) people of evident refinement or distinction
(2) New Englanders of many generations
(3) law-enforcement officers
(4) Israeli journalists and intellectuals
(5) men. (85)

The young women in *Rabbit, Run* also become inarticulate when "in the wrong" with a man who is ever "right."

In contrast to and in compensation for the verbal incapacity he shares with his female characters, Updike successfully pursues the opposite extreme of the spectrum of verbal power as a male writer, the implications of which have been discussed. Updike admits that "central to my artistic impulse" was "the papery self-magnification and immortality of printed reproduction—a mode of self-assertion that leaves the cowardly perpetrator hidden and out of harm's way" (*SC* 108). Not only is his "captive tongue" released through the assumption of masks, but because of his highly developed stylistic skill, his voice achieves the "legitimacy" and authority the stutterer's lacks (86). Updike says that "I continued . . . to get the words out—to get them out in the specialized sense of words to be printed, as smooth in their arrangement and flow as repeated revision could make them, words lifted free of the fearful imperfection and impermanence of the words we all, haltingly, stumblingly, speak" (102).

Because Updike experiences the helplessness and invalidation of the inarticulate as well as the power and self-magnification of the literary, he is especially sensitive to both the positive and negative aspects of verbal power. This awareness has contributed to his artistic theory and choice of form. Updike understands that imposing one's imaginative construction of reality is both a creative and coercive act. The character Ellelloû in *The Coup* can, for example, shape a nation and a history by asserting his perspective (by means of language through his storytelling), but in order to do so, he must disregard, in fact destroy, all competing perspectives (Newman 115–19). In order to counter this destructive potential, Updike strives in his work to faithfully "particularize" the "apprehended real" (*SC* 103) in the manner described by Peter Caldwell in *The Centaur*: "It came upon me that I must go to Nature disarmed of perspective and stretch myself like a large transparent canvas upon her in the hope that, my submission being perfect, the imprint of a beautiful and useful truth would be taken" (218). In an address entitled "Why Write," delivered in 1974, Updike speaks of his own development from a desire for celebrity to a desire for this transparency.

> Beginning with the wish to make an impression, one ends wishing to erase the impression, to make of it a perfect transparency, to make of oneself a point of focus purely, as selfless as a lens. One begins by seeking celebrity and ends by feeling . . . an impatience

with everything that clouds and clots our rapt witness to the world that surrounds and transcends us.[4] (*PUP* 54)

More recently, in "Getting the Words Out," Updike continues with this theme:

> My own style seemed to me a groping and elemental attempt to approximate the complexity of envisioned phenomena and it surprised me to have it called luxuriant and self-indulgent; self-indulgent, surely, is exactly what it wasn't—*other*-indulgent, rather. My models were the styles of Proust and Henry Green as I read them (one in translation): styles of tender exploration that tried to wrap themselves around the things, the tints and voices and perfumes, of the apprehended real. (*SC* 103–4)

FIVE

Rabbit Redux

TEN YEARS later Rabbit, now called Harry, is living in the Brewer suburbs with Janice and Nelson. In the years following his return, he has been a steady worker, a faithful husband, and a political conservative, but his quiet life is now disturbed by the fact that his mother is dying and his wife is having an affair. When Janice leaves, Rabbit is left to care for Nelson, with whom he has not had a good relationship. Rabbit soon expands the household to include Jill, a young runaway and former drug addict, and Skeeter, a black militant "outlaw." Thirteen-year-old Nelson flounders as sex, drugs, and violence pervade the home and all conventionality is discarded, until finally arsonists (probably white neighbors) burn the house down and Jill dies in the fire. Rabbit returns to his parents' home, is fired from his obsolete job, and tentatively reconciles with Janice.

Much of the criticism on *Rabbit Redux* focuses on the novel's record of the social and political turmoil of the sixties and on Harry Angstrom's reactions to dislocation in a changing society. The discussion here, however, looks at Rabbit's family relationships to establish that Rebecca's death has left him more insular, defensive, and controlling than he was in *Rabbit, Run*. Moreover, this discussion makes a connection between these attitudes and the role of technology and violence in Rabbit's personal life with the purpose of revealing that Updike links Rabbit's gender identity (and its manifestations at home) to the national character.

Although they may differ widely in their explanations, sociologists, anthropologists, psychologists, historians, and even biologists have all seen connections linking male aggression, sexual violence, racial oppression, economic oppression, aspects of technological and scientific advancement, and international strife. Since 1969, the year in which *Rabbit Redux* is set, a great deal has been written on these subjects, and by now the notion that many of our social problems are related to masculinity is a familiar hypothesis.

Psychologists speculate that the human desire to control environment arises from the initial long experience of helplessness. The child's survival depends on developing self-sufficiency, and its world-shaping capacity also compensates for the loss of continuity with the mother. According to Dorothy Dinnerstein (136–49), although these impulses ("the impulse to console oneself for a loss and the impulse to affirm self-sufficiency" [139]) are the benign result of dependency, they may take pathological forms. Our repaying our losses "by the exercise of competence and will" (121) may express grievance and rage rather than authentic consolation for a deeply felt but accepted loss. Furthermore, if in the pursuit of competence, one fails to locate the source of continued limitation and vulnerability within, and identifies woman, nature, or any blameless other as the source of danger (139–49), then one may, like Rabbit (and like the society represented in *Rabbit Redux*), spend a great deal of energy in avoidance and denial of the truth of the human condition and array these world-shaping capacities against imagined enemies. Politics may devolve, like Rabbit's, into sexism, racism, and nationalism. Science and technology may become preoccupied with evasive questing, or worse, with death dealing.[1]

In his interpretation of the first two Rabbit novels as "Updike's treatment of the theme of freedom," George Slethaug uses the analogy of a pebble dropped in water forming ever-widening concentric circles (237). Rabbit's flight radiates consequences: "His initial leap toward freedom in *Rabbit, Run* begins like a pebble dropped in the water, a tight circle concentrated around his own character, and then expands outward to include and involve his family, representatives of his cultural milieu, and finally the nation as a whole" (237–38). Although I emphasize a different aspect of Updike's work, I find that Slethaug's analogy perfectly describes the development in the two novels. Rabbit's flawed orientation toward self and other is the pebble dropped in water. The effect is at first "concentrated around his own character." He is unable to mature, to face his own death, to develop spiritually. Fearful and self-protective, he cannot form and sustain the intimate relationships he desires. His lovers and children wither and die, whether literally or metaphorically. Now we see that his society is plagued by manifestations of the same arrested development. The same aggressive self-interest and lack of compassion, the same fear and anger erupt in sexual violence, racial oppression, and war. Updike writes in the tradition of Whitman, who insisted that the failure to come to terms with the physical-spiritual nature of the self will be reflected in society. For this reason, Updike draws the elaborate correspondences between national events and occurrences in Rabbit's private life. Many critics, noting these correspondences, see Rabbit as merely a reflection of his troubled times, a hapless victim once more. Updike, however, again suggests a causal relationship—America is the way it is because Rabbit, a representative American man, is the way he is.

Rabbit Now

What kind of man is Rabbit now? The opening paragraphs of *Rabbit Redux* depict Rabbit Angstrom as one of the ghostly inhabitants of Brewer, Pennsylvania, "the land of the living-dead."[2] Updike initiates *Rabbit Redux* by reintroducing, but adjusting, the themes and imagery of *Rabbit, Run*.

> Men emerge pale from the little printing plant at four sharp, ghosts for an instant, blinking, until the outdoor light overcomes the look of constant indoor light clinging to them. In winter, Pine Street at this hour is dark, darkness presses down early from the mountain that hangs above the stagnant city of Brewer; but now in summer the granite curbs starred with mica and the row houses differentiated by speckled bastard sidings and the hopeful small porches with their jigsaw brackets and gray milk-bottle boxes and the sooty ginko trees and the baking curbside cars wince beneath a brilliance like a frozen explosion. The city, attempting to revive its dying downtown, has torn away blocks of buildings to create parking lots, so that a desolate openness, weedy and rubbled, spills through the once-packed streets, exposing church facades never seen from a distance and generating new perspectives of rear entryways and half-alleys and intensifying the cruel breadth of light. The sky is cloudless yet colorless, hovering blanched humidity, in the way of these Pennsylvania summers, good for nothing but to make green things grow. Men don't even tan: filmed by sweat, they turn yellow.

> A man and his son, Earl Angstrom and Harry, are among the printers released from work. The father is near retirement, a thin man with no excess left to him, his face washed empty by grievances and caved in above the protruding slippage of his bad false teeth. The son is five inches taller and fatter; his prime is soft somehow pale and sour. The small nose and slightly lifted upper lip that once made the nickname Rabbit fit now seem, along with the thick waist and cautious stoop bred into him by a decade of the linotyper's trade, clues to weakness, a weakness verging on anonymity. (Redux 3–4)

We meet Rabbit again on his way home from work at day's end. He now seems unexceptional among the lifeless men released from the plant at four o'clock. His soft, pale, sour flesh and "cautious stoop" are clues to his spiritual condition. The younger Rabbit was repulsed by the false teeth that made his father's mouth move "like an old woman's" (*Run* 211), suggesting powerlessness and a lack of vitality, but now Rabbit's physical difference from his father is less striking than the impression of a shared "weakness verging on anonymity."

A number of the images in this passage have been carried over from *Rabbit, Run*. The "desolate openness" of the dying city recalls Rabbit's wasteland vision of "a huge vacant field of cinders" at the end of Summer Street (*Run* 283). Its "weedy and rubbled" parking lots recall the overgrown gardens that symbolized spiritual decline in the earlier novel, although in *Rabbit Redux* the Angstroms' scruffy suburban plot also refers to their neglected relationships and abandoned commitments. The "frozen explosion" recalls Rabbit's icebox dream of death and sexuality. This image ties in with the coldness that spreads through Rabbit's veins at the first hint of Janice's affair and with Earl's idea that Mary should "put herself in deep freeze" until a cure for Parkinson's disease is found (*Redux* 6, 8). Markle notes the use of coldness and whiteness throughout *Rabbit Redux* to suggest sterility and death (9–10, 151–52).

Images of light and vision have been carried over. The man who squinted to set his sights for the perfect basketball shot at the opening of *Rabbit, Run*, now blinks from the physical discomfort of trying to see things in a new light. Rabbit will experience internal discomfort throughout this novel as he sees, and is himself seen, in a variety of perspectives. The factory light is artificial, but it feels like "cream to his eyes" because it shows everything in the clear black-and-white dichotomies to which he is accustomed and because it introduces "no problem of fidelity" (*Redux* 30). This light is contrasted with the troublesome lights at home that burn out, cast dirty shadows, produce unwanted reflections, and blind with glare (30). Rabbit struggles to adjust, but typical of his problem, light (like perspective and vision) is more complicated than it was a decade earlier; the encouraging spiritual glow that once suffused the church window has become an enigmatic glint on the madhouse windows.

Finally, the otherworldly quality of the opening passage initiates the analogy between Rabbit's journey and return and that of U.S. astronauts aboard *Apollo 11* during July 1969. Detweiler and others have explored Updike's "orchestration" of the space and space exploration imagery extensively.[3]

Clearly, Rabbit now is spiritually depleted. His loss of vital power is contrasted with, and perhaps balanced against, the increase of energy, vision, and authority in those around him—in women, blacks, and even children.[4] These others have grown to fill the vacuum created by Rabbit's passivity and now demonstrate autonomy. Before, Rabbit dictated the terms of his relationships with women and abandoned his partners when they failed "to pay his price" (*Run* 136). Now Jill and Janice set conditions, take new partners, and, along with Peggy and Mim, try to define their own sexuality. Rabbit has lost touch with God as a result of Rebecca's death, but Janice (whom critics widely interpreted as antispirit in *Rabbit, Run*) and Jill now have religious experiences and possess the gift of life that once distinguished Rabbit (*Run* 207). "Stupid" Janice and "dumb" Jill seem more insightful and articulate than Rabbit himself. And Janice and Mim act purposefully at the novel's end to reestablish the Angstrom marriage. All of these women now have the confidence and conviction to stand up to Rabbit as only Ruth could in *Rabbit, Run*. Others, including Nelson and Skeeter, make a stand. Skeeter, for example, begins by telling Rabbit, "You are white but wrong," and ends by undermining his position, usurping his home and his lover, and dominating his life (*Redux* 234). The children, Nelson and Jill, not only share a loving, supportive bond that is beyond Rabbit's capacity, but they must remind this grown father of how to care for and protect them when he seems to have no clue.

Perspectives on Passivity

While unique in its circumstances, Rabbit's case nevertheless represents a perceptible social phenomenon. In 1963, just a few years before *Rabbit Redux* was written, anthropologist Margaret Mead delivered a lecture in which she reportedly claimed that "American men had been so effectively domesticated by their women that they had too little time and energy to engage in the national and communal tasks which needed doing" (Tiger 51). Mead not only observes the problem but seems to assign the responsibility to women. Updike spoke of the phenomenon himself in reference to *Couples*, the novel immediately preceding *Rabbit Redux*, and his comments are insightful. He says:

> While the women in that book are less sensitive perhaps to this oppressive quality, of cosmic blackness, and it is the women who do almost all of the acting. I don't want to say that being passive, being inactive, being paralyzed, is wrong in an era when so much action is crass and murderous. I do feel that in the generations that I've had a glimpse of—I can see my grandfather at one end, and I can see my boys coming up—there has been a perceptible loss of the sense of righteousness. But many evils are done in the name of righteousness, so perhaps one doesn't want it back. Nevertheless, I suspect that the vitality of women now, the way many of us lean on them, is not an eternal phenomenon but a historical one, and fairly recent. (*PUP* 484)

Kathleen Verduin, in her excellent article, "Fatherly Presences," examines this loss of a sense of empowering righteousness in Updike's father-protagonists. She does not, however, suggest, as Updike does here, that such a loss may be justified or beneficial. A failure of faith in the traditional way of ordering the world—that is, in "the right way and the good way" of *Rabbit, Run* (283)—may result in a loss of confidence and a disinclination to act, but the tyranny of that old way had fatal results.

Rabbit's passivity and paralysis have stimulated controversy. Paul Theroux gave *Rabbit Redux* a scathing review when it appeared in 1971, calling Rabbit "too passive and inarticulate to count" (Rev. of *Rabbit Redux* 3), and since that time, the subject has generated diverse opinions. Edward Vargo answered Theroux's objection by arguing that Rabbit's passivity is the central to the novel. Vargo sees Rabbit as "caught between *why* and *why not?*" (149–50), but he also observes that "Harry's passivity is really a cover for his fear or anger" and that "passivity numbs pain" (157, 156). Markle says that Rabbit, who was once a life-giver himself, "has become one of the burnt-out cynics—the washed-out, dissipated Americans in need of a priest and life-giver" (149).

Rabbit's passivity is ambiguous and depends upon context, motivation, and perception. When Peggy Fosnacht, the mother of Nelson's friend Billy and a sexual partner to Rabbit on the night of the fire, tells Rabbit, "You're much too passive," he responds, "Yeah. Or something" (*Redux* 253). Depending on one's viewpoint, the acceptance of a sacrificial role, or the patient endurance of trials, can be considered as either active or passive behavior. For example, critic Donald J. Greiner finds Rabbit's "stagnation" a form of rebellion, but he also finds some growth in Rabbit's resignation and acceptance of time at the novel's end (*John Updike's Novels* 73, 80). On the other hand, the protagonist's aggressive, defensive behavior can be understood as a form of paralysis, reflecting his inability to progress beyond the oppositional framework or to envision new solutions; or his paralysis may be reflecting his lack of the necessary spiritual resources to move forward. Furthermore, superficially passive behavior may be manipulative. Rabbit continues to play the powerful victim in this novel; he admits, for example, that he courts danger so that Janice will save him (*Redux* 212). Thus, Greiner finds Rabbit's passivity a form of resistance to change; and critics Charles Samuels and Mary Allen find collusion in his passivity regarding Jill's destruction.

Other critics identify causes. Wayne Falke sees Rabbit as left behind by a changing world, a boy who "learned his catechism and was a faithful servant of the Protestant ethic" but now finds "his knowledge is suddenly irrelevant" (72). George Hunt says he is a "WASP version of Bech," "a victim of cultural change made passive and inarticulate by onrushing political and social currents" (*Updike* 165). Robert Detweiler finds Rabbit "caught in the tension between continuity and change, between a stubborn worship of the [American] dream and a first hand experience of its dissolution" (*John Updike* 135).

George Searles observes that *Rabbit Redux* depicts the "collective spiritual emptiness" of contemporary society, "a kitsch-strewn vista bare of moral guideposts" (24–25). Philip Vaughan says, "Rabbit feels trapped in a meaningless present filled with synthetic articles and gadgets" (58). Furthermore, Vaughan maintains that Rabbit shares his creator's conservative sense that institutions "are outcroppings of human nature, . . . that in general when you destroy one set of institutions you get something worse" (72). Under these circumstances, all action is suspect, if not futile. Yves Le Pellec suggests Rabbit is paralyzed because "the notion of travel is infected by the remorse Harry nurses over the death of his daughter" (99).

According to Robert Alter, the "central awareness . . . is a white failure of nerve, or at least a flagging sense of white identity in the face of black assertiveness" (41). When "angry blacks force upon white consciousness the bitter knowledge of their collective pain and degradation. . . . the white man responds with guilt and a concomitant feeling of obligation and, above all, with an apocalyptic fear that such suffering must issue in a destructive rage of unimaginable proportion and effect" (41).

Judie Newman (like Detweiler) sees Rabbit as a Gutenberg man in Updike's thematic exploration "of technological evolution and its consequences, with special reference to the theories of Marshall McLuhan" (40). She says Rabbit is introduced in the first section as the product of this cultural phenomenon:

> Harry Angstrom as Gutenberg Man, [is] sensually deprived and passively dependent upon the machine. A social conformist and ardent supporter of state intervention in Vietnam, Harry lives his life by outdated rules, values order and neatness, and is isolated from his fellows to the point of racism. Sex has lost its charms for him, he no longer plays contact sports. (43)

Charles Samuels, an early reviewer, sees Rabbit's passivity as both a social and a personal phenomenon. He says Rabbit has changed from "a man in conflict with his culture" in *Rabbit, Run* to a "perfect example of its repressiveness" ("Updike on the Present" 64). Samuels also sees Rabbit as personally paralyzed by guilt over his earlier flight. However, he notes that these causes fail to account for Rabbit's sinister passivity regarding Jill's destruction. He suggests that Rabbit's "failure with Jill escalates into active collusion in destroying her" although his motive is unclear (66).

Samuels's insight is shared by Josephine Hendin and Mary Allen who try to identify the motive. Hendin observes that "Rabbit is the dark side of any man that realizes his ideals and power are gone" and "takes out his rage on women" (101). Mary Allen believes that Rabbit is "callous to the point of cruelty" with Jill because "he is glad to see this particular girl suffer" (91–92). Allen maintains that Updike and Rabbit dislike the intelligent "new woman" enough to allow (in the author's case to arrange) her destruction.

Suzanne Uphaus says that "emotional emptiness makes Rabbit a passive observer" and then "makes him feel guilty in retrospect" (82). According to Uphaus's sociopolitical reading, "Updike thus implies that the 'silent majority' did indeed remain passive through the sixties and . . . contributed to the chaos in this country" (82–83).

The combined insight of critics is sometimes more valuable than their individual opinions. According to this survey, Rabbit's passivity is socially induced, the consequence of sweeping changes in a society that has abandoned old institutions, values, traditions, and rituals. These social, political, and technological changes devalue Rabbit as an American, a white, a male, a husband, and a worker. His confidence is further undermined by his sense of individual and communal guilt. Rabbit is haunted by the fatal consequences of his earlier "inner light trip" and no longer trusts the instincts he followed in *Rabbit, Run*. Thus, he is left having to deal with revolutionary change without the benefit of guidelines and without confidence in his own intuition. Unable to move decisively in any direction, Rabbit becomes increasingly desperate as his position erodes. His passivity masks fear and anger. He becomes alternately and futilely nostalgic, evasive, defensive, aggressive, and destructive. And here, the circle comes around, for the America that induced this behavior, the America seen on the evening news, manifests in macrocosm the same motivations and the same limited range of response.

Unresolved Problems

Without at all diminishing these insights, I want to suggest that Rabbit's passivity, his "deadness," is also the direct result of his continued failure to resolve the problems encountered in *Rabbit, Run*. In that novel, acting out of a fear of self-compromise, Rabbit adopts the culturally supported defensive attitudes and behaviors. He perceives the world in the oppositional and hierarchical frameworks of patriarchy, and he tries desperately to control the other he found in God, nature, death, and woman in order to reduce a perceived threat to himself. He projects, denies, bullies, manipulates, charms, flees, and even destroys the other rather than risk the self-surrender essential to relationship or transcendence. Now, ten years later, he still wants to dominate in personal and social relationships, and he is still unwilling to engage, surrender, or commit. What is new, however, is that Rabbit has added withdrawal and passivity to his repertoire of avoidance strategies. He no longer flees physically; but where he cannot control, he flees within, hoping to elude death and the other, not by running, but by standing absolutely still within a confining web of defenses. Peter Rabbit has become "Br'er Rabbit" (*Redux* 123; Slethaug 251). What is also new is that the novel's broader scope invites us to observe the public ramifications of Rabbit's attitudes and behaviors.[5]

Interpretations of Rabbit's passivity are obviously diverse. For the purpose of this discussion, I use the concept of deadness to refer to all of the behaviors arising from Rabbit's spiritually frozen condition, including not only avoidance and withdrawal but controlling, even aggressive, behaviors that reflect his resistance to growth. Furthermore, the illustrations used here have been selected because they tie in these behaviors with sexism, racism, nationalism, militarism, scientism, and technology. It is insufficient, for example, to say that Rabbit withdraws from demanding relationships and difficult questions without observing that he often withdraws *into* technology (Newman 44–45). Technology offers a form of control over the physical world and tends to express power rather than acceptance. Like Rabbit, the nation, too, has become preoccupied with technology in the form of space exploration (evasive questing) and militarism (coercion) while avoiding momentous questions at home.[6]

Mom

Rabbit's withdrawal is evident in his relations with women. When Janice and Rabbit "re-dock" at the novel's end (Vanderwerken 73), she asks him:

"Who matters more to you, me or Nelson?"
"Nelson."
"Nelson or your mother?"
"My mother."
"You are a sick man." (*Redux* 399)

Obviously, Mary continues to be the most important person in Rabbit's life. Rabbit is "still too much a son" (*Redux* 91); he loves Mary more than anyone else and believes that "in this whole rolling-on world his mother is the only person who knows him" (166).

In the opening pages, Earl Angstrom asks Rabbit to visit Mary, who is slowly dying of Parkinson's disease and who has recently been troubled by rumors of Janice's affair. It is apparent that Rabbit rarely visits Mary, although he feels guilty about his neglect. Of course, Mary has never been an easy woman to deal with. In *Rabbit, Run*, she threatens to overwhelm Rabbit's sense of identity with her powerful personality and her need to prolong his infantile relationship. He still remembers the "demands and impossible expectations" that dominated his childhood and recalls that instead of the usual childish gifts, "he gave her himself, his trophies, his headlines" (197, 89). Rabbit also resents the damage she has done to his relationship with Nelson and is aware of her continued attempts to undermine his marriage.

It is not for any of these reasons, however, that Rabbit withdraws from his mother when she needs his compassionate support.

> Rabbit's mind, as the bus dips into its bag of gears and surges and shudders, noses closer into the image of her he keeps like a dreaded relic: the black hair gone gray, the mannish mouth too clever for her life, the lozenge-shaped nostrils that to him as a child suggested a kind of soreness within, the eyes whose color he had never dared to learn closed bulge-lidded in her failing, the whole long face, slightly shining as if with sweat, lying numbed on the pillow. He can't bear to see her like this is the secret of his seldom visiting, not Janice. The source of his life staring wasted there while she gropes for the words to greet him. And that gentle tawny smell of sickness that doesn't even stay in her room but comes downstairs to meet them in the front hall among the umbrellas. (*Redux* 12)

Although Rabbit's mind typically "slides away from her" or "offers to hide her in darkness," Mary's encroaching death contaminates his life as the odor of sickness contaminates the Angstrom house (5). Rabbit has withdrawn from Mary because he fears death.

On his first night with Ruth in *Rabbit, Run*, Rabbit has a dream in which Mim opens the icebox door, and he discovers the adult secrets of love and death. The dream reveals Mary's desire to perpetuate Rabbit's childhood and, more important, reveals Rabbit's refusal to claim this adult knowledge, his refusal to accept his maturity and his share in the human tragedy. I have interpreted Rabbit's behavior as a flight from these realities, a flight which led, paradoxically, to Rebecca's death. Now Mary Angstrom reminds us of this dream in *Rabbit Redux* with one of her L-Dopa nightmares in which she too opens an icebox and finds the frozen corpse foreshadowing her death (194). Rabbit also inadvertently recalls the dream when Mary refuses to acknowledge that Janice and Nelson have legitimate claims on her son. Rabbit thinks: "This is her falsity, that she forgets what time creates, she still sees the world with its original four corners, her and Pop and him and Mim sitting at the kitchen table. Her tyrant love would freeze the world" (197). Rabbit not only fears Mary's death, but fears his own death in hers. Furthermore, as in *Rabbit, Run*, he fears the existentialist's version of death, that is, annihilation. He dreads the "unblinking ungathering gaze into space that lifts her eyes out of any flow and frightens Rabbit with a sense of ultimate blindness, of a blackboard from which they will all be wiped clean" (*Redux* 92–93). Updike conveys this dread in images so morbid they might have come from Edgar Allan Poe. Rabbit speculates on whether a woman's hair continues to grow after she is dead, filling her coffin like a mattress (94). Mary describes a series of nightmares in which her dead children ask for food or she is buried alive in trash (194–96). The most interesting of these dreams introduces the vision of a technologically induced, government-supported "living death." Mary tells Rabbit:

> "The worst is Earl and I go to the hospital for tests. All around us are tables the size of our kitchen table. Only instead of set for meals each has a kind of puddle on it, a red puddle mixed up with crumpled bedsheets so they're shaped like. Children's sandcastles. And connected with tubes to machines with like television patterns on them. And then it dawns on me these are each people. And Earl keeps saying, so proud and pleased he's brainless, 'The government is paying for it all. The government is paying for it.' And he shows me the paper you and Mim signed to make me one of—you know, *them*. Those puddles."
> "That's not a dream," her son says. "That's how it is." (196)

Mary and Rabbit understand, on some level, that efforts to overcome nature or death by force and manipulation are not only doomed to failure but produce aberrations more frightening than death itself. Nevertheless, as in *Rabbit, Run*, Rabbit fails to live according to his wholesome intuitions. Although he is angered by Mary's wealthy, detached doctor, who offers pills but never feels or expresses compassion or solidarity, Rabbit similarly withdraws from his mother rather than face his own vulnerability. When he is forced to return home following the fire, his daily contact with Mary takes the edge off his terror, and his mother improves as a result of increased family involvement. Both characters benefit from the "unifying dimensions" of daily routine, suggesting that engagement, not withdrawal, from the human family eases the acceptance of our limitations (Detweiler, *John Updike* 134).

Mary Angstrom is peripheral to the plot of *Rabbit Redux*; nevertheless, she appropriately initiates its action by questioning Janice's fidelity. She remains central to Rabbit's dilemma. As she is the source of his life, she is also the source of his death—the floodgate of the physical world. Furthermore, she initiated the complex emotional problems that motivate Rabbit's defensive behaviors. Updike identifies the powerful mother as the origin of the feelings of helplessness Rabbit guards against in all of his relationships.

In *The Second Sex*, Simone de Beauvoir speaks of the link between mother and wife. She says that

> what man cherishes and detests first of all in women—loved one or mother—is the fixed image of his animal destiny; it is the life that is necessary to his existence but that condemns him to the finite and to death. From the day of his birth man begins to die; this is the truth incarnated in the Mother. In procreation he speaks for the species against himself: he learns this in his wife's embrace; in excitement and pleasure, even before he has engendered, he forgets his unique ego. Although he endeavors to distinguish mother and wife, he gets from both a witness to one thing only; his mortal state. He wishes to venerate his mother and love his mistress; at the same time he rebels against them in disgust and fear. (165–66)

In *Rabbit, Run*, Rabbit transfers his fear and antagonism to the younger women whom he finds dangerous because of their desire for intimacy, their capacity to limit his freedom, and their role as death bearers. In *Rabbit Redux*, Rabbit also continues to fear the "little deaths," the vulnerabilities required by intimacy and sex, and he has become plainly obsessed with woman as the source of physical life and death. Earlier, he projected a greedy skull onto the twenty-three-year-old Janice, and Rebecca June's drowning has apparently reinforced this connection in his mind.

Nevertheless, Updike and Rabbit make an important distinction between mother and wife. Rabbit loves and fears Mary, but because she retains the residual psychological power established in his childhood, she is impossible to control. This is especially true in *Rabbit, Run*, where Rabbit foresees no resolution except in Mary's death: "He comes to the conclusion that either he or his mother must die" (266). The situation with the younger women is different because they lack the immemorial power of the mother. He *can* deal with the younger women, wife and lovers, by making them the victims of his need to control what he fears.[7]

Janice

In *Rabbit Redux*, we see that in the arrangement of his marriage, Rabbit has externalized death, identified Janice as its source, withdrawn from intimacy with her, and made it the business of his marriage to control her. In the decade since his return, Rabbit has taken his wife "for granted" to the extent that he cannot imagine she is interesting enough to stimulate gossip or attract another man: "Janice, who'd have that mutt" (6; Allen 87). He and Janice drink a lot, have little communication and no sex. Rabbit has not only refused to ease Janice's despair over Rebecca with another child, but he has also made her live in guilt, by associating her sexuality with death (Slethaug 238). He thinks:

> Since he refused to get her pregnant again the murder and guilt have become all his. At first he tried to explain how it was, that sex with her had become too dark, too *serious*, too kindred to death, to trust anything that might come out of it. Then he stopped explaining and she seemed to forget: like a cat that sniffs around in the corners mewing for the drowned kittens a day or two and then back to lapping milk and napping in the wash basket. Women and nature forget. (*Redux* 36–37)

Although he mistakenly thinks that he alone remembers and grieves, he continually reminds Janice that she's "the girl that's good at death" and that "any dying I've been doing around here, you've been helping it right along" (48, 74). When the couple does have sex on the night before Janice leaves home, "her appetite frightens him, knowing he cannot fill it, any more than Earth's appetite for death can be filled" (40).

Rabbit not only sees death in Janice's sexuality, he sees it as a hungry, carnivorous beast: "It had all seemed a pit to him then, her womb and the grave, sex and death, he had fled her cunt as a tiger's mouth" (27). Elsewhere Rabbit thinks, "Mouths munch. Cunts swallow. Monstrous" (134). The old "myth of *vagina dentata* . . . derived from a paralyzing fear of female genitalia" is telling in a novel preoccupied with oral sex (Dworkin, *Pornography* 107). In a later variation, Rabbit associates Jill with Chinese women who "put razor blades in their cunts in case the Japanese tried rape" (*Redux* 140), and "he never forces his way into her without remembering those razor blades" (157).

Rabbit perceives Janice and Jill as enemies; so his relations with them, especially sexual relations, are frequently presented in terms of violence and warfare. Rabbit gets high when he beats his wife and thinks, "So it's war," when she charges expensive clothing for Nelson (203). Eventually, he imagines his semen is napalm that will burn Jill's skin (157). And he repeatedly translates marital and sexual disputes and rivalries into rancorous arguments over Vietnam.

Because Rabbit sees Janice as the vehicle of death, he has withdrawn from any personal or sexual intimacy with her. Despite his withdrawal, however, he is impelled to dominate Janice. He keeps her sexuality "locked up" in order to contain her destructive potential (56). Janice's interior monologue reveals that she understands why he "tried to make a box for her to put her in like they put Rebecca in when the poor little baby died" (57). He apparently dominates Janice in other ways as well, using strategies he perfected in *Rabbit, Run*. According to Nelson, he ridicules her. According to Janice, he calls her dumb "every hour on the hour" and denies her a voice (75). And he is still capable of intimidation and violence when she crosses or rejects him.

Rabbit is both overtly controlling and secretly manipulative. His passivity in allowing Janice to leave arises in part from guilt over his abusive treatment of her. Indeed, he regrets his oppression: "Poor mutt, he somehow squelched her potential. Let things bloom" (147). As Greiner notes, he is also afraid of failing Janice sexually and remains guarded to the last scene: "You can get in [bed] but don't expect anything, I'm still pretty screwed up (*John Updike's Novels* 73; *Redux* 403). Still, Mim and Janice's lover, Stavros, are perplexed by his behavior; Stavros speculates that Rabbit would have welcomed "any disaster" that set him free (*Redux* 366). The uncertainty surrounding his motives arises from the fact that Rabbit, miscalculating a power play, effectively pushes Janice out when she is willing to end her affair; and later, during his interview with Stavros, Rabbit sets unreasonable conditions for her return. Mary Allen maintains that author and protagonist both want Janice back but only as demoralized as she was before. Allen sees Janice's return as a humiliating defeat: "Janice's lover soon tires of her, and she returns from her affair mellowed but not buoyed up. More dependent on Harry than ever, she now knows that no one else will have her. The return to him comes about with none of the style she was beginning to show when she left. Once again she is dowdy Janice, properly humbled and inept" (88). Although most critics disagree with Allen that this is the Janice who returns to the marriage, her perception that this is the Janice that Rabbit (at least) prefers is accurate. This is the Janice, "humbled," "dowdy," "inept," and "dependent," that Rabbit in his seeming passivity manipulates to regain (88). It is symptomatic of his deadness that he is frightened by any growth in Janice and by any revision of the terms of their marriage.

When Janice initially determines to break with Stavros, Rabbit tells her to keep him. She asks, "Aren't you going to stop me?" but he answers, "See him if you want to" (*Redux* 78). His controversial reaction involves more than hurt feelings or injured pride. Rabbit's relationships are power struggles and even after ten years of marriage, he is unwilling to empower Janice with the knowledge that she is loved or even wanted. Remember that his mother played the same miserable game with Earl in *Rabbit, Run*: "I didn't want *you*; you wanted *me*. Or wasn't it that way?" (154).

As soon as Janice leaves, Rabbit begins to play the part of the innocent victim: "Janice went first. I keep inviting her back" (*Redux* 166). As in *Rabbit, Run*, however, he continues to be a powerful victim who covertly manipulates for advantage. When he agrees to let Skeeter stay, the narrator asks, "Why has he invited this danger?" and answers, "To get Janice to rescue him" (*Redux* 212), and later that night, Rabbit tells Jill he has let Skeeter stay because

> "Janice has been doing some things out of the way, so I have to do things out of the way."
> "To pay her back."
> "To keep up with her." (215)

The interview with Stavros confirms not only Rabbit's appalling devaluation of Janice ("So now you've tried her in all positions and want to ship her back. Poor old Jan. So dumb" [181]). The interview also confirms how far Rabbit will go to force his wife to accept his valuation as reality. Because he wants Janice back demoralized and dependent, he insists that Stavros reject and throw her out, without any assurance that she is wanted at home. When Stavros asks, "If I kick her out, will you pick her up?" Rabbit snaps, "Kick her out and see" (181). He realizes this maneuver is evil:

> There is a depth of suffering, of toothsore reality, beneath this finagle, that makes it silly, worse than silly, evil. His bladder gets a touch of that guilty sweetness it had when as a child he was running to school late, beside the slime-rimmed gutter water that ran down from the ice plant. He tries to explain. "Listen Stavros. You're the one in the wrong. You're the one screwing another man's wife. If you want to pull out, pull out. Don't try to commit me to one of your fucking coalition governments." (181)

Mary Angstrom and Mim also manipulate on Rabbit's behalf. Mim announces she has come "to help her [Mom] help *you*" and reassures Rabbit that "we'll get her back" (368, 360). And despite his verbal snipes at Mim for sleeping with Stavros, he thinks of his sister as the Angstroms' "secret weapon," "a gaudy knife into the heart of the Springer empire" (364–65), and he benefits from her strategy to end the relationship in a way that undermines Janice's position. As noted, critic Allen believes that Janice returns weaker than she left, although most critics find her much improved. Andrew S. Horton, for example, says that "Charlie 'remakes' Janice so she feels ready to return home" (576).

The contrast between Charlie Stavros and Rabbit is illuminating. The two characters manifest the difference Updike sees between "those for whom nothingness is no problem, and those for whom it is an insuperable problem" (*SC* 229). Because Charlie has had a rheumatic heart since childhood, he has internalized and accepted death as part of his human condition. As a consequence of his acceptance— that is, because death is not something for which he needs to assign blame—Charlie loves life, nature, and sex. Janice describes him to Rabbit: "He has a gift, Charlie does, of making everything exciting— the way food tastes, the way the sky looks, the customers that come in. . . . He loves life. He really does, Harry. He loves life" (*Redux* 73). Also as a consequence of his acceptance, Stavros sees and relates to people as people rather than as projections of fear. Mim tells the Angstroms that Charlie treats Janice as a person. She says:

> "I thought he was sweet. And quite intelligent. And *much* nicer about you all than you are about him. He was very thoughtful about Janice, he's probably the first person in thirty years to give her some serious attention as a *per*son. He sees a lot in her."
>
> "Must use a microscope," Rabbit says. (366)

The mean-spiritedness of Rabbit's belittling attitude is striking when set beside Stavros's generosity.

Critic Falke observes that Stavros has divine associations. His name means "cross" in Greek, and Janice regains the gift of life only after nailing herself to his body in an effort to save him (71). Despite this association, however, Stavros does not want to save Janice in the long term, because she interferes with his own need to "keep things orderly" (*Redux* 388). Nevertheless, since he does not externalize death, Stavros is not, like Rabbit, angry or violent or racist or nationalistic; he does not "hate sex" or find "technology that sexy," and this distinction between the men continues to be important in subsequent novels (*Redux* 57, 42).[8]

Stavros brings Janice to life like "mud made radiant," while Rabbit, who cannot accept death, leads his young lover to destruction

(382). Elizabeth Tallent observes that Updike's protagonists have an uncanny ability to turn lovers into wives (4). As we shall see, what this odd capacity finally means is that "when they find the woman of their dreams they invariably begin to hate her" (Hendin 102). Indeed, as with Ruth in *Rabbit, Run*, Jill is transformed into a mirror image of Janice at her worst, and then Jill is allowed to die in the bed she shares with Rabbit.

Nelson

Just as daily contact eases Rabbit's relationship with his mother, his care of Nelson in Janice's absence brings him closer to his son. He is finally able, on the day of the fire at least, to identify with Nelson and feel overwhelmed by love. As they walk to Peggy's apartment,

> Rabbit is struck, seeing their elongated shadows side by side, by how much like himself Nelson walks: the same loose lope below, the same faintly tense alertness of the head and shoulders above. In the shadow the boy, like himself, is tall as the giant at the top of the beanstalk, treading the sidewalk on telescoping legs. Rabbit turns to speak. Beside him, the boy's overlong black hair bounces as he strides to keep up, lugging his pajamas and toothbrush and change of underwear and sweater in a paper grocery bag for tomorrow's boat ride. Rabbit finds there is nothing to say, just mute love spinning down, love for this extension of himself downward into time when he will be in the grave, love cool as the flame of sunlight burning level among the stick-thin maples and fallen leaves, themselves flames curling. (*Redux* 309)

The passage looks back to *Rabbit, Run*, where Rabbit imagines "the vertical order of parenthood, a kind of thin tube upright in time in which our solitude is somewhat diluted" (228). For the most part, in that novel, Rabbit sees his children in an oppositional framework; their lives have cut him off from his own childhood, signaling his adult responsibilities and eventual decline. So his positive identification with his son here is a significant step forward, although it comes too late to help Nelson.

Nelson is at crucial point in his development. He stands at the edge of manhood needing "something" to affirm his "specialness" in order to move forward confidently (*Run* 120). In earlier days, Rabbit himself had been affirmed by an adoring, if oppressive, mother; by his faith in a God "he [was] the apple of the eye of"; by being "first-rate" at basketball; and by being a "winner" with Mary Ann (*Rich* 302; *Run* 101, 184). Just the opposite conditions now shape Nelson's future—Janice abandons him; he looks, as he has been taught, "no higher than his father's head" (*Redux* 325); he is unsuccessful in sports; and he is powerless to save the young woman he loves from destruction. If Nelson is devalued and misguided by society, and if he cannot look to God either for affirmation or for a confirmation of his place in the order of things, then his father's approval and support become all the more critical to his progress. The bitterly unhappy young man of years to come remembers this summer as the turning point in his life, and he remembers that his father failed him.

What Nelson thinks he needs is a minibike. As soon as Rabbit comes home from work, Nelson begins pressing him for one like Billy Fosnacht's. Nelson has picked up on the pervasive cultural message that material possessions (especially cars for men) will provide the boost he needs in status and self-esteem. Rabbit feels guilty that he can't afford the bike, but he does explain that "the reason Fosnacht keeps getting Billy all this expensive crap is probably he feels guilty for leaving him" (*Redux* 17). His insight is accurate; the bike is a material, mechanical, cheaply made substitute for a relationship. However, Rabbit, who has withdrawn from his family emotionally despite having become a steady provider, fails to apply this insight to his own relationship with Nelson. The issue of the bike underlines the fact that these adolescent boys need more from their fathers than material benefits, although years later, in *Rabbit Is Rich*, Rabbit will still regret not having bought Nelson a minibike.

Rabbit, in fact, sees that Nelson is in trouble and wants his son to have "something" (now called "bliss") to sustain him through life. He wonders, "How can he get the kid interested in sports? If he's too short for basketball, then baseball. Anything, just to put something there, some bliss, to live on later for a while. If he goes empty now he won't last at all, because we get emptier" (*Redux* 25). Unfortunately, according to Rabbit, basketball has lost its magic ("everything the jump shot, big looping hungry blacks" [18]), and Nelson is too short for the game anyway. But a day at the ballpark also proves disappointing: "The spaced dance of the men in white" fails to "enchant" or "yield its meaning" (18). What baseball used to represent to Rabbit was a combination of perpetual youth, idealism, ritual, grace, and the American Dream, but the listless men on the field now seem little different from enervated factory workers. Each player has his mind on "the own-your-own-bowling alley money" that goes along with "making it into the big leagues" (83). The "bliss" of sports has been drained by greedy materialism. Both the fact that it *could* be drained, however, and the fact that Rabbit himself has grown "emptier" over the years suggest that such bliss was never sufficiently grounded to provide an enduring hedge against despair. So perhaps it is not worth passing on to Nelson, though in a world of "slippery disposable gloss," Rabbit can find nothing else to sustain himself and his boy (25).

Like his own father, Rabbit now lacks a vision worth passing on. His confusion reflects a general cultural incapacity to identify and provide what a child, or anyone else, needs to sustain psychospiritual life. In addition, as Rabbit's own masculine identity is undermined in this novel, his uncertainty about guiding Nelson is understandable. At this point, these impediments become secondary to the fact that Rabbit remains profoundly ambivalent toward the boy. Rabbit still dislikes Nelson and has withdrawn to the extent that he doesn't know who the boy is, let alone what he might need.

What Rabbit dislikes in Nelson is Janice or, more precisely, his sense of other in the boy. Perhaps Mary Angstrom triggered this reaction. The narrator says Mary has never forgiven Nelson "for not being another Rabbit" and mentions an incident in *Rabbit, Run* in which she emphasizes Nelson's resemblance to the Springers, saying that the three-year-old could not grow up to be a ball player like his father because "he has those little Springer hands" (*Redux* 93; *Run* 211). At that time, Rabbit thought, "It shouldn't matter what size hands Nelson has. Now he discovers it does matter; he doesn't want the boy to have his mother's hands, and . . . likes [him] a little less" (*Run* 212). Over the years, Nelson has grown more like his mother who is also small, unathletic ("clumsy"), dark, and feminine: "Nelson, at thirteen, is under average height, with his mother's dark complexion, and something finely cut and wary about his face that may have come from the Angstroms. His long eyelashes come from nowhere, and his shoulder-length hair is his own idea. Somehow, Rabbit feels, if he were taller it would be all right, to have hair so long. As is, the resemblance to a girl is frighteningly strong" (*Redux* 16). The relationship between athletics and masculinity in *Rabbit, Run* continues to be important here because Rabbit not only tries unsuccessfully to relate to the boy in terms of sports but, more important, measures his son by an athletic standard and finds him lacking. Jill accurately observes that Rabbit treats the boy like a "failed little athlete because he's not six feet six" (*Redux* 191).

What is worse for Nelson is that his father, and much of his society, correlates athletic ability with masculinity. Rabbit thinks, "A few inches. In a world where inches matter. Putts. Fucks. Orbits.

Squaring up a form. He feels bad about Nelson's height" (*Redux* 18). Measurement of some kind is paramount in a hierarchical system, and areas of male competition tend to overlap. Putts, "fucks," orbits, and squaring translate into athletics, sex (penile length [18, 134]), technology (control), and work. In Rabbit's mind, the lack of those crucial inches means Nelson is a failure both as an athlete and as a man.

The competitive athletic model not only ritualizes contests for dominance and measures (scores) the results but also furnishes participants with clearly defined identities, roles, relationships, and rules. Playing basketball allowed the younger Rabbit to withdraw from the complex human world and to safely and successfully negotiate a constructed one. Furthermore, Rabbit was mistakenly assured by Tothero that the competitive athletic model was an adequate representation of the "game of life" (*Run* 62). To a significant extent, Rabbit's own masculine identity, his perceptions of the world, and his responses to it conform to that model. Nelson's physical measurements have determined that he will never be "first rate" in basketball, but his even more discouraging lack of interest or ability in any sport makes Rabbit question his son's masculinity, as he will continue to do, with damaging results, in the next two novels. And, finally, as noted earlier, athletics are an important means of inculcating boys as workers. At one point in this novel, Rabbit's boss Pajasek delivers a locker room pep talk, encouraging Rabbit to conform: "We have a team here, we're in a highly competitive game, let's keep up our end, what do you say?" (*Redux* 216). Later, of course, Pajasek summarily fires Rabbit and advises him to look out for "Number One" (342). The point, nevertheless, is that athletics are so intimately related to masculine identity for Rabbit that to see his son as unathletic is to see him as not masculine.

Rabbit's perception of Nelson as feminine is emphasized several times. The boy looks, Rabbit thinks, "like a sulky girl" (25), and "it unsettles Harry, how in the corner of his eye, once or twice a day, he seems to see another woman in the house, a woman who is not Janice; when it is only his long-haired son" (25). What Rabbit fears in Mary's or Janice's femininity may be its power, but what he fears in Nelson's is its powerlessness. Some theorists believe man fears the power of woman and renders her powerless in response. Then he fears being like her *because* she is powerless. In other words, our "*inferiors*" "expose us to the reality of our own powerlessness" (Astrachan 18). Such an interpretation is consistent with Rabbit's perception of weakness in Nelson:[9] "The kid's face is tense. Mom was right, too delicate, too nervous. Thinks the world is going to hurt him, so it will. The universal instinct to exterminate the weak" (*Redux* 225). Rabbit's observation not only hints at the cultural prejudice that associates the feminine with weakness, but more disturbing, his observation acknowledges the cultural impulse to repress (or exterminate) the feminine or, conversely, to feminize what is to be destroyed. Identifying Nelson as feminine and as victim arouses in the father both a dislike for the boy and a desire to protect him. This mixed attitude and its consequences for Nelson unfold in the subsequent novels.

Finally, Nelson is dark like his mother. To Rabbit, dark people—Janice, Tonto, Stavros, Skeeter, blacks, or Vietnamese—are always radically other. Regardless of origin or citizenship, they are aliens who arouse fear and hatred. For example, "[Rabbit] stares at Janice and she is dark and tense: an Indian. Massacre this squaw" (*Redux* 50). He thinks of the young blacks on the bus as taking over America and usurping his place in the order of creation.

> They are a strange race. Not only their skins but the way they're put together, loose-jointed like lions, strange about the head, as if their thoughts are a different shape and come out twisted even when they mean no menace. It's as if, all these Afro hair bushes and gold earrings and hoopy noise on buses, seeds of some tropical plant sneaked in by birds were taking over the garden. His garden. Rabbit knows it's his garden and that's why he's put a flag decal on the back window of the Falcon. (13)

All of the dark people in this novel, including Nelson, challenge Rabbit's conception of the world, but it is ultimately their darkness, their otherness, that fascinates and frightens him. When he reads from one of Skeeter's books, "It frightens him, as museums used to frighten him, when it was part of school to take trips there and to see the mummy rotting in his casket of gold, the elephant tusk filed into a hundred squinting Chinamen. Unthinkably distant lives, abysses of existence, worse than what crawls blind on the ocean floors" (227).

To summarize, Rabbit admits that he loves Nelson second only to his mother, but he has nevertheless withdrawn from the boy. Unable to encompass that Springer otherness in his son, he withholds the affirmation that Nelson desperately seeks. As with Janice, Rabbit invests Nelson with negative values that obscure his real identity and needs. Lacking the necessary knowledge and vision, Rabbit is unable to provide for Nelson or to encourage his maturation. In addition, in this novel Rabbit begins to see Nelson as a sexual rival.

In Jill Pendleton, Nelson finds a sister, a friend, and a potential lover willing to "treat him like a human being" (191). Jill rejects the materialistic conception of humankind that Nelson has struggled under and opens new possibilities for self-definition. Furthermore, she flatly rejects the competitive athletic model of masculinity that has devalued and humiliated Nelson. Her transforming influence can be seen in the fact that Nelson, in the face of imposing destructive forces, assumes a nurturing, protective role that is decent, mature, and "masculine." When Rabbit disregards Nelson's pleading, allows Jill to be enslaved and destroyed, and belittles Nelson's grief by calling it "self-pity," the damage is irreparable (363). With Jill dies Nelson's hopeful manhood, and in the next two novels, we find him imprisoned in anger and powerlessness.

At one point in the novel, Nelson declares that he wants to grow up to be like his father. Unfortunately, Nelson *does* grow to resemble Rabbit as another case of arrested development. This is quite evident in *Rabbit Is Rich* where, when Pru asks Nelson, "Why don't you grow up?" he gives his pregnant wife "a little vengeful shove" down a staircase (although he cannot remember it clearly later), nearly repeating his family history by destroying his own daughter (315).

Rabbit's deadness, then, is manifested in emotional detachment from Nelson and anyone else who matters (Slethaug 244). Despite some progress, he continues to regard Nelson as a threat and is unable to encourage or affirm his son's development either as a person or as a man. He has withdrawn from personal and sexual intimacy with his wife, having also identified her with nature and death. He has devoted himself to controlling her by undermining her confidence. He has neglected his stricken mother because he fears the implications of her death. He has lost touch with his sister Mim. He has almost no ties with the larger community. At work, he has no friends except for Earl; he has no companions, and he knows none of his neighbors.

Technology

Part of Rabbit's deadness is his refusal to participate in life at the risk of facing and enduring the inevitable, frightening compromises involved in living and dying. The other part of his response, the flip side of withdrawal, is his desperate need for control. Beginning with his wife Janice, he seeks to control the world that threatens him. It is important to note that when Rabbit withdraws, he tends to withdraw into areas that reinforce his sense of power (Newman 44–45). For example, when Janice comes to bed after working late with Stavros,

Rabbit touches her to confirm his suspicions but instantly retreats from the truth: "His fingers search lower, . . . discover a moistness already there. He thinks of feathering the linotype keys, of work tomorrow, and is already there" (*Redux* 27). Frightened and hurt, Rabbit immediately withdraws to his work and his machine. Similarly, responding to pressure from Earl to visit Mom and unnerved by his discovery that Janice lied to him, Rabbit explodes, "'Goddammit Pop I have a family of my own to run! I can't do everything.' He returns to his machine gratefully. And it fits right around him, purrs while he brushes a word from his mind ('Poconos'), makes loud rain when he touches the keys, is pleased he is back" (31). Critics who see Rabbit solely as a victim of technological progress fail to acknowledge that he himself is a technological man and that his involvement sheds light on the national penchant as well as the reverse. Rabbit's machine

> stands tall and warm above him, mothering, muttering, a temperamental thousand-parted survival from the golden age of machinery. The sorts tray is on his right hand; the Star Quadder and the mold disc and slug tray on his left; a green-shaded light bulb at the level of his eyes. Above this sun the machine shoulders into shadow like a thunderhead, its matrix return rod spiralling idly, all these rustling sighing tons of intricately keyed mass waiting for the feather-touch of his intelligence. Behind the mold disc the molten lead waits; sometimes when there is a jam the lead squirts hot out; Harry has been burned. But the machine is a baby; its demands, though inflexible, are few, and once these demands are met obedience automatically follows. There is no problem of fidelity. Do for it, it does for you. And Harry loves the light . . . that nowhere casts a shadow, light so calm and fine you can read the glinting letters backwards at a glance. It contrasts to the light in his home, where standing at the kitchen sink he casts a shadow that looks like dirt over the dishes, and sitting in the living room he must squint against the bridge lamp Janice uses to read magazines by, and bulbs keep burning out on the stair landing, and the kid complains except when it's totally dark about the reflections on the television screen. In the big room of the Verity Press, ceilinged with fluorescent tubes, men move around as spirits, without shadows. (29–30)

The narrator's description refers obliquely to the significant determinants of Rabbit's behavior—the desire for a comforting mother rendered as helpless and easily controlled as a baby, the need to escape from the human complications and demands at home, the desire for power satisfied by tons "awaiting the feather touch of his intelligence"

(*Redux* 29–30; Newman 44). Like the simple math he was good at in school and like the basketball he excelled at, the machine (and by extension technology in general) is yet another constructed world into which Rabbit can withdraw and whose relatively simple rules he can master to achieve security and control. The price he pays, however, is that of becoming one of the enervated "spirits" or automatons featured in the opening paragraphs of the novel.

With this machine, Updike demonstrates that withdrawal into technology is both ineffective and dangerous. Humankind cannot escape its conflicts because, as Jill points out, "whatever men make . . . what they felt when they made it is there" (*Redux* 158). Her insight is verified when Rabbit's emotional upset over a telephone altercation with Janice produces errors in his text. Furthermore, it is Rabbit's initial withdrawal from Janice and his neglect of family concerns that eventually leads to his newsworthy catastrophe. The connection between Rabbit's individual and public life is emphasized when he sets the newspaper piece reporting the fire and death at his home. And, finally, Updike suggests that, far from enhancing Rabbit's security or power, technological advances (in photo-offset printing) ultimately make his job obsolete, reducing him to the condition of a dependent adolescent in his parents' home. On another level, the evasive, questing technology symbolized by the moon shot involves Brewer components whose manufacture contaminates the local river. And the power-seeking technology that makes America's "patient bombing" for freedom possible also defoliates Vietnam and threatens humankind with extinction (*Redux* 47).

Judie Newman's excellent work, *John Updike*, develops these relationships at length (39–61) by applying the insights of Marshall McLuhan, a theorist on the role of media in Western culture. Like Robert Detweiler, she sees Rabbit as a Gutenberg man whose Linotype machine reflects his habit of seeing the world in simplistic, oppositional, black-and-white terms. The "fastidious" boy of *Rabbit, Run* still wants control; he wants a rigid, orderly, linear, nonthreatening world. Newman's argument connects the Gutenberg man's controlling tendencies with violence and militarism. She says that "McLuhan envisages war as a reaction to a threatened sense of self and an attempt to reassert identity in new forms" (54).

And finally, a technology that marginalizes or exploits human needs cannot satisfy them authentically. Dehumanizing labor, polluted environments, chemically tainted food, bad mass-produced art (and even mechanical sex) leave the characters depleted rather than renewed. When he tries to find an appropriate gift for his dying mother, he thinks, "What a lot of ingenious crap there is in the world," yet "the pain of the world is a crater all these syrups and pills a thousandfold would fail to fill" (*Redux* 90).

Violence

Updike establishes a similar pattern of relationship connecting Rabbit's evasive and controlling impulses, his personal violence, and the Vietnam War. This connection is generally overlooked, as many critics feel no need to account for the fact that Rabbit beats people who are weaker than himself. Whether critics in the past felt that a certain level of violence at home (and particularly against women) was normal or felt that Rabbit's pain and confusion constitute extenuating circumstances, avoiding the issue of Rabbit's violence diminishes the import of the novel.

There are too many graphic descriptions of Rabbit's abuse to ignore. For example, when Janice denies her infidelity, Rabbit beats her:

> "You dumb bitch," he says. He hits her not in the face but on the shoulder, like a man trying to knock open a stuck door.
> She hits him back, clumsily, on the side of the neck, as high as she can reach. Harry feels a flash of pleasure: sunlight in a tunnel. He hits her three, four, five times, unable to stop, boring his way to that sunlight, not as hard as he can hit, but hard enough for her to whimper; she doubles over so that his last punches are thrown hammerwise down into her neck and back. (*Redux* 64)

He stops when "astonished by the beauty expressed in her abasement" and carries her into the living room with "zombie-strength" (65).

Unlike Janice, Skeeter baits Rabbit by attacking his white, middle-class, American male values. Skeeter insults Rabbit's mother, his father, and his God without result, but when he unzips his fly, asserting himself sexually, Rabbit's anger is touched with fear:

> Rabbit's time has come. He is packed so solid with anger and fear he is seeing with his pores. He wades toward the boy deliciously and feels his fists vanish, one in the region of the belly, the other below the throat. He is scared of the head, whose glasses might shatter and slash. Skeeter curls up and drops to the floor dry as a scorpion and when Rabbit pries at him he has no opening. . . . He

wants to pry this creature open because there is a soft spot where
he can be split and killed; the curved back is too tough, though
knuckles slammed at the hole of the ear do produce a garbled
whimper. (210–11)

In both cases, Rabbit's behavior is partly an evasion. He attacks as an alternative to absorbing, or even acknowledging, hurt, confusion, anger, or fear. His violence seems to him like a way out, like "sunlight in a tunnel" or wading toward something (64).[10] His wish to find holes in or to open his victims connects this behavior with need to find escape holes in the nets of *Rabbit, Run*.

Edward Vargo suggests that, at least in respect to Janice, Rabbit achieves through violence an ecstasy he once sought in sex (155). Whether that ecstasy arises out of the relief produced by direct action or out of the assertion of power, there is nothing else in the novel like the weird euphoria of Rabbit's personal violence but the description of America's role in Vietnam: "America is beyond power, it acts as in a dream, as a face of God. Wherever America is, there is freedom, and wherever America is not, madness rules with chains, darkness strangles millions. Beneath her patient bombing, paradise is possible" (*Redux* 47). Rabbit's violence, more obviously, allows him to reassert control when he feels threatened. Vargo also notes that the "whimper" of submission offered by Janice and Skeeter is important to Rabbit because it confirms his domination (161). As soon as the token is given, Rabbit retreats. Jill, however, who recognizes and who is unwilling to appease his need for power, incites "cold fury" (169). Rabbit sees in "her thin disdainful face with its prim lips and its green eyes drenched so dark in defiance their shade is as of tree leaves, a shuffling concealing multitude, a microscopic forest he wants to bomb" (169). Rabbit here links the national violence with his own.

The Lone Ranger

The extended analogy drawn between Rabbit and the Lone Ranger incorporates the relationship linking evasion, control, violence, technology, sexuality, racism, the American Dream, and masculinity. The Lone Ranger scene occurs early in the novel when Rabbit spends the evening alone with Nelson, watching a comedy skit on *The Carol Burnett Show* in which the Lone Ranger's wife complains to him of her drudgery and loneliness. She reproaches him for disappearing and for only giving silver bullets to her as gifts. During the skit, the wife opens a closet where the silver bullets are stored, and they spill out onto the stage and remain underfoot. Tonto, played by a black actor, quips that the next time the Lone Ranger should "put-um bullet in gun first" (*Redux* 23). The wife turns on Tonto for not returning their dinner invitations. He replies that if she came to his home, she would be kidnapped by braves. Interested, she says, "Let's go" (23). At the end of the skit, the wife tells the Lone Ranger to choose between Tonto and herself; he tells Tonto to saddle up and leaves. His wife then changes the phonograph record from the *William Tell Overture* to "Indian Love Call"; Tonto returns and embraces the wife.

The skit proves to be ironic because Rabbit loses both of his women to dark men, Janice to the Greek "spic," Charlie Stavros, and Jill to black Skeeter. Of course, as the skit (and later Stavros) suggests, the loss has less to do with the dark man's treachery than with the hero's neglect. Ironically, Rabbit calls Stavros, who becomes his faithful companion in *Rabbit Is Rich*, Tonto.

Critic Horton reminds us that although the Ranger "defends the middle class institutions of home, the family, and womanhood, and is 'fair' to all racial and religious groups," as his mask and name suggest, he is an outsider who is unable or unwilling to live in the society he protects (571). Like other American heroes including Rabbit, he rejects woman and other and, because of his withdrawal, is entirely ignorant of their identities or needs. As he watches the skit, Rabbit realizes that "he understands nothing about Tonto" (*Redux* 23). This idea is developed later by Jill who tells Rabbit that "the reason Skeeter annoys and frightens you is he's opaque" (229), and by Skeeter himself, who confirms, "Some white man see a black man he don't see a man he sees a *symbol*, right? All these people around here are walking around inside their own *heads*, they don't even know if you kick somebody else it *hurts*" (242).

Horton's essay, "Ken Kesey, John Updike, and the Lone Ranger," stresses that the Lone Ranger was the most popular and influential radio hero during the time when Rabbit grew up. So, Rabbit nostalgically recalls that the summer evenings of his childhood were interrupted at half past seven for *The Lone Ranger*, and he associates the program with the national self-confidence that prevailed during World War II: "In the days of the war no one asked" which was "the side of right" (*Redux* 24). Like childhood and like the American Dream, the Lone Ranger represents a comforting but arrested, overly simplistic conception of reality. According to Horton, the Ranger operates in a world where good and evil are "readily identifiable forces," "might and right are on his side," and violence is the only law (571). Jill, however, explains that although the habit of translating instinct into immediate action worked in the "frontier moment," that moment has passed. Jill tells Rabbit, "Because of the competitive American context, you've had to convert everything into action too rapidly.... But now, you see, we must [give thought], because action is no longer enough, action without thought is violence. As we see in Vietnam" (*Redux* 228–29).

Even as he watches the skit, Rabbit begins to question the Lone Ranger's perspective. He thinks, "The Lone Ranger is a white man, so law and order on the range will work to his benefit, but what about Tonto?" (24). Times have changed, and the order that once seemed absolute is now subject to scrutiny and even ridicule. The icon of Rabbit's childhood, whom Nelson barely knows, has been reduced to a cuckold in a comedy routine. Rabbit must adjust to this changed world and, according to Horton, "the whole novel deals with Rabbit's attempt to come to an understanding of the problems raised by this skit" (575).

All of the themes just discussed are unified in the symbolic silver bullet. Horton believes that the silver bullet represents the material possessions ("security, job, money" [577]) that Rabbit and the Lone Ranger give to their wives instead of a relationship (suggesting both what is given and what is withheld). The phallic bullet also recalls fatherhood described as a "thin tube" in *Rabbit, Run*. Rabbit now withholds not only sex but children from Janice. In addition, the bullet is a spacecraft, a product of evasive, questing, "frontier" technology. And it is literally a bullet, a product of the technology of coercion and death. It looks and travels like the bombs or silver canisters of napalm that fall over Vietnam. Tellingly, Rabbit and Stavros speak of the Vietnam War as if it were a "Cherokee uprising" (*Redux* 49; Horton 575). The bullet also suggests the silver bullet that Rabbit asks his boss for in his dream and that Pajasek presumably fires when he lets Rabbit go. Finally, the bullets that spill from one reality to another are tokens suggesting the interrelatedness of Rabbit's life.

While it is a particularly illuminating example, the Lone Ranger skit is only one of many links between Rabbit's personal life and the national life. Detweiler writes of what he calls the novel's "orchestration of tropes" (127), an arrangement in which images and metaphors arising from Rabbit's life and from the national life

> merge, blending in and out of each other, to produce a sense of interconnectedness and interchangeability that gives the book its

> integrity and vast allusiveness. Moreover the big subjects of war, sex, violence, space exploration, drugs, American polarization and loss of self-confidence are related better than ever to the Middle-American milieu. (*John Updike* 130)

Markle suggests that Updike's characters are "microcosms of the United States as a whole," and she notes his sense that "society even reflects each presidential administration" (147, 148). The discussion here, and in the following chapters, insists on a causal relationship between private and public life. That is, Updike does not present Rabbit *merely* as an "American 'everyman' caught in the midst of events over which he has no control" (Uphaus 80), nor is this novel weak "in fathoming causes" or "mute about questions of motivation" (Samuels, "Updike on the Present" 64–65). Updike has a coherent vision, similar to Whitman's, from which the correspondences flow, that Rabbit and his problems and the nation and its problems are all one. Causes and motivations are revealed *in* correspondences, and although time does not permit tracing every strand, the threads of relationship in *Rabbit Redux* are drawn from the skein of the masculine self and woven into a single cloth.

SIX

Life in Furnace Township

IN THE interim between Rebecca's death and burial in *Rabbit, Run,* when Rabbit is overwhelmed with guilt and grief, two older men, both pragmatists and materialists, offer advice. Marty Tothero arrives to disclaim any responsibility for the Angstroms' tragedy and to coach his "greatest boy" in the game of life one last time (46). He says: "Right and wrong aren't dropped from the sky. We. We make them. Against misery. Invariably, Harry, invariably . . . misery follows their disobedience. Not our own, often at first not our own. Now you've had an example of that in your own life. . . . When I'm dead and gone, remember how your old coach told you to avoid suffering" (*Run* 257–58). According to Tothero, Rebecca's death followed from Rabbit's having violated the man-made rules that limit misery, and he can only avoid further suffering for himself and his family by keeping those rules— the conventions of right and wrong—more closely in the future. Later, Fred Springer, who understands the "business" of life, tells Rabbit that, since everything has been smoothed over with the coroner, "the question is, How do we cut the losses from here on in?" (*Run* 264).

The opening chapter of *Rabbit Redux* reveals that following his flight at the end of *Rabbit, Run,* Rabbit has returned home yet again, this time stoically determined to cut his losses by minimizing his, and his family's, vulnerability. He has committed himself to a dreary life of scrupulous conformity to "forms without substance" (Slethaug 243). He now thinks, for example, that "life is quicksand. You've got to find a straight path and stick to it" (*Redux* 37). And he perfectly understands Jill's mother Mrs. Aldridge's need "to stay out of harm's way" and "not to have to apologize to any heavenly committee" following Jill's death (*Redux* 347). As Jill points out, however, Rabbit's conformity, his fidelity in marriage, his devotion to work, and his political conservatism are all products of "fear" and "tired pragmatism" rather than of inspiration, let alone love (228). He seems to have made a pact under which he agrees to scrupulously obey all the rules if chaos and death and suffering will leave him and his alone.

Until the opening of *Rabbit Redux*, Rabbit has been fairly successful at keeping disaster at bay and has even achieved a kind of psychological stasis. Still, it has been only a precarious truce—his mother has been slowly dying, and although he doesn't know it, trouble has been brewing at home. It has also been a "stale peace" (6); Janice feels like she's been put into a box and Nelson fails to thrive. Janice admits, "There've been a lot of days . . . when I was sorry you came back that time. You were a beautiful brainless guy and I've had to watch that guy die day by day" (74). Even Rabbit, who still has reliable intuitions, has been hoping for a way out. Janice tells Stavros, "He came back to me, to Nelson and me, for the old-fashioned reasons, and wants to live an old-fashioned life, but nobody does that any more, and he feels it. He put his life into rules he feels melting away now. I mean, I know he thinks he's missing something, he's always reading the paper and watching the news" (53). He has been on the lookout for "a new combination [that] might break it open, this stale peace" (6).

Updike associates Rabbit's refusal to engage with the notion of the "living dead" and presents this condition as an aberration worse than death itself (Markle 41). Indeed, Updike has mentioned elsewhere that he sees conflict, not stasis, as the natural human condition: "A person who has what he wants, a satisfied person, a content person, ceases to be a person. . . . Yes, I guess I do feel . . . that to be a person is to be in a situation of tension, is to be in a dialectical situation. A truly adjusted person is not a person at all—just an animal with clothes on" (*PUP* 485). According to Updike, life resists the kind of sterility and immobility Rabbit has imposed on himself and his family. Nature is all flux and process, as the black nightclub performer, Babe, reminds Rabbit in her song. The God of Ecclesiastes, whose purposes Babe celebrates, allows everything its season—but nothing beyond. In this novel, the ten-year "stale peace" ends, and Rabbit is "sent on a quest against his will" (Detweiler 134).

In order to live again, Rabbit must, inevitably, undergo exactly the process he has sought to avoid. Metaphorically at least, Rabbit endures death, submits to chaos, and suffers the loss of his identity.

The death is quick; when Janice admits her affair, "he remains stiff when she pulls at him, he is dead, she has killed him" (*Redux* 66). The process of decomposition is more complex. It is presented in terms of madness, oxidation, and conflagration in the metaphor of the madhouse windows that haunts this novel (14, 26, 98, 346) as the rose window haunted *Rabbit, Run*. Riding home on the bus the first day, Rabbit catches a "glimpse of the sunstruck windows, pumpkin orange blazing in reflection of the tall new wing of the County Hospital for the Insane" (14). The building can be seen from different parts of town. Rabbit thinks of the window when he tries to explain Jill's death to her mother: "But it is all life, sex, fire, breathing, all combination with oxygen, we shimmer at all moments on the verge of conflagration, as the madhouse windows tell us" (346).[1]

Rabbit must endure chaos before regaining life. As many critics have noted, his journey parallels the astronauts' journey to the desolate moon. His journey also conforms to the pattern of descent described by Northrop Frye in *The Secular Scripture* and already discussed in relation to *Rabbit, Run*. Once again, Rabbit loses an old identity, receives a new name (Skeeter calls him "Chuck") and a map, and travels through an instinctual underworld with, in this case, several guides. A sacrifice of innocent blood, Iphigenia's again, facilitates Rabbit's ascent. He returns with valuable information and regains his identity. As in the earlier novel, his progress coincides with a seasonal change; *Rabbit Redux* begins in late summer and continues through autumn. This pattern is worth noting, as so many critics have focused predominantly on the novel as a contemporary social document; Detweiler argues that *Rabbit Redux* is Updike's attempt to replace "myth supported fiction" (*John Updike* 126). He says, "Updike settles on two of the alternatives to a fiction supported by myth: on the stress on contemporary world events and on the orchestration of images" (126; Uphaus 7).

Updike also alludes ironically to Dante's journey in the *Inferno*.[2] When Rabbit sleeps, he dreams that Stavros (like Virgil) gives him a map, and the two of them leave a forest and approach "The Rise." In the *Inferno*, carnal sinners are blown about like leaves in the wind, an image that corresponds to Updike's use of weightlessness in his sexual descriptions. Dante's journey also incorporates lectures and education, and of course, when Dante reaches the frozen center of hell, he finds the vilest sinners to be those who betrayed innocent blood. The allusions serve as an ironic contrast. Not only is contemporary life hellish near Furnace Township, but in Dante's God-centered universe, even hell is better organized. Although Rabbit's journey is part of an old and respected tradition, his hell is more chaotic, his way is less clear, his guides are less reliable, and his end is less certain.

The Fixed, Fluid, and Disintegrating Self

Updike presents the self as a fluid as well as a fixed phenomenon. The first time Rabbit visits his mother, he ponders old photographs of Mim and himself. The crooked photographer who took those shots "by the somersault of time had become a donor of selves forever lost" (*Redux* 95). When he visits her again, he feels threatened by her suggestion that he "pray for rebirth" (198). Rebecca's death has left him so rigid with guilt and fear that he now believes "growth is betrayal" (78), and he wants his own identity to remain fixed: "He feels she is asking him to kill Janice, to kill Nelson. Freedom means murder. Rebirth means death. A lump, he silently resists. . . . An old lump whose only use is to stay in place to keep the lumps on top of him from tumbling" (198). Because of Janice's decisive action, however, Rabbit has no choice but to endure the change that follows, despite his fear.

Updike also distinguishes, as he did in *Rabbit, Run*, between the authentic self and the self assigned and defined by society. When Rabbit returned home and began to follow Tothero's athletic model again, he not only committed himself to a life of perfect conformity to rules as a way of avoiding penalties but also to an identity predicated upon his role and function in society. (As noted earlier, Tothero's model not only enabled the adolescent Rabbit to play it safe but it also furnished him with a clear, if limited, identity and with a set of prescribed relationships.) Two problems follow. On the one hand, as Rabbit discovered at the ballpark, filling assigned roles without passionate commitment produces listless frauds instead of baseball heroes. On the other hand, and more to the point at the moment, a prescribed identity not only may obscure the authentic self (so that Mim's publicity photograph is "less Mim than the men posing her" [*Redux*] 195) but also can only be maintained with the cooperation of the other players on the field. That is, social definitions require the concurrence of a partner or partners in relationship. In order for Rabbit's identity as a husband, worker, member of a privileged sex and race, or citizen of a dominant America to remain fixed, all other identities must remain fixed as well. The wife must consent to remain the wife and the underdog, the underdog; the employer must continue to employ and so on. The whole system of relationships must remain frozen. Rabbit recognizes this rigidity in his mother's unwillingness to accept Janice and Nelson; he thinks, "Her tyrant love would freeze the world" (197). On the other hand, Skeeter's readings from Frederick Douglass emphasize that when the slave, claiming a more authentic identity, refuses to be a slave, the whole system of relationships based on this fixity begins to crumble (283).

Almost everyone in Rabbit's life and society is changing. Janice sounds like someone else as her language and thoughts reveal Stavros's liberating influence. She gains confidence and resists continuing in the marriage under the old terms. Mrs. Angstrom has changed physically and lost her former vitality and power due to age and illness. Innocent Mim has become a prostitute. Nelson grows three inches as he enters adolescence. Sexually and racially "inferior" people refuse to be cowed. Pajasek no longer guarantees Rabbit's identity as a worker-provider. Even the Vietnamese refuse to be overwhelmed. Though she sounds painfully trite, Janice gives Rabbit good advice when she tells him that he too should search for "valid identity" (104).

One by one, the old tethers of Rabbit's identity are loosened, and he becomes unhinged. The experience is analogous to weightlessness or madness or oxidation. His predicament is neither entirely unique in literature nor exclusively contemporary. King Lear, discussed earlier as an archetype of the powerful victim, similarly anchors his identity to a network of unauthentic relationships and becomes unhinged, subject to madness and the wind, when he discovers those relationships are as insubstantial as his power. Granted that Lear's experience is more extreme and that the king attains tragic stature while Rabbit remains sad and foolish; nevertheless, these protagonists share a common delusion and the painful but liberating experience of disintegration.

Rabbit continues to be both the victim and the perpetrator of social definitions. Although he himself lacks a valid identity, that experience does not keep him from ruthlessly forcing his own and society's projections onto Janice and others. His dilemma is intimately related to the problem of freedom as presented in *Rabbit, Run* and discussed previously. The epigraph to *Of the Farm*, taken from Sartre and cited earlier, suggests that to be free, one must allow the freedom of others. Similarly, to be an authentic self, one must allow and relate to other authentic selves. Rabbit has consistently denied the identities of others. Now, by disowning their projected identities, they destabilize Rabbit's. And, just as Lear's madness has a counterpart in civil and international strife, so does Rabbit's.

The news on television, reports in the *Vat* (the newspaper Rabbit typesets), and the general gossip tell of civil rights unrest, the unsuccessful war, and the anti-Vietnam protests, and Janice's affair reflects both the sexual revolution and the rise of feminism. Each of these movements represents one aspect of a general challenge to the tyranny of the imagination imposed by the patriarchal order, and each movement contributes to the destabilization of the whole system. Updike clearly presents the challenge as necessary and potentially beneficial; nevertheless, as Gerda Lerner observes, "To step outside of patriarchal thought means: Being skeptical toward every known system of thought; being critical of all assumptions, ordering values and definitions" (228). To step outside of the patriarchal order means to step into revolution and chaos.

Chaos and Disintegration

One of the metaphors for Rabbit's flight in *Rabbit, Run* involves the earth's revolution around the sun. Rabbit throws the marriage out of balance as he pursues the course of self-interest to its furthest extreme. *Rabbit Redux* begins a decade later, during the period of imbalance and "tilting" following the summer solstice in July, when Janice pursues her own interests and throws the marriage out of balance in the opposite direction. The novel proceeds through the autumnal equinox, when balance is restored, However, the restoration of balance in the Angstrom marriage is also poignantly associated with the autumnal change and with the fiery death of young Jill, whose eyes are the color of "August grass" (*Redux* 129).

The moment Rabbit gets an inkling of Janice's infidelity, he feels "the world turn" as he watches the "Schlitz spinner doing its polychrome parabola over and over" (6). Later, at night, alone in bed, he dreams about his marriage going out of control: "He was dreaming about a parabolic curve, trying to steer on it, though the thing he was trying to steer was fighting him, like a broken sled" (26). When Janice joins him, however, "her being in the bed changes its quality, from a resisting raft he is seeking to hold to a curving course to a nest, a laden hollow, itself curved" (27). Once Janice leaves to join Stavros, Rabbit's bed remains tilted until the end of the novel. Jill is symbolically too light to restore the natural balance, and with her, Rabbit often wakes "to find himself nearly pushed from the bed by this inequality" (213). Part of the comfortable feeling of "nestling" with Janice in the Safe Haven Motel at the end arises from a restored equilibrium that is confirmed by Rabbit's ability to ride the "inward curve" to sleep (407).

This space metaphor is, of course, overshadowed by the metaphor of space exploration in which Rabbit and the astronauts travel through chaos to a barren moon and return home. Nevertheless, the equinox-solstice metaphor is a useful starting point for this discussion because in this novel, Rabbit's marriage represents traditional values and established order, and when Janice leaves and chaos floods in, Rabbit loses control.

Rabbit is surrounded and overwhelmed by utter confusion. Boundaries that were once rigidly maintained are no longer secure. Several critics have noted that the characters exchange roles and that fixed identifies disintegrate. Wives, lovers, sisters, and daughters begin to overlap as do lovers, husbands, and fathers. Rabbit becomes Chuck, Chuck is Charlie, Charlie is the Viet Cong and everyone else. Children are mature; parents, childish. The "refugee" guests usurp Rabbit's home and authority, and his younger sister saves her former protector.

Order collapses. The young die while the old live on, unable to die. Rabbit struggles with impotence while his dying mother is aroused by her medication. Gender identifications are confused. Nelson seems like a girl; Jill looks boyish; and Rabbit is attracted to Skeeter. Sex is angry and desperate, conveyed through images of war.

Mental faculties decline as the result of confusion and drugs. Without reliable guidelines, Rabbit is unable to make necessary distinctions or sound judgments. Good and evil, Jesus and Satan, seem to merge. Inertia overwhelms. Jill lacks the will to survive, and Rabbit lacks the will to protect the young. Inhibitions weaken. Passions fly out of control.

A sense of physical distress mounts. The smell of sewage permeates Rabbit's neighborhood as the smell of disease fills Mary's home. Mary's medications have frightening side effects. Sleep is troubled. Chemically tainted food and unappetizing meals are inedible. Characters get dizzy, lethargic, and queasy on marijuana. Drug hangovers last all day. Jill rots with Skeeter's "luminous poison" (254). She loses interest, stops eating, and vomits from heroin. This cumulative tide of nausea rises until Nelson finally retches after the fire.

Of particular interest to this discussion is Rabbit's loss of control over perspective and language, which contrasts with the rigid control he exercises in *Rabbit, Run*. Technical adjustments from *Rabbit, Run* to *Rabbit Redux* suggest the rippling effect. In the first novel, Rabbit's consciousness is the urgent, nearly exclusive focus of attention, and his vision dictates meaning and value. Now, as Updike's interest widens to include American society, Rabbit must share the reader's attention with sympathetic characters who challenge his worldview. His loss of control over perspective and language radically diminishes his authority. For Rabbit, the established order not only has the advantage that it is orderly but that it places him as the dominant male, in control of that order at least within his own home. Indeed, it is his repressive vision that drives Janice away. Previous discussion has established Rabbit's control of perspective, and following from that, his control of language in *Rabbit, Run* as an important manifestation of his gender-based power. *Rabbit Redux*, in many ways a mirror image of the earlier novel, now demonstrates that the overthrow of the established order, specifically the erosion of white male power, is manifested in a loss of control over perspective and language. Thus, when Janice rebels, Rabbit finds his first disturbing clues in her expanded vocabulary and "foreign" ideas and in the sound of "another voice in hers" (*Redux* 20). Once displaced, he "has this sensation of nobody hearing him" (35).

Rabbit's loss of control over perspective is incorporated into the structure of *Rabbit Redux* from the outset. While Updike continues to use the historical present to "reinforce the continuation of the earlier novel's action" (Detweiler, *John Updike* 134), he also modifies the narrator to serve a radically different purpose. The camera-eye narrator of *Rabbit, Run* reflects the tyranny of Rabbit's imagination by presenting his perspective almost exclusively. A manifestation of his solipsism, Rabbit's perspective dominates the novel to the extent that Updike must devise ways of revealing his fallibility indirectly. Now, a new "tricky narrator" further erodes Rabbit's authority by commenting on his actions and thoughts (Cox 135). Critic George Hunt dislikes the final effect of this shift and feels that because Updike assumes the "sociologist's stance," "the novel's tone is altered, becoming overly discursive instead of descriptive, unified more often by argument than by sensibility" (*Updike* 169). If, however, the novel is *about* the overthrow of one dominating perspective, then the technical adjustment is entirely appropriate.

Not only has the narrator been modified; so has the physical format. *Rabbit, Run* more or less simulates the continuous flow of Rabbit's sensibility. *Rabbit Redux*, however, is divided into four chapters,

"Mom/Pop/Moon," "Jill," "Skeeter," and "Mim." The first chapter reveals current situations and introduces challenges by Janice and Stavros, while each of the last three chapters presents the featured character's challenging worldview.

Because Rabbit dominates the perspective in *Rabbit, Run*, anyone who differs with him (e.g., Janice, Margaret) tends to be invalidated, but in *Rabbit Redux*, characters with differing interpretations of reality are, to use Updike's phrase, "considered respectfully" (*PUP* 490). He says, "I try to love both the redneck and the flower child, the anarchist bomb thrower" (*PUP* 490). To illustrate, Janice is seen in a purely negative light in the earlier novel by readers who accept Rabbit's hostile valuation of her without question. Now her sympathetic Molly Bloom monologue immediately wins our interest, sympathy, and respect.[3]

Not only does Rabbit lose control of perspective, but as a consequence, he also loses control over language itself: "All around him, Harry hears language collapsing" (*Redux* 150). And as Vaughan observes, "Updike goes to great pains to illustrate in stressing the point about the decline of language" (62). In one sense, Vaughan is entirely right—the *Vat* specializes in printing trash, Nelson curses, Mary's speech is distorted, and Janice sounds trite and trendy. However, the very notion of decline depends upon the position of the language user within the system. Rabbit thinks of language as in decline partly because it no longer exclusively projects his white male vision.

An interesting example of Rabbit's disempowerment is revealed in his verbal interaction with a coworker, Buchanan, and the black community. Recall that in *Rabbit, Run*, the first time Rabbit thinks Janice is "dumb," it is because she fails to get his joke about the MagiPeel Kitchen Peeler, and indeed, Janice does look stupid to many readers in that context. Because Rabbit controls perspective, we hardly stop to think that male humor is a linguistically "restricted code" that excludes and denigrates women.[4] In *Rabbit Redux*, however, Updike indicates Rabbit's loss of power by putting him in Janice's old position. In relation to the black community, Rabbit is the linguistic outsider who cannot catch the nuances, get the jokes, or be sure he is not being ridiculed. When Buchanan approaches, the narrator tells us, "Harry has known the other man by sight and name for years but still is not quite easy, talking to a black; there always seems to be some joke involved that he doesn't quite get" (*Redux* 101). "Their speech is so strange" to Rabbit that "he wonders if this is how they really talk" (117). Unsure of how to take Buchanan and the others, he does not know what is expected of him. This linguistic uncertainty puts Rabbit off balance and makes him feel, interestingly enough, *feminine*: "Distaste and excitement contend in Harry; he feels tall and pale beside Buchanan, and feminine, a tingling target of fun and tenderness and avarice mixed" (103).

The notion that Rabbit loses control over language is consistent with the interpretation that he is a Gutenberg man. Detweiler says Rabbit is comfortable only with "the linear thought and sequential action to which the printed page has accustomed him. As a conservative, he thinks not only within the framework of the old content of Western society, but also naturally enough, in terms of its patterns" (*John Updike* 136). One might add that the patriarchal culture that produced the printing press exploited its potential for control of perspective by limiting who might write or publish, or, as Skeeter notes, who might read. Now Jill and Skeeter introduce books about "distant lives" and revolutionary ideas—"stuff that makes Rabbit feel sick" (*Redux* 227). Jill expects Rabbit to learn rather than teach, and Skeeter selects the readings and dominates the discussions.

Even while Rabbit clings to the solid, actually leaden, written word, his Linotypist's trade is becoming obsolete.[5] The Gutenberg man and his way of seeing and saying are challenged by a multiplicity of mediums and messages (Newman 43–61). Thus, Updike incorporates not only a perceived decline but an increase in language and communication possibilities. *Rabbit Redux* includes typeset newspaper items, television interviews, simulations, spacecraft transmissions, game shows, comedy skits, movies, phone calls, notes, songs, cartoon drawings, ideographs, and spray-paint graffiti. Language may be "collapsing" from Rabbit's perspective (*Redux* 150), but it is also expanding exponentially. Everyone has something to say, and everyone, even Nelson, contradicts Rabbit.

To summarize, Rabbit suffers a metaphorical death, submits to chaos, and endures a loss of identity. He loses his wife; his name; his son; his surrogate daughter, Jill; his home; and his job. His faith in God has been shaken by Rebecca's drowning, and now his confidence in America and its institutions is undermined as well. His sense of place in society and in the family, which he derived from those beliefs, is compromised, and the authority of his position is diminished. He loses control of his faculties; his mind, judgment, and will are impaired by drugs, confusion, and fascination. His sexual identity is compromised. He loses control of perspective and language. When Rabbit finally "re-docks" with Janice at the Safe Haven Motel, he is a disempowered and diminished self (Vanderwerken 73), yet a number of critics have recognized the motel scene as a tentative beginning for the Angstroms:

> He slides down an inch on the cool sheet and fits his microcosmic self limp into the curved crevice between the polleny offered nestling orbs of her ass; he would stiffen but his hand having let her breasts go comes upon the familiar dip of her waist, ribs to hip bone, where no bones are, soft as flight, fat's inward curve, slack, his babies from her belly. He finds this inward curve and slips along it, sleeps. He. She. Sleeps. O.K.? (406–7)

The encouraging nature of this conclusion is clarified by reference to the situation it parallels in *Rabbit, Run* on the night preceding Rebecca's death when Rabbit demands that Janice "roll over" for masturbatory purposes, "thumps" her when she refuses to cooperate, and leaves in a rage (229). Rabbit has lost much, including his earlier assertiveness, but to use Updike's phrase, "perhaps one doesn't want it back" (*PUP* 484). And in exchange for the confidence, status, and power Rabbit has lost, he has gained new perspective and tolerance. For her part, Janice's identity is more secure, and she will continue to be less easily repressed in the future. So the Angstroms are better matched; their bed is balanced, judging by their comfortable nestling and by Rabbit's ability to ride the inward curve (a reference to the earth's elliptical path) to sleep. Furthermore, by shedding the limitations signified by their ill-fitting high school clothing, Rabbit and Janice prepare to begin anew.

Of course, even with this guardedly hopeful ending, Updike leaves a number of questions unanswered, once again submitting them to his readers for speculation. Two innocent female children are dead. The less optimistic critics have questioned whether the education, the humanizing of Rabbit Angstrom, or the restoration of the Angstrom's marriage is worth their sacrifice. And, as the marriage represents the established order, is Updike exposing the fact that patriarchal culture lives by the sacrifice of women?[6] The "resisting reader" has additional questions. Has Updike, like John Fowles, shown us that, while the male protagonist is humanized by his experience, his education depends upon women? And if so, is Rabbit or the reader in any real sense liberated from the old myths, or are they merely reimposed in a new form? Does the novel presume or expose the presumption that, as Fetterley observes in her study of Hemingway, "male life is what counts," while female life is supportive and expendable (71)? Or does Updike, as Mary Allen's work suggests, and as the reproduction of Frye's pattern of descent and ascent suggests, shore up by example the existing social order that he prefers or sees as inevitable? As with *Rabbit, Run*, Updike does not supply unambiguous or "right" answers, but he certainly raises the pertinent cultural and political questions.

SEVEN

Revolution and Chaos

THE POLITICAL aspects of *Rabbit Redux* are of particular interest in exploring several of the questions just posed. These aspects include Updike's ambivalent attitude toward revolution, arising from his belief that human institutions reflect human limitations, and his representation of two levels of political conflict. The first and more superficial conflict is between the established order and the peace and civil rights movements of the sixties. Updike uses this conflict to explore the weaknesses of each political faction while expressing reservations about the revolutionary process in general. The second conflict, less obvious but more disturbing, reenacts the perennial Freudian revolution of sons against their fathers and includes the unconscious (but not necessarily unintentional) use and destruction of Jill. The collapse of the old order leaves Rabbit, Skeeter, and even the suspected arsonists Showalter and Brumbach without any "moral guideposts" (Vaughan 25). With nothing to inhibit their destructive impulses, they revert to the most primitive level of political action, something on the order of William Golding's lost boys. The quest for validation and power, the accompanying increase in aggression, and the tendency toward scapegoating, which Tiger claims are characteristics of male group bonding, are acted out in the murder of Jill Pendleton–Iphigenia. In the myth, as in the novel, the perpetrators claim an innocence that, according to Edith Hamilton, was spurious even to the Greeks (248).

Several critics believe that *Rabbit Redux* is a "thesis novel" about the decline of America and death of the American Dream (Hunt, *Up-*

dike 169). Eugene Lyons argues that *Rabbit Redux* incorporates a number of clichéd observations on American life (44–59), and Wayne Falke says it is "curiously old-fashioned," dealing as it does with "America's heightened consciousness of wrong-doing, at home in its oppressive treatment of blacks, and abroad in its waging so futilely so brutal a war" (62). He says, "Updike . . . deals with the loss of the American dream though for students of American culture it seems bizarrely late to risk so threadbare a theme" (62).

Certainly, Updike makes it clear that the American Dream has ended and that Rabbit and his recalcitrant ilk are among the last conservatives to awaken. Both Jill and Skeeter articulate at some length the novel's overall impression that the seeds of materialism and injustice, sown in the heart of the prevailing system, have contributed to its decline. Updike himself said of *Rabbit Redux* that "revolt, rebellion, violence, disgust are themselves there for a reason, they too are organically evolved out of a distinct reality, and must be considered respectfully" (*PUP* 490). Rabbit's conception of America as a divinely instituted agent of righteousness needs to be balanced against (if not overthrown by) Skeeter's reality. Rabbit remembers that "when he first heard the phrase [American Dream] as a kid he pictured God lying sleeping, the quiltcolored map of the U.S. coming out of his head like a cloud" (*Redux* 114). And in his argument with Stavros, he imagines: "America is beyond power, it acts . . . as a face of God" (47). To Skeeter, the American Dream is a lie generated by white male interests. His experience confirms that

> the thing about these Benighted States all around is that it was never no place like other places where this happens because that happens, and some men have more luck than others so let's push a little here and give a little there; no, sir, this place was never such a place it was a *dream*, it was a state of mind from those poor fool pilgrims on, right? Some white man see a black man he don't see a man he sees a *symbol*, right? All these people around here are walking around inside their own *heads*, they don't even know if you kick somebody else it *hurts*, Jesus won't even tell 'em because the Jesus they brought over on the boats was the meanest most deballed Jesus the good Lord ever let run around scaring people. (242)

Rabbit's conception needs to be challenged even though, as Sheila Rowbotham claims, "any challenge to the prevailing order of fantasy is a political struggle" (425).

On the one hand, Updike makes no attempt to justify Rabbit's resistance to change that enhances justice in society or at home and pictures his protagonist as frightened, defensive, unpleasant, and occasionally ridiculous in his vituperative arguments. Actually, although he learns belatedly and imperfectly, Rabbit learns authentically, and Updike himself counts this capacity as a saving grace. In the Kakutani interview, he says that Rabbit, "like me, has been taught a lot not only by individual instructors, but by the times" ("Turning" 14). Not only is change presented as necessary for renewal and development on both the personal and national level, but unyielding resistance to change, exemplified in the presumed arsonists, Showalter and Brumbach, is revealed as murderous.

On the other hand, Updike and his protagonist have similar apprehensions regarding the revolutionary process. As he explores the nature of revolution and chaos, examines the forces at work to formulate a new order, and estimates the best outcome that can be expected, Updike, like Rabbit, is profoundly aware of the destructive possibilities unleashed by chaos, and he is convinced of the perversity of human nature. Updike claims not only a Quaker's suspicion of all but "interior revolutions" but also a Lutheran's deeply ingrained distrust of the works of men (SC 129, 130). In his chapter "On Not Being a Dove" (SC), Updike quotes from Tillich's paraphrase of Luther's "positivistic authoritarianism" in *History of Christian Thought* (SC 130). The passage assumes that given fallen human nature, even an imperfect state serves higher purposes by inhibiting the worst human capacities, thereby creating an environment in which charity is possible:

> The power of the state, which makes it possible for us to be here or for works of charity to be done at all, is a work of God's love. The state has to suppress the aggression of the evil man, of those who are against love; the strange work of love is to destroy what is against love.... The whole positivistic doctrine of the state makes it impossible for Lutheranism, from a theological point of view, to accept revolution. Revolution results in chaos; even if it tries to produce order, it first produces chaos and disorder increases. (qtd. in SC 130)

Elsewhere, Updike suggests that his profession reinforces this skeptical attitude. He says:

> There may be something also in the novelist's trade which shades you toward conservatism. Things exist because they evolved to that condition; they cannot be lightly or easily altered. It is my general

sense of human institutions that they are outcroppings of human nature, that human nature is slow to change, that in general when you destroy one set of institutions you get something worse. (*PUP* 489)

Rabbit already knows from tragic experience that a "mess" can lead to disastrous consequences (*Redux* 172). In addition, Updike continues to represent Rabbit as good at reading people and allows him to accurately assess the weaknesses and mixed motivations of other characters. Described as "alert" and "wary," Rabbit has an instinctive distrust of human nature and anticipates self-interest and a capacity for evil in others, and like his creator, he has the ability to cut through pretense. Rabbit and Updike seem to work together to deflate the pretensions of both conservatives and revolutionaries; Updike undermines Rabbit while Rabbit undermines the liberals. One wry example of Updike's use of the undercut involves a television interviewer and a rioter. The scene in which they appear concludes with this exchange:

"I see. Your aim then by smashing windows, is to curb a runaway technology and create the basis for a new humanism."
The boy looks off-screen blearily, as the camera struggles to refocus him. "You being funny? You'll be the first up against the wall, you—" (*Redux* 276)

Neither Updike nor Rabbit believes this approach will work. Nevertheless, despite all reservations, change is inevitable, for "at all times, an old world is collapsing" (*HTS* 230).

The First Level: A Parable of Revolution

The dangers inherent in revolution and the struggle between competing forces are played out in Rabbit's home. Skeeter's role is analogous to that of Richard III; his character involves fusing a representation of possibly divine wrath with a representation of the agent of unfolding political realities in combination with an individualized personality. Jill's doubleness is more on the order of Billy Budd's, although not all critics find Jill appealing or agree that the doubleness of these two characters works successfully (Detweiler, *John Updike* 135).

Jill is an eighteen-year-old runaway from upper-class life in Stonington, Connecticut. Like Janice and Ruth in *Rabbit, Run*, Jill is crippled by the absence of paternal support and suffers from a lack of ego strength that leaves her dangerously vulnerable to exploitation and abuse by men—Freddy (her former drug-addicted boyfriend), Rabbit, and Skeeter. A flower child, Jill has rejected a system that she sees as exploitative, and she opposes the war in Vietnam, which Rabbit and Skeeter support. In *Self-Consciousness* Updike admits that he prefers peace-loving women, even when he differs with their politics: "I expected dovishness and liberal sentiments in women, as part of their nurturing, pitying nature. . . . and once had to control a shudder of revulsion when an adored beauty confided to me, from her side of the bed, an intention to vote for Goldwater" (135). As Allen points out, Jill is also a "new" woman—intelligent, articulate, and courageous in her resistance to Rabbit's domination (94). Sexually experienced and formerly addicted, Jill is nevertheless almost childishly innocent and idealistic; she wants to reorder the world by replacing the fear that Skeeter and Rabbit believe runs the world, with love.

Jill may seem merely to depict the "goodness and light" faction, but her program, though vague, accurately represents a political movement specific to the sixties and early seventies. *The Greening of America* by Charles A. Reich was an enormously popular manifesto of that movement published the year after *Rabbit Redux*. Reich's description of "Consciousness III," a new level of enlightenment that once achieved would automatically transform the world, is basically consistent with the ideas and attitudes espoused by Jill (Reich 217–63). Although almost none of the movement's expectations have been realized, Jill's perspective and teachings still represent authentic values as well as the human capacity for idealism, hope, and courage—the essence of all "interior revolutions" (*SC* 129). Like Stavros, Jill is doomed yet has the gift of life. She can sing, draw cartoons (like Updike), befriend Nelson, and cook appetizing meals. She reawakens the "sensually deprived" Gutenberg man, reviving his sexual interest (Newman 43). She opens his mind and challenges his prejudices. And she is able, as Ruth was, to read Rabbit's behavior and speak the truth. Updike's great affirmation of Jill follows her death, when she is resurrected in Rabbit's dream (380–81).

On the other hand, Updike sees the enlightenment movement and Jill as foredoomed by an almost culpable ignorance of the grim realities of life and of the perversity of human nature. In *Self-Consciousness*, Updike explains the attitude his anti-Vietnam friends found so puzzling:

> To be alive is to be a killer; and . . . there is really no hiding what every meal we eat juicily demonstrates. Peace is not something we are entitled to but an illusory respite we earn. On both the personal and national level, islands of truce created by balances of terror and potential violence are the best we can hope for. Pacifism is a luxury a generous country can allow a small minority of its members, but the pacifism invoked by the anti-Vietnam protests was hypocritical and spurious. (131)

Rabbit also believes in the "dog eat dog" nature of the world (*Redux* 77) and makes a similarly grim observation as he eats dinner at Peggy's, just before the fire:

> Peggy feeds them, a casserole of chicken legs and breasts, poor dismembered creatures simmering. Rabbit wonders how many animals have died to keep his life going, how many more will die. A barnyard full, a farmful of thumping hearts, seeing eyes, racing legs, all stuffed squawking into him as into a black sack. No avoiding it: life does want death. To be alive is to kill. (311)

One cannot help but note that Rabbit's diet is exclusively feminine and that Jill is about to be served up in a green body bag to enhance the quality of his life through education. That issue aside for the moment, Updike's comment is that to ignore the realities is to risk being destroyed like Jill, who tries to "rise above eating" because "it's one of the uglier things we do" (*Redux* 140). Updike's perspective is not merely Darwinian but has a theological foundation in Barth and Kierkegaard from whom Updike had learned "to say the worst about our earthly condition" (*SC* 149). He explains:

> There was a theological animus; down-dirty sex and the bloody mess of war and the desperate effort of faith all belonged to a dark necessary underside of reality that I felt should not be merely ignored, or risen above or disdained. These shameful things were intrinsic to life, and though I myself was somewhat squeamish . . . they must be faced, it seemed to me, and even embraced. It was the reality-embrace—the admission, from all doves however vehement and wives however sleepy that we had been led into the Vietnam mire plausible step by step, that the mire was U.S., us. (*SC* 135)

Trusting in the kindness of strangers, as Jill does, is a perennially fatal activity, and from Milton forward such ignorant innocence seems to stir up the agents of evil. The first scene at Jimbo's Lounge reveals Skeeter's fierce animosity toward Jill, which later unfolds in his degradation and enslavement of her (*Redux* 122). Rabbit responds similarly to Nelson's innocence. When Skeeter kisses Jill in order "to be a man," Rabbit sees that Nelson's eyes "are warm watery holes so dark, so stricken he would like to stick pins into them, to teach the child there is worse" (250). Rabbit demonstrates both a perverse desire to puncture such innocence and a protective wish to force Nelson into the "reality-embrace."

Jill assumes the significance of Rabbit's lost daughter and Nelson's sister, Rebecca, and she also temporarily becomes Rabbit's lost wife, Janice. Just as the reason for the failure of his marriage in *Rabbit, Run* was revealed in the subplot with Ruth, the secret behind Rabbit's loss of these women is now revealed in his incapacity to love and thus save Jill. Rabbit's reaction to his dream about Jill clarifies his earlier behavior; Rabbit acknowledges both "her daughterly blind grass-green looking to him" for love and his own retreat into deadness and "hardness of heart" (*Redux* 380–81). On the one hand, without empathy, Rabbit is subject to what Updike sees as a natural preference for mischief ("He loves destruction. Who doesn't?" [*PUP* 490]) and can observe the progress of Jill's devastation with fascinated detachment. When Nelson begs him to protect Jill, and his father claims helplessness and disavows responsibility, the boy's response is insightful: "We *could* if you . . . If you cared enough" (*Redux* 292).

On the other hand, Rabbit's behavior toward Jill is motivated by self-interest from the outset, despite his later claim that he acted as a "Good Samaritan" (358). He dons a "sharkskin" suit and goes to Jimbo's Lounge looking for sexual adventure in order to "screw Janice" (104). He brings Jill home partly to make Janice feel displaced (156), and he then allows Skeeter to join the group in order to make Janice rescue him (212).

In Jill's introduction, Updike emphasizes that "she's a poor child needs a daddy" (134): "Jill's lemonade arrives. She is still girl enough to look happy when it is set before her: cakes at the tea party. Her face lights up" (127). Jill is just a girl not old enough to drink, who looks like an adolescent boy and barely has breasts. Both Rabbit and Skeeter complain that her "cunt" is so tight it "stings" (209, 157), and Rabbit "cannot overcome his fear of using her body as a woman's" (157). He and the others keep to the letter of the law; Jill cannot be served alcohol, but she is old enough for sexual exploitation.

When she first meets Nelson, Jill comments that he is fortunate in having "such a protective father" (151). But in fact, Rabbit continues to play the careless Agamemnon, risking the welfare of his children, Jill and Nelson. Several critics presume that because Jill is sexually experienced, she has no claim to the protection afforded the young, but this presumption conflicts with Rabbit's regret following Jill's dream appearance and with Updike's reference to Jill as Iphigenia (*HTS* 859). Even though Jill expects to pay her way with sex, she is nevertheless remarkably innocent, idealistic, generous, and vulnerable even in her sexuality—"waiting to learn the words by hearing them spoken" (381). But Rabbit's rejects Jill's "call," pursues "angry sex," and betrays her into Skeeter's care (380; Vargo 157). He not only does not give Jill the consideration one owes a child or a lover, but as Samuels observes, by allowing her enslavement, he fails to display even "the minimum of responsibility we feel for another human being" ("Updike on the Present" 66).

Again, because of his own limitations and susceptibilities, Rabbit fails to love Jill adequately as either a father or a lover. He continues to see relationships as power struggles. He sees Jill, like Janice, as the other he imagines to be his enemy and with whom he engages in acts of warfare rather than love. In addition, he dislikes Jill for her independent wealth, her threatening competence, her political difference, and her refusal to be cowed. All of these limitations inhere in Rabbit himself and work against a loving and protective relationship. Thus, even before Skeeter arrives, Rabbit himself has already frightened, beaten, and berated Jill and has begun the process of turning her into Janice.

Jill is the victim of her own ignorant innocence, of Rabbit's limited capacity for good, of his susceptibility to evil, of his "hardness of heart" (epigraph to *Rabbit, Run*) and, eventually, of Skeeter's capacity for malice and hatred. In addition, however, Jill's history suggests that she, like Ruth and Janice before her, is also the victim of her own lack of the ego strength necessary for survival. She practices an ego-negating philosophy and shows a fatal willingness to accommodate the men, at the risk of her own welfare (*Redux* 159, 214). Thus, Mim's comment that Jill "let herself die" is partly accurate (361). In this novel, Updike suggests, as he did in the dream of converging circles in *Rabbit, Run*, that a strong ego is essential to life and contributes to successful union because it limits the destructive capacity in others. It is for this reason that Janice's newfound confidence is a hopeful sign for the continuation of the Angstrom marriage.

Unlike Jill, Skeeter rises to the surface of revolution like Robespierre. Rabbit returns from work one day to find the black militant installed in his home, and when he asks what is going on, Skeeter tells him, "Hell, man it's revolution, right?" (*Redux* 205). Skeeter has jumped bail for drug dealing and Jill has offered him a haven to escape being "crucified" by the white system of justice (208). Uphaus sees the relationship between Jill and Skeeter as "a temporary alliance of the rich white radical youth with the black militant to overthrow the 'System'" (85–86). Rabbit represents the system for Skeeter, who says, "He is the Man" (*Redux* 225), and indeed, the two radicals cooperate in initiating his reeducation (Uphaus 86). Despite the fact that he is "known far and wide for his lack of sympathetic qualities," Skeeter is also a charismatic figure who radiates the vitality that Rabbit and his society have lost (*Redux* 206). Skeeter also has a compelling vision of history. He explains that "there are two theories of how the universe was done" (261), and he prefers the version that says that "everything is expanding outwards"; "it does not thin out to next to nothingness on account of the reason that through strange holes in this nothingness new somethingness comes pouring in from exactly nowhere" (261).

The local hole, he says, is where "God is pushing through" and "the world is redoing itself" (261). These holes are rather like our contemporary "windows of opportunity." Skeeter believes that corrupt systems contain the seeds of their own downfall and that the chaos of their collapse creates an opportunity or "space" that can be used for renewal. One such opportunity, he says, was lost following the Civil War, when America took that "greedy turn" (235).

> The Southern assholes got together with the Northern assholes and said.... Why'd we ever care, free versus slave? Capital versus labor is where it's at, right?... You screw your black labor and we'll screw our immigrant honkey and Mongolian idiot labor and, *whoo-hee!* Halleluiah.... The South got slavery back at half the price, it got control of Congress back by counting the black votes that couldn't be cast, the North got the cotton money it needed for capital, and everybody got the fun of shitting on the black man. (232)

The establishment of a corrupt new system guaranteed still another revolution. Thus, Skeeter tells Rabbit, "We are what has been left *out* of the industrial revolution, so we are the *next* revolution, and don't you know it?" (235).

Furthermore, according to Skeeter, the war in Vietnam and the civil unrest at home are producing a new chaos, and following this violence will come a "great *calm*" (245) that can be used to establish a new order: "The problem is really, when the gangsters have knocked each other off, and taken half of everybody else with them, to make use of the *space*" (246). Skeeter promises to fill that space, declaring that he is the future.

The possibility of his divine affiliation aside, on a secular level, Skeeter possesses exactly what Jill lacks. Having been victimized by oppression, he is familiar with the grim realities and is suspicious to the point of cynicism about human nature. In addition, he clearly has the instinct for survival, even at the expense of others. On the other hand, perhaps having suffered too much both from racism and the war, Skeeter has lost what Jill has to offer—the capacity to risk loving even the radically other. Babe, the singer at Jimbo's, identifies Skeeter's problem when she says, "A boy like you with hate in his heart, he needs to wash" (121). Because he lacks the capacity to love, Skeeter cannot use the calm space well. He is destined to repeat all of the old mistakes and sow the new seeds of corruption in his own quest for power. Although he complains that white men see blacks as symbols, he himself sees Jill as a symbol of the white man's power and makes her serve a symbolic function in appeasing his anger. Emerging from a history of slavery and degradation himself, he nevertheless sets out to enslave and degrade Jill, reproducing another manifestation of the old system. Nothing changes but the faces of the victims and the oppressors.

Uphaus sees Skeeter's revolutionary activity in a slightly different light. She says that "the blacks find the rich white radicals . . . as expendable as they themselves were for whites throughout American history" (86).

> If the conservative white element can be used by "reeducating" him to the black militant's point of viewpoint, well and good. But if the education proves to have only minimal effect on the beliefs of the middle class . . . its destruction lies in its unwillingness to change, to relinquish past values and ideals. Thus Rabbit's neighbors set fire to a house that is . . . identical to their own, and inadvertently kill, not the black, but the rich white radical youth. (86)

Actually, at least in terms of the novel's events, not just any whites are expendable, only Jill, and there is a disturbing alignment of the masculine forces against her. The rippling effect is evident again. If Rebecca June's death signified Rabbit's repression of the feminine in Rabbit's personal and interior life, then Jill's death, through the unwitting cooperation of all male political factions—Skeeter, Rabbit, and the presumed ultraconservative arsonists Showalter and Brumbach—signifies the repression of the feminine and the suppression of the capacity to love the radically other in a patriarchal society. To Rabbit-Agamemnon's pleading, "You don't think it was just bad luck?" (*Redux* 235), the real Iphigenia still replies, "It is the men of this land who are bloodthirsty and they lay their own guilt on the gods" (Edith Hamilton 250). In the aftermath of his dream of Jill's return, Rabbit admits that "he had retreated into deadness and did not wish her to call him out. . . . Let black Jesus have her, he had been converted to hardness of heart" (*Redux* 380). Rabbit not only lets the enigmatic Skeeter have her, he pays him the usual thirty-dollar fee for her betrayal (335).

The Second Level

Three critics, Samuels, Hendin and Allen, have been especially sensitive to the sinister machinations below the surface of this novel. Although an early reviewer, Charles Samuels raised a number of critical questions that have yet to be adequately addressed. He says, "As his [Rabbit's] failure with Jill escalates into active collusion in destroying her, his motivation becomes less clear" ("Updike on the Present" 66):

> Skeeter seems less interested in changing the world than in playing out a psychodrama in which Harry is forced to atone for white racism by voluntarily witnessing the humiliation and destruction of a white woman by a black man. Why does Harry watch this so willingly? Why doesn't he reject Skeeter, since not only Jill but his son fears the man? Unacknowledged national guilt may predispose him to hear Skeeter out, but what dark bond draws him into nearly sexual identification with his sinister guest. . . . And what explains his failure to recognize that Skeeter is hooking Jill despite the many hints that she and the child provide? Perhaps he hates Jill, who is upper class, out of a resentment parallel to Skeeter's resentment of whites . . . perhaps he sacrifices her to his own yearning to recontact God . . . perhaps, like America itself, he is merely an exhausted being who can only be quickened by cruelty? We can never sort these possibilities out. . . . This obscurity makes Updike's final refusal to pass judgment particularly disturbing. (66)

Josephine Hendin also suspects that Rabbit "takes out his rage at women by passively letting him [Skeeter] kill the girl" (101). Mary Allen develops the argument that Rabbit's particular resentment against the new woman "makes him fascinated with Skeeter's schemes to destroy her" (91), and she adds that Updike "allows his bias in behalf of the stupid-sexual woman to intrude to the point of forcing a violent death (and violence is not usually his subject) upon this intelligent girl whom he dislikes and cannot deal with" (91). The following discussion, which addresses the issues raised by these critics, recognizes a good deal of ambivalence in the male author who examines masculinity, without supporting Allen's complete identification of Updike with his protagonist.

In addition to sensing that something sinister is going on in the novel, critics have also registered discomfort with a certain unreality or altered reality, especially in Skeeter's chapter. Vargo says Rabbit, Jill, and Skeeter participate in "rites of rage and death" that become "orgiastic," lead "deeper and deeper into chaos," and "are reflected in the disjointed sequence of events through this entire section" (168). Vanderwerken, Falke, and Alter use the word *apocalyptic* in their descriptions; and Detweiler says, "Skeeter is an incarnation of the fearful shapes that have transformed the American dream into a nightmare" (*John Updike* 135).

The notion of Harry's journey through chaos as a kind of madness from which he is eventually "restored to health" (one meaning of *redux*) is extremely helpful in understanding the impression of heightened reality each of these critics registers in the chapters focusing on Jill and Skeeter. The line between reality and madness (and between realism and surrealism) blurs as Rabbit suffers from destabilizing trauma, culture shock, personality disintegration, and mind-altering drugs. It is not that Rabbit, like Ellelloû in *The Coup*, imagines, hallucinates, or dreams what happens, but rather that the events that do occur take on the weird aspect of psychodrama. Reality becomes nightmarish, assuming the significance that Rabbit's own mind might invest it with, *if* he were dreaming. Two critics use the word *psychodrama* specifically to describe Skeeter's reenactment of black degradation with Jill (Vargo 166; Alter 41), but the word seems appropriate to describe large portions of the second and third chapters. The success of this technique depends on our accepting Jill and Skeeter as projections of Rabbit's mind, as reflections of American society, and as believable, individualized characters. Updike, remember, makes the political intensely and painfully personal; and the real horror of the novel depends upon our being able to relate to the victim of

Rabbit's psychodrama—and the victim of society's ritual sacrifice of innocent blood. Moreover, the horror depends on relating to the victim not in terms of an anonymous or undeveloped scapegoat (in which case, Jill's death might be merely cathartic) but in relation to a real and sympathetic person. In this case, Jill's death becomes appalling.

In this sense, Jill and Skeeter are Rabbit's mental figments come alive. Jill is his best dream, and Skeeter is his worst nightmare. When Rabbit meets Jill, she is, though he is unaware, everything he wants, or at least, everything that he complained Janice was not in *Rabbit, Run*. She is fair while Janice is dark, and a "girl" while Janice's aging face had reminded him of a death's skull. She is physically strong where Janice had been depleted, and slender and flexible where Janice had been lumpy and clumsy. Jill comes to him in the white wedding dress Rabbit had projected onto Ruth. Jill is both accessible and virginal. Unlike Janice, she never rejects sexual advances. She is cheerful where Janice had been sullen and unhappy. As soon as she enters his home, Jill takes him to the bath, like the Venus he prefers, and then voluntarily kneels to give him the oral sex he had demanded of Ruth. Jill has independent interests and does not watch television like Janice. She is intelligent instead of dumb, articulate instead of silent. She cooks well. Unlike Janice, who is an alcoholic, Jill is recently recovered from her addiction. Where Janice seemed aligned with nature, Jill is unearthly and spiritual; she has seen God. She is wealthier than Janice, but where Janice's smile had been greedy, Jill renounces materialism. Finally, Jill has no interfering parents and no institutional claim on Rabbit.

The reader knows that Jill is everything Rabbit ever thought he wanted and everything that Western culture taught him to want, and *still he hates her*. Is Updike's plan for the Angstrom marriage that Rabbit should finally reject this idealized projection of woman, the questing for which has caused so much restlessness and disappointment in *Rabbit, Run*? Or does Updike suggest that by acting out, by exorcising once more, his rage toward women through Jill, Rabbit will be able to move forward to a more positive relationship with Janice? Is the relative harmony that we see in *Rabbit Is Rich*, the balance between Rabbit's fondness for Janice and his desire to pound her skull, achieved through Jill's sacrifice? Perhaps Jill's death is the recurring forfeit demanded by the id for its unnatural domestication (Newman 39).[1] Certainly, Jill's death represents the suppression of the feminine that is the cost of maintaining a patriarchal society.

Once Skeeter arrives, the progress of Jill's destruction accelerates, but Rabbit actually initiates her downfall himself. Despite Jill's charm, intelligence, and culinary skill, all of which seem to revive Rabbit, there are a number of things he dislikes about her that point back to the general resentment he harbors against all women. He thinks she adopts a superior attitude (his usual stance). She is perceptive and vocal. She does not hesitate to comment on faults or on his impotence. She is not easily frightened or coerced. She is not exclusively loyal. He cannot control her mind or her behavior. Furthermore, he cannot forgive her for being wealthier, which to him means more powerful, than himself. In brief, Jill is the threatening other he cannot control, and given his oppositional framework, he must therefore overwhelm and destroy her (see Allen, "John Updike's Love"). Rabbit accomplishes this end in much the same way he did with Janice and Ruth in *Rabbit, Run*. By withholding love, by undermining her confidence, and by verbally and physically abusing her, he begins the process that Skeeter, his opposite number, will complete. Jill is transformed into Janice and then left for dead in the bed she shares with Rabbit. Before she dies, Jill becomes a slovenly, "dumb mutt," who is incompetent and cooks worse than Janice (*Redux* 307, 269, 257). She becomes drug dependent, loses interest, and loses touch with God. Her skin becomes "tight" on her face like Janice's (295). She is so "needy" that she loses the capacity for independent speech and must ask Skeeter, "Isn't that what you want me to say?" (257, 300). Prior to her death, Jill is completely overwhelmed, completely silenced, and completely resigned. Like Rebecca, the "Daddy" she calls to abandons her (256). And like Rebecca, Jill seems dead even before her actual death, an impression Skeeter confirms when Rabbit tells him Jill is dead. Skeeter responds, "Poor bitch, doubt if she knows the difference" (334). Only Nelson tries ineffectually to stop this incredible destruction.

Another Metaphor of Failed Union

Jill and Skeeter fit together, as in a union of self and other, which Updike usually expresses as a possibility in terms of male-female relationships but here expresses in terms of race as well. Black and white are attracted to each other, just as Rabbit is attracted to Skeeter and to women. In his letter to his mixed-race grandsons, Updike explains the mysterious and potentially beneficial attraction of racial opposites. He says:

> If some day, you come to read in its entirety this book dedicated to you, and not just this grandpaternal letter, you will notice in every chapter a touch or two of this pressing issue within the American psyche—the matter of the blacks brought here against their wills, and confined to the slave quarters of the society, and that yet fascinate us whites as a people strikingly other, with an otherness that perhaps we need. There is a floating sexual curiosity and potential love that in your parents has come to earth and borne fruit and that the blended shade of your dear brown skins will ever advertise. (*SC* 196)

As in *Rabbit, Run*, Rabbit intuitively seeks union and resolution and senses the potentially saving nature of the attraction of the radically other. In this context, the image of Jill and Skeeter engaged in "interracial fellation" (Vargo 166) is similar to the metaphors of union in *Rabbit, Run* (the earth's revolution, the dream of converging sun and moon, and the garden). Like the earlier metaphors, this one also suggests the haunting possibility of union and resolution while providing a measure of how sadly distant from this aspiration the characters stand. This passage recalls the references to flowers and blending in the metaphors of *Rabbit, Run*:

> What he sees reminds him in the first flash of the printing process, an inked plate contiguous at some few points to white paper. As his eyes adjust, he sees Skeeter is not black, he is a gentle brown. These are smooth-skinned children being gently punished, one being made to stand and the other kneel. Skeeter crouches and reaches down a long hand, fingernails like baby rose petals, to shield Jill's profile from the glare.... An inch or two of Skeeter is un-enclosed by her face, a purplish inch bleached to lilac, below his metallic pubic explosion....
> "You're beautiful," Rabbit says. (*Redux* 297–98)

Locked together, the two characters resolve several dichotomies. They are visually reminiscent of both of the cosmic metaphors in *Rabbit, Run* and of the symbolic union of yin and yang. They unite self and other, black and white, man and woman. In terms of character, they reconcile the capacities for love and mercy with justice and wrath. As in *Rabbit, Run*, however, Rabbit and his surrogate, Skeeter, violate the model of union by entering the relationship seeking to dominate and exploit. Like the forcing of oral sex on Ruth, which this act parallels, Rabbit and Skeeter use Jill for self-assertion and self-aggrandizement. Therefore, they make, not a new religion or even a new beginning, but a travesty, as Rabbit did in *Rabbit, Run*. The vision of this failed hope returns to haunt Rabbit when, after Jill's death, he tries to recall the union, but the figures fly apart.

The observation that Skeeter becomes Rabbit's surrogate needs clarification. Initially, Skeeter appears to be an enemy. Rabbit knows from his visit to Jimbo's that Skeeter is a black radical with a hostile manner. When Skeeter appears in Rabbit's home, Rabbit begins to look at the young man with dread, discovering "a pit of scummed stench impossible to see the bottom of" (*Redux* 208). He subsequently beats Skeeter to assert his domination yet then allows Skeeter to stay, even though Rabbit expects to be murdered in his sleep. It is Jill who identifies Rabbit's fear of Skeeter, a fear stemming from ignorance of the black man's history or motivations. Robert Alter develops the argument that Rabbit (like Lesser in Malamud's *The Tenants*) responds "with an apocalyptic fear that such suffering must issue in a destructive rage of unimaginable proportion and effect" (41).

Rabbit's fear is allayed by daily contact and reeducation. In *Rabbit Is Rich*, Rabbit remembers having been flattered by Skeeter's interest, and certainly, Rabbit is mellowed by marijuana use. More than any of these factors, however, Rabbit's animosity is dissipated by a process of identification that begins with his fascinated attraction and is guided and nurtured by Skeeter, who is a master manipulator. Watching television one night, the little group watch a skit in which Sammy Davis, Jr., and Arne Johnson play dirty old men. The point is made that although the two look different, they are identical: "They are like one man looking into a crazy mirror" (*Redux* 247).

Critics have noted that Rabbit's association with Skeeter is beneficial; Rabbit learns much, including some respect and tolerance. But Updike is not one to feed us platitudes about universal brotherhood. A closer look reveals that an important basis for identification between the two men is shared pathologies. Although he has been forced to the bottom of the hierarchical ladder, Skeeter is also the product of a patriarchal society. He, too, is made in its image despite his efforts to be free. More fundamental than their racial difference is the common stereotypical masculinity of Skeeter and Rabbit.

Though for ostensibly different reasons, Skeeter, like Rabbit, is motivated by an overwhelming fear of the other and, like Rabbit, believes that fear runs the world (170, 241). His lifelong experience of powerlessness has taught him to enter every situation and relationship defensively. Skeeter cannot love anyone and lets no one pierce his metallic exterior. He hides behind many voices and identities. He keeps running away. He fears intimacy and seems to Rabbit like "a finely made electric toy" that will shock whoever touches it (251). Skeeter constantly pursues the goal of enhancing his power by achieving dominance and control. Skeeter's ego, like Rabbit's in the earlier novel, is demanding and insatiable. He has little care for the intrinsic value of others and perceives them according to the part they play in his struggle for self-aggrandizement. Having successfully entrapped Jill, he gloats, exactly as Rabbit did with Ruth, that "he has her" (264).

Less and less content to manifest God or to represent the principle of divine justice, Skeeter eventually insists that he *is* God, just as Rabbit, at the height of his egotism in Rabbit, Run, claimed to be a mystic. Like Rabbit, he is "stuck inside his own skin" (*Redux* 335). Like Rabbit, Skeeter is centered in fear, anger, and hatred of others, and hardened in that condition, he too becomes "Mr. Death" (*Run* 279).

Male Bonding

Beneath the parable of the sixties revolution, the deeper political drama unfolds, manifesting the rage at the center of Rabbit's masculinity. The constraints imposed upon men by a hierarchical system in which they are forced to accept the self-negating domination of those higher up on the ladder of power have already been discussed. In *Rabbit Redux*, Rabbit and Skeeter bond into a revolutionary force that seeks to overthrow the powerful males who dominate society. In narrative terms, those men are the wealthy upper-class whites of Penn Park–Stonington, but in psychological terms, they represent Laius or, in Lacan's terms, "the Law of the Father" or the will of absent patriarchs encoded in a culture that subjugates angry sons. Jill Pendleton, the daughter of those powerful, upper-class men, becomes the medium for the younger men's rebellion. At the same time, the bonded males avenge their old grievance against the powerful mother when they enslave and degrade Jill. Finally, in psychological and concrete terms, Rabbit and Skeeter reassert male dominance over the body and spirit of the emerging autonomous woman.

In 1969 anthropologist Claude Lévi-Strauss identified a phenomenon in which women are "reified" or dehumanized to serve as a medium of exchange in transactions between males or male groups. He found, according to Gerda Lerner, that this "exchange of women" is the "leading cause of female subordination" (Lerner 46–47). The phenomenon is evident in numerous tribal practices including ritual rape, the sharing or sale of women, and bride stealing (all of which occur in *Rabbit Redux*). Lévi-Strauss's work enabled subsequent feminist anthropologists and historians to "see" patriarchal culture as "homosocial," a term that describes a "total relationship of exchange . . . not established between man and woman but between two groups of men, [in which] the woman figures only as one of the objects in the exchange, not as one of the partners" (Lévi-Strauss 115). Homosocial activity establishes and fosters "interdependence and solidarity among men that enable them to dominate women" (Hartmann 177).

This cultural paradigm has proven useful in analyzing literature. For example, using the notion that patriarchal culture is homosocial, Eve Kosofsky Sedgwick has been able to better explain incidents of homosexual panic that turn up in the work of male authors. She explains that a homosocial society generates homosexual panic in heterosexual males because, on the one hand, it requires men to engage in close, intense contact with other males (in school, sports, the military, business, etc.), and, at the same time, maintains taboos and penalties for homosexuality. The homosocial requirement that men be *very* close but not *that* close to other men creates substantial anxiety, not, in fact, for homosexual men but for *heterosexual* men (Sedgwick, "The Beast in the Closet" 245–46). This anxiety-provoking uncertainty is built into the system as a means of control; the less certain one is of the lines of demarcation and the more terrible the penalties, the more scrupulously one conforms: "An endemic and ineradicable state of what I am calling male homosexual panic became the normal condition of heterosexual entitlement" (245). Thus, Rabbit, who is in the process of bonding with Skeeter, runs from the room terrified when the black man masturbates because he experiences the kind of homosexual panic Sedgwick has observed elsewhere. The paradigm of a homosocial society has a wider application to this novel, however. The emphasis on adult male transactions, and particularly on male bonding, is striking in a novel where Rabbit has emotionally withdrawn from women and children.

Despite the ten years of accelerated change, Pennsylvania remains a man's world. Janice herself expresses Lévi-Strauss's concept when she thinks about Stavros returning her promptly to meet Rabbit: "He paid the bill and dropped her off under the marquee as promised. Men are strict that way, want to keep their promises to each other, women are beneath it, property" (*Redux* 52). Stavros is equally clear in his negotiations with Rabbit over the return of Janice. He asks: "What do *you* want? You're sitting there twitching your whiskers watching me squirm, so how about it? If I throw her out, will you pick her up?" (181). Rabbit deals with Buchanan over the disposition of Jill. And Skeeter has no hesitation about using Jill as a pawn to secure safe shelter from Rabbit. Later, Rabbit and Skeeter share Jill as a means of bonding. They also use her body as the medium in their quest for God and as the vehicle for their revenge against the white establishment males of Penn Park–Stonington, of America.

Competition with other males has become less enjoyable to Rabbit in this novel, whether because of his age or his passivity. He is willing to engage in grim conflicts if necessary, as when he prepares to fight the young blacks who follow him from Jimbo's (138) or when he lashes out at Skeeter to assert his dominance. But Rabbit doesn't look for opportunities for individual competition as he used to when, for example in *Rabbit, Run*, he sparred with Ronnie Harrison at the Chinese restaurant. In *Rabbit Redux*, Rabbit lets Stavros have his wife too easily and later becomes impotent with Peggy when he "feels himself competing" with the "presences" of the other men she has known (313).

On the other hand, Rabbit sometimes anticipates and enjoys bonding with men through the bodies of women. In *Rabbit Run*, he feared Ruth's sexual vastness (73) and was infuriated by seeing his sister with a date, but in *Rabbit Redux*, he is fascinated by Mim's sex life, and when he greets his sister, "he holds her wanting to feel all the hundreds of men who have held her before" (352). Similarly, where we might expect him to feel only jealousy or anger toward Stavros, in fact, he also feels solidarity with a brother engaged in the common male project of controlling the "ancient craziness" of women (284): "But, far from feeling Stavros as one of the enemy camp, he counts on him to keep this madwoman, his wife, under control. Through her body they have become brothers" (157). In *Rabbit Is Rich*, long after the affair, "Harry thinks of Charlie's prick inside Janice and his feeling is hostile and cozy in almost equal proportions, coziness getting the edge" (6), and he later thinks his wife has "accrued" value by having been shared. As we shall see in subsequent novels, Rabbit develops a pattern of sharing women with the men with whom he unconsciously wants to bond.

Another anthropologist, Lionel Tiger, proposes that specialization for hunting widened the gap between male and female behavior by "favoring those 'genetic packages' which arranged matters so that males hunted cooperatively in groups" (44). Successful group hunting required enhanced cooperation and the inhibition of violence within the group. He describes male bonding as the process arising from this primitive need; and he maintains that it is still operative in contemporary society, wherein individual males recognize other males "as directly and distinctly relevant to themselves" (Tiger 21) and derive power not only from individual strengths but by drawing on the support of other males. According to Tiger, this bond is not only *stronger than the sexual bond with women* but characteristically stimulates aggression against outsiders. He asks, "Does it matter if male bonding is a function of aggression or if aggression is a function of male bonding? It is impossible in practice to separate the two processes" (166).

What is relevant in Tiger's work is less his argument that present cultural institutions have a biological basis than the striking similarity between his descriptions of the practice, process, and purpose of male bonding in contemporary secret societies and voluntary organizations and what occurs between Rabbit and Skeeter in *Rabbit Redux*. Tiger observes that initiations in male organizations of this kind "have the aspect of male-male courtship" and an emphasis on "symbolic eroticism" with "homoerotic implications" (146). Initiation involves education and ordeals of some kind. Professions of faith and loyalty are usual, and detachment from parents and family may be required. According to Tiger, a secret society disassociates itself from the mainstream culture and, therefore, will eventually attract the interest and hostility of the established authority (in *Rabbit Redux*, Showalter, Brumbach, and the police). Once formed, the male bond is outer-directed, often stimulating aggression that easily turns into violence, especially in the face of an "external threat or a perceived possibility of advantage" (172, 183). Finally, Tiger tries to account for the bonded group's ability to overcome inhibitions against in-species killing through a process of "reverse anthropomorphism," of transforming people into animals or "pseudo-species" (167). This process is common in warfare and sounds similar to reification in that both involve dehumanization for the purpose of facilitating destructive behavior. Rabbit, of course, is already in the habit of imagining his enemies as beasts.

Rabbit is a likely initiate. Having been rejected by Janice and displaced by his society, he needs the validation and enhanced power that bonding provides. He is already fascinated by the radical otherness of the blacks on the bus and at Jimbo's. He is sexually interested as well; he wonders how the black bride on television would be and speculates on the potency of black males. Skeeter is especially attractive to Rabbit because he is a visionary. When Rabbit remembers

Skeeter in *Rabbit Is Rich*, he regrets that "a certain light was withdrawn from the world, a daring, a promise that all would be overturned" (28).

Although his manner is abrasive, Skeeter nevertheless courts, educates, and initiates Rabbit. He introduces Rabbit to black history and has him identify with a black perspective by having him read the texts aloud. Skeeter encourages Rabbit to participate and compliments his performance: "Oh, you do make one lovely nigger" (*Redux* 283). The two men also bond through shared interests. Skeeter, like Rabbit, believes in the U.S. role in the Vietnam War and shares his experiences. (Interestingly, Skeeter emphasizes male bonding as one of the redeeming aspects of war because it transcends racism.) The two also bond when they play basketball together. Finally, Skeeter reawakens Rabbit's interest in the quest for God.

Rabbit and Skeeter have another shared interest in their antagonism toward women. Agamemnon is a careless father not only in that he is incautious and places his daughter at risk but also in that he does not care for her. Rabbit's background needs no further elaboration on this point. We know very little of Skeeter's relations with women before he comes to Rabbit's home, but he very apparently hates them as much as, or more than, Rabbit does. We do know that he feels rejected by black women, for which he blames the white males who would not allow him to "be a man" (*Redux* 250). And, when Rabbit tells him to "go ahead" and "be one," he does so by abusing Jill (250). Skeeter has also been rejected by white women in the sense that his access has been restricted by a prohibition that characters Showalter and Brumbach want to perpetuate. Furthermore, as Angela Davis explains: "Sexual coercion was . . . an essential dimension of social relations between slavemaster and slave. In other words, the right claimed by slaveowners . . . over the bodies of female slaves was a direct expression of their perceived property rights over black people as a whole" (175). Thus, Skeeter negotiates his equality and revenge by enslaving and sexually dominating Jill, and the more vicious and dehumanizing his behavior, the better it serves his underlying purpose. He reifies Jill toward this end by referring to her almost exclusively in terms of sexual function ("Hey you cunt" [*Redux* 257]). Jill tries to overcome Skeeter's resentment with sexual accommodation but only succeeds in further infuriating him. Instead, Skeeter sees her openness as promiscuous and condescending, and she remains for him a symbol of the effects of white male power.

Like other initiates, Rabbit submits to ordeals that confirm his loyalty, his faith ("I do believe" [*Redux* 277]), and his ability to inhibit his aggression against the dominant male. When Skeeter introduces drugs or kisses Jill or attempts rape or frightens Nelson, he watches to see that Rabbit remains passive. Rabbit demonstrates his loyalty to Skeeter in this way: he not only breaks the law by sheltering Skeeter and by permitting the escalating drug use in his home, Rabbit also abandons his parental responsibility by siding with Skeeter against the interests of Jill and Nelson. The little group holds ritual ceremonies that Vargo discusses at length (149–71). These "rites of death" have religious overtones that include sharing marijuana, the "nightly sacrament" of "brotherhood and communion" (Vargo 162). Everyone participates initially, but the two young characters sense the danger in their progressive exclusion from the male bond; Jill tells Rabbit she is afraid of Rabbit and Skeeter together (251).

According to Tiger, male bonding is always outer-directed, requiring a "consummatory stimulus" or goal, "which is the functional equivalent to the prey animal in the dynamics of the group" (184). Of course, the stimulated aggression can be channeled constructively, as in the case of the Rotary Club to which Rabbit belongs in *Rabbit Is Rich*. But often, as in this case, the aggression turns into violence directed toward a perceived enemy or out-group. The specification of a common enemy is crucial.

In the course of his initiation, Skeeter awakens Rabbit to his own suppressed hatred for the wealthy, white, establishment Penn Parkers (Uphaus 86–87). Rabbit particularly imagines the insensitive doctor who attends Mary Angstrom and whose handshake conveyed the message: "*I am strong, I twist bodies to my will. I am life. I am death*" (*Redux* 249). Between Rabbit and Skeeter, the powerful Penn Parkers are identified as the common enemy, especially since Skeeter sees racial oppression as economically motivated.

The resentment of both men harkens back to the masculine dilemma previously discussed: the hierarchical system gives men power over those below but forces them to submit to the domination of those higher up on the ladder of force. Both men identify Jill as the daughter of this powerful group and express their rebellion and revenge by destroying her. Updike's selection of Jill as their symbolic victim has a historical basis in fact: "With the development of private property and class stratification. . . . [u]pper class families used their daughters to consolidate their social and economic power" (Lerner 111); so there is an ironic justice (or injustice) in the notion that angry oppressed classes will now use the symbolic daughter against upper-class male power. There is also an appropriate historical connection between sexism, racism, and class oppression that makes Jill a particularly apt victim. Lerner, writing seventeen years after the publication of this novel, also expresses the intricate relationship between these forms of oppression and, like Updike, finds an enslaved woman at the heart of the matter. She says that early on,

> women themselves became a resource, acquired by men much as land was acquired by men. Women were exchanged or bought in marriages for the benefit of their families; later, they were conquered or bought in slavery, where their sexual services were part of their labor.... In every known society it was the women of conquered tribes who were first enslaved, whereas men were killed. It was only after men had learned how to enslave the women of groups who could be defined as strangers, that they learned how to enslave the men of those groups and, later, subordinates from within their own societies.
>
> Thus, the enslavement of women, combining both racism and sexism, preceded the formation of classes and class oppression. Class differences were, at their very beginnings, expressed in terms of patriarchal relations. Class is not a separate construct from gender; rather, it is expressed in genderic terms. (213)

On the night that Skeeter and Rabbit act out their psychodrama of class, racial, and gender hostility by dominating and degrading Jill, a face at the window interrupts their ritual. As Lionel Tiger predicts, the subversive group eventually attracts not only the interest of the neighborhood adolescents but the suspicion and hostility of the establishment. Rabbit understands the danger when he thinks, "They are at war. They have taken a hostage. Everywhere out there, there are unfriendlies" (*Redux* 300). Eventually, the establishment takes action; Showalter and Brumbach (the presumed arsonists) have accurately interpreted Skeeter's sexual involvement with Jill as a threat to their power, and they in their turn reassert their dominance and transact their revenge, unwittingly, through the body of Jill Pendleton.

Thus, what emerges is a situation in which all of the males in the society, regardless of their relative positions on the hierarchical ladder of privilege and power and regardless of their politics, are blindly unified in their domination of woman. By reifying and using Jill as the medium of their transactions with one another, the male characters also assert their domination over her and literally and symbolically destroy her in the process. And that, of course, means that they suppress not only the feminine perspective but the feminine capacities within themselves and within their society. To cite Updike again: "The cost of the disruption of the social fabric, was paid as in the earlier novel, by a girl. Iphigenia is sacrificed" (*HTS* 895).

Rabbit's collusion in Jill's destruction not only manifests the antagonism he has always felt against powerful males but once again manifests his antagonism toward the powerful mother. Dinnerstein and others observe that initiation and woman-sharing ceremonies have much in common and are sometimes combined: "The shared woman . . . usually has no claim on any man's fidelity. She is the captive and derogated mother, the dethroned tyrant, the defiled goddess, communally possessed in a spirit of ritual counter-assertion against the sexual rivalries that weaken male solidarity" (58). Rabbit and Skeeter not only sacrifice exclusive claims on Jill as a way of solidifying their bond but also as a way of acting out their antagonism toward women. Dinnerstein adds, woman sharing serves the additional function of permitting "male homoerotic impulse some expression in a safe context of triumphant, harsh masculinity" (59).

It is important to note here that, by her passivity, Jill also cooperates in destroying the feminine. As noted earlier, possibly as a result of the female monopoly on child rearing, men and women both fear the power of woman and cooperate to control it. By submitting to woman sharing, "the woman participates vicariously in the act of humiliating the mother, against whom she also has a grudge. . . . And at the same time she has a chance to relive directly the situation of the humiliated child, this time of her own accord" (Dinnerstein 58). Jill may well have internalized her anger against the powerful mother she has fled. She has clearly bought the cultural stereotype of woman as victim; for example, where Rabbit interprets the word *immolating* actively to mean "burn," Jill interprets it passively to mean "sacrificing" (*Redux* 244). With Jill's passivity, Updike again suggests that women also perpetuate the patriarchal order either by aligning themselves with male power givers as Mary Angstrom does or by inviting and submitting to victimization as Jill does. Updike avoids the usual error of idealizing the oppressed (women and blacks) and, at the same time, presents a systemic problem.

Finally, Rabbit and Skeeter use Jill as the medium in their quest for God, a theme that merits some attention as Rabbit is the third man to want to enslave Jill for this purpose. When Jill tells Rabbit that Skeeter is bringing her "mesc" so that she will tell him about God, he is intrigued: "'That's crazy.' But exciting: maybe she can do it. Maybe he can get music out of her like Babe out of the piano" (251). In *Rabbit, Run* Rabbit used the bodies of women to quest for "something," and in *Rabbit Redux* he and the others are intent on tapping

Jill's spiritual capacities for the same purpose. In both novels, aggressive male questing after God is unsuccessful because Rabbit, Eccles, Freddy, and Skeeter are so preoccupied with imposing their projections onto God that they lack the openness essential to revelation—expectation being a form of projection.

In *Self-Consciousness*, Updike conveys his own feeling that uncertainty concerning God is inevitable and appropriate. He says: "The sensation of silence cannot be helped: a loud evident God would be an insecure tyrant, an all-crushing datum instead of, as He is, a bottomless encouragement to our faltering and frightened being" (229). A number of Updike's characters, however, are unwilling to accept this silence and try, like Piet Hanema of *Couples* (1968), to force God's hand in the form of retribution or, like Dale Kohler of *Roger's Version* (1986), to trick him into self-revelation. Others, like Rabbit and Skeeter, begin by questing and end, because of the nature of projection, by proclaiming their own divinity. Updike suggests, that these are especially destructive and futile forms of behavior. As Rabbit will remember in *Rabbit Is Rich*, every time he has approached the invisible world in this aggressive way, "someone has gotten killed" (150).

Men have historically defined God, but according to Lerner, since post-exilic times, they have more or less exclusively controlled "transactions" with the *male* deity (161–98), a prerogative that has been vigorously and violently protected. The doctrine of "resemblance" is still used to exclude women from some priesthoods (Kolbenschlag 170), as character Peggy Fosnacht observes in her harangue against the pope in *Rabbit Is Rich* (267). In *Rabbit Redux*, however, Babe, Janice, and Jill all have direct experience of God and, in consequence, possess (in Janice's case, reclaim) life-giving power. Women who have direct access to the supernatural, however, "steal" power from men, and the traditional punishment for this crime is burning. One of the secrets of this novel is that Jill is punished because the men are jealous of her spiritual power.

At first, Skeeter wants to use Jill to see God, but later, he forces her to say she sees God *in* him. The real quest is not for God but for a magnified and powerful version of the self. Updike has cited Barth emphasizing that "one cannot speak of God by speaking of man in a loud voice" (*AP* 280). The real quest is for male power, which is not to say that God, however silent, may not be active in the world of the novel but only that questers cannot find him.

After the fire, once Jill's body is found, Nelson goes with the police to his grandmother's: "The boy, his hair hanging limp and his tears flowing unchecked, seems relieved to be at last in the arms of order, laws and limits" (*Redux* 326). Nelson's relief that order has finally been reestablished to check the destructive impulses set loose in chaos recalls Ralph's relief at the end of Golding's *The Lord of the Flies* (1954). Later, as Rabbit stands alone amid the rubble, "pain moves upward from his shins through his groin and belly to his chest and out. A demon leaving" (*Redux* 331). The revolutions fail; the demon departs; the fevered madness passes; and the protagonist reawakens to his old identity. Nevertheless, the damage done in the atmosphere of chaos to Jill, Nelson, Rabbit, Skeeter, and the whole society is irrevocable.

Rabbit ponders the fate of the nation as he lies in bed with Janice in the Safe Haven Motel. With the failure of Jill's idealism and Skeeter's justice and with the final suppression of the feminine, what will become of America? The novel's last chapter is named for Rabbit's sister, Mim, who returns to Brewer to help put the Angstroms' marriage back together; whereas Rabbit is "Mister Muddle," she is "little Miss Fix-It" (*Redux* 369). Mim is an appealing prostitute who has charmed a number of critics with her frankness, competence, good intentions, and filial affection. Despite these qualities, however, Mim is also a completely nonspiritual, amoral person who represents the pragmatism, materialism, and even brutality (gangsterism) overtaking America. She warns Rabbit about

> the way it is out there. They're not bad people. They have rules. They're not very interesting rules, nothing like Stick your hand in the fire and make it up to Heaven. They're more like, Ride the exercise bicycle the morning after.... They're survival rules, rules for living in the desert. That's what it is, a desert. Look out for it, Harry. It's coming East. (359)

Mim belittles Rabbit's little remaining faith in "ghosts" and "old Jack Frost" (356). Like Tothero, although without his high-toned hypocrisy, she believes exclusively in arbitrary rules. Her sexuality is not only uncomplicated by spirituality, it is completely depersonalized. She keeps her emotional distance by sleeping with clients only three times; she is described as mechanical and "inhuman" (366, 352). Mim admires the younger generation's stoical acceptance of a diminished human condition, and she believes that the way to live in the desert is to "be a cockroach" and "live on poison" (361).

Following Rebecca's death in *Rabbit, Run*, Rabbit had a dream of reconciliation. He wanted to found a new religion but was unable even to incorporate the dream message into his own waking life. Now Rabbit has another dream of reconciliation in which Jill appears at his bedside and touches him. He recognizes her beauty and value, accepts his responsibility, and grieves. Rabbit wants to tell Nelson that "she had been here, her very breath and presence" (*Redux* 381), but Updike suggests that Rabbit once again misses the opportunity for healing and renewal: "On this resolve he relaxes, lets his room . . . be coupled to an engine and tugged westward toward the desert, where Mim is now" (381). The American wasteland portrayed in the next novel, *Rabbit Is Rich*, is the direct result of the betrayal and loss of the feminine capacities represented by Jill.

EIGHT

Is Rabbit Rich?

Rabbit Is Rich opens during the last weekend of June 1979 at the height of the oil crisis. The famous opening phrase, "Running out of gas," reestablishes the correspondence between the condition of American society and its declining Everyman. Ten years have passed since the events of *Rabbit Redux*. After the fire in which Jill died, Janice's father, Fred Springer, took on Rabbit as a salesman at Springer Motors and brought him, with Janice and Nelson, into his home, where they have lived ever since. Five years later, Fred had "the kindness to die," and Rabbit began running the dealership that Fred left in the control of Janice and her mother (*Rich* 2).

Rabbit is now "king of the lot" and enjoys the benefits and privileges that signify "the Brewer gentry" (3, 371). His success is reflected in traditional male terms of power and status: he has "money to float in," a wife who can "sign chits like a Du Pont," a respected place in the business community, and the social acceptance of friends at the Flying Eagle Golf Club. Even his formerly shaky marriage now seems successful, for, although Janice continues to drink and remains a marginal housewife, she has aged nicely, plays tennis well, and fits in at the country club.

Despite the emblems of success, Rabbit senses a lack. He is older now and feels the mortality, which has haunted him through the earlier novels, closing in. His time, like the nation's oil, is running low. His feelings are further complicated by the arrival of Nelson, who has left college and who, as it turns out, has impregnated a young woman named Teresa (called Pru), whom he eventually marries. Rabbit goes on vacation soon after Nelson's arrival and swims and runs every day, gathering his strength for the confrontation he anticipates. He feels that "there's people out to get me. I can lie down now. Or fight" (132). When Janice asks who his attackers are, Rabbit responds, "You hatched him" (132). Caught in the oppositional framework of his relationship with Nelson that has been developing in the previous novels, Rabbit experiences the fears and dissatisfactions of his own situation in terms of the son who is reaching his masculine prime and crowding out his father.

These two themes, the corrupting power of money and the ambivalence of paternity, which were introduced in the first two novels, are now taken to their logical extremes in *Rabbit Is Rich*. Updike's approach to both subjects remains consistent as he continues to unfold the consequences of Rabbit's attitudes and behaviors. It will therefore be helpful to this discussion to bear in mind previous discussions of the relationship connecting masculinity, power, money, and women; on Rabbit's tendency to see his children in an oppositional framework; and on hierarchical competition.

Rabbit-Babbitt

The connection between *Rabbit Is Rich* and *Babbitt* is well known and acknowledged by Updike in his choice of an epigraph from Sinclair Lewis's novel.[1] A look at the relationship between the novels will be useful because the authors adopt a similar perspective in satirizing the "current ideal of material progress" (Parrington 67) but also because Rabbit's world evolves from Babbitt's, is, in fact, the inevitable progression of Babbitt's. The automobile industry, introduced in *Babbitt*, now dominates the American scene, and Rabbit is a Toyota salesman in a world that is running out of gas. The optimistic materialism of *Babbitt* is nearing exhaustion and ennui. And Babbitt's combination of smug respectability and shady business practices evolves into Rabbit's expedient business ethics, which in turn eventually culminate, in *Rabbit at Rest*, in Nelson's white-collar crime, embezzlement.

Rabbit Is Rich and *Babbitt* also share a number of structural similarities, and of course, the protagonists, who are also mentally and physically similar, find themselves in similar predicaments. George F. Babbitt is immersed in the "religion of business and its paunchy priesthood" (West 24). The hedonistic religion Updike showed us in *Couples* reappears in *Rabbit Is Rich*, combined now with the religion of capitalism or business. Even when they are not actively engaged in money-making, Babbitt and Rabbit are preoccupied with related activities, like talking shop, scrutinizing the financial news, or lunching with the Rotarians. As masculine self-esteem in this culture depends primarily on the capacity to make money, the protagonists' unusual success has given both men an inflated sense of power and self-importance, which their authors deflate. Despite their success, both men are frustrated and uneasy. Rabbit says, "The trouble with consumerism is, that the guy next door always seems to be doing better at it than you are" (385). In addition, by confining their attention to business, they have lost emotional touch with their families.

Both protagonists enjoy the status that accompanies success, but the members of their social groups have little in common and share no real warmth. Babbitt's friendships tend to be "mechanical" (Whipple 74), and Rabbit's social interaction seems to focus on competition and sexual opportunism. Rabbit's conversations at the country club, like his story of the murdered goose, are rehearsed performances delivered for effect like Babbitt's speeches (Whipple 74). Both protagonists, however, find solace in the companionship of noncompetitive, doomed male confidants; Babbitt has Paul and Rabbit has Stavros. According to T. K. Whipple, the men in Babbitt's society have denied themselves everything to get up in the world, and "instincts that can't be entirely suppressed, such as sex, begin to take on queer distorted forms" (75). This tendency is even more pronounced in Updike's novel where, as we will see later, heterosexual relations have become pornographic, mechanical, and infantile, and homosexuality is presented in lurid, even sadistic, terms that suggest culturally induced self-loathing.

Despite their initial smugness, Rabbit and Babbitt "suffer from an obscure but acute dissatisfaction" (Whipple 75), a "loathing at the smooth surface of . . . standardized life" (West 25). They experience ambivalent feelings toward their families, especially their rebellious sons, and eventually look outside of their marriages for emancipation and renewal with younger women.

As Whipple observes, in Babbitt's society, "the men are ruled mainly by the desire to get rich, and the women by the desire to rise socially, but the two are ultimately the same" (75). The Victorian legacy controls their lives. The men have exchanged their freedom for the prize of a domestic life that no longer seems worthwhile. Increased self-esteem and social privilege reward their diligence as worker-providers, and their masculinity is certified by their wealth and women. Unfortunately, having struck this bargain, the men no longer want what they have. Male resentment against confining wives is reflected in Babbitt's own, and his troubled friend Paul's, intense dislike for Paul's wife, Zilla, and in Nelson's grudge against his wife, Pru. And although Rabbit's marriage seems solid, he recurrently fantasizes about bashing his wife's skull with a decorative glass egg. These feelings are not merely the harmless discontents of youth or middle age; Paul shoots his wife, and Nelson (possibly) shoves Pru, who is pregnant, down the stairs, breaking her arm. Newman observes that while the women in *Rabbit Is Rich* are preoccupied with the domestic sentimentality of television programs (*The Waltons, The Jeffersons*), the men, Rabbit and Nelson, are preoccupied with images of television violence (*The Amityville Horror, Charlie's Angels*) (68).

The ideology at the heart of American society in both of these novels combines patriarchy and capitalism and was expounded by Rabbit's coach, Tothero, in *Rabbit, Run*. It is power and the hierarchical status that goes with it that are all important, but women and money are the "counters" for male power (Fetterley 73). As suggested earlier, in this system, wives tend to be valued either for the money they bring to the marriage (Janice's case) or for the money required to win and maintain them (Babbitt's wife Myra's case). Nelson thinks he might have been mistaken in not marrying Melanie, because her father had been a corporation lawyer and her brother "played polo" (*Rich* 304). And in fulfillment of Veblen's theory, while the husbands are profiting at work, their wives attest to their success (and masculinity) by their indolence and conspicuous consumption. In this novel, Rabbit values Janice because she has brought him her father's wealth; he is proud that she plays tennis daily and signs chits at the club, but he is still, like Babbitt, critical of his wife's indifferent homemaking, because part of what he contracted for was "*a haven in a heartless world*" (Osherson 84). Furthermore, when he thinks of all that he will never do, he still resents his entrapment.

Both Rabbit and Babbitt face the challenge of resolving conflicts with their rising adult sons. Here, too, Tothero's ideology strains an already difficult human situation. As the paternal characters increasingly withdraw from the home into the world of work, they lose touch with the members of their families, becoming "absent fathers" who lack the knowledge and sympathy necessary to help their sons. In addition, a system that teaches competition as the dominant model for male interaction makes it especially difficult for fathers to accept, let alone foster, their sons' development. As Nelson realizes, with "any other man around . . . [Rabbit] gets nasty" (*Rich* 293). Babbitt's resolution with his son is easy and optimistic; Rabbit's unresolved conflict with Nelson is more wrenching and honest.

Perhaps the most important similarity between the two novels is in their notion that "to be rich is to be poor" (*Rich* 351). Both draw a detailed portrait of American society and suggest that to profit in such a society a man must sell his soul both in the marketplace and at home. As Lewis demonstrates with Babbitt, Updike, too, shows that Rabbit's wealth and power are tainted and illusory at worst, fleeting at best. Updike's character, however, suffers more intensely than Lewis's from the intrinsic natural losses associated with middle age—declining vigor, waning power, and diminishing potential (especially sexual potential). In this novel, Updike uses being rich, especially being a rich *man*, as a metaphor for human mortality, for at the moment that Rabbit crests in life, he is most vulnerable to the inevitable hurt and humiliation of loss and most bitterly aware of his vulnerability.

The challenge of middle age requires that Rabbit accept his losses, modify his self-concept, revise his expectations, reviews his values, and move in new directions. As he struggles to make these adjustments, he considers the alternatives represented by the materialism and hedonism of the Murketts, friends from his country club gang, and the more enduring values offered by his three guides, Melanie, the first girl Nelson brings home; Stavros; and Thelma Harrison, another member of the country club gang, who is dying of lupus and with whom Rabbit will have a crucial sexual encounter. The role of masculinity continues to be a significant issue in the Rabbit novels. Rabbit's gender identity shapes his present spiritual crisis, his relationships with women past and present, and, increasingly important, his relationship with Nelson.

Rabbit in 1979

With the failure of the revolution against the old order and with the suppression of the feminine in *Rabbit Redux*, we find at the opening of *Rabbit Is Rich* that the America of 1979 continues to be dominated by the wealthy white patriarchs who are conducting business as usual. The sign in the Toyota franchise window ironically proclaims, "You asked for it, we got it" (10).

Rabbit and Charlie discuss whether the oil crisis means that the earth is being exhausted by economic exploitation or whether the crisis has been manufactured to gouge the consumer. Worst of all, they observe that the greed motivating those at the top of society has trickled down to the common man and woman and become a feature of daily life as people squabble over the little gasoline still available. Critic Dilvo I. Ristoff suggests that Rabbit is relieved by the news that Skeeter has been shot by the police because the black radical believed that system, from which Rabbit now profits, "was essentially wicked" (116). The only blacks mentioned in this novel are employees or potential customers (the country club set is exclusively white). Rabbit is now so much a part of the wealthy white establishment he once despised that he will eventually move into Penn Park himself on the profits he makes trading South African gold. As Ruth tells him toward the end of the novel, "That's just where you belong, with those phonies" (*Rich* 419).

Andrew Tolson has observed that male power and privilege are the carrots that culture uses to lure boys into a certain kind of labor and domesticity (46). Rabbit Angstrom has been bought; after twenty-three years of marriage, he is a tame, "domestic rabbit" who loves his privileges yet continues to resent the price he paid for them (Ristoff 40). He blames Janice for "the entire squeezed and cut-down shape of his life ... at every turn she has been a wall to his freedom" (*Rich* 38). Babbitt also blames Myra for the narrow domesticity of his life; however, an important difference between the novels, as far as masculinity is concerned, is that in 1922 it was possible for both the author and the protagonist to maintain, without reservation, the attitude that dull, demanding women are to blame for male bondage and unhappiness.

As one might expect, by 1979, even if the characters operate under this illusion, the author sees the problem as more complex. The characters hold varying opinions as to who are the victims and who are the oppressors in society. Ironically, Rabbit and Nelson each see the other as benefiting from the exploitation of women and himself as the victim of female oppression. Nelson thinks, "I can't stand him, the way he sits there in the living room hogging the Barcalounger. He ... just sits there in the middle of the whole fucking world, taking and taking. ... being a lousy husband to my mother. That's all he's done to deserve all this money: be too lazy and shiftless to leave my mother like he wanted to" (*Rich* 123). And Rabbit thinks

> of poor Pru lying there with a snivelling baby burying his head in her side instead of a husband, of Melanie slaving away at the Crêpe House for all those creeps from the bank that lunch downtown, of his own sweet hopeful daughter stuck with that big red-faced

Jamie, of poor little Cindy having to put on a grin at being fucked from behind so old Webb can have his kicks with his SX-70, of Mim going down on all those wop thugs out there all these years, of Mom plunging her old arms in gray suds and crying the kitchen blues until Parkinson's at last took mercy and got her upstairs for the rest, of all the women put upon and wasted in the world as far as he can see so little punks like this can come along. (325)

Rabbit does not include himself in this group. Elsewhere, he and Mim give the moral edge to men, believing, as their mother did, that women understand the system better than men who are more innocently duped. They see Janice's and Pru's pregnancies as deliberate entrapments. Of course, this perception is balanced for the reader by having seen Rabbit (and Skeeter) knowingly entrap and triumph over women in Jill. Interestingly, when Rabbit's lesbian neighbors offer good luck following the wedding, he thinks it is Nelson who needs good luck; they think it is Pru. With these and other diverging opinions, Updike reflects the rising awareness of gender issues in the society he represents.

Unlike his characters, Updike suggests that men and women are both victims and supporters of the system. Rabbit's loss of power is due less to the ascendancy of matriarchs than to the terms he accepted in accessing his power. His "transaction," ostensibly with the women, was, in reality, negotiated with the absent patriarchs, that is, with the patriarchal will encoded in the culture. To illustrate, when Rabbit comes home from work, he finds that Janice and her mother have been fighting. Janice asks him to go out to the garden to gather lettuce for dinner. He does so, "glad to escape" from any family unpleasantness (41). Gardens stand for spiritual life in *Rabbit, Run* and for relationships in *Rabbit Redux*. In *Rabbit Is Rich*, Rabbit has now given up gardening altogether, presumably in favor of cultivating "business" at his "acre of asphalt" (3). He now only gathers from this garden that was planted by Janice (though she neglects it as she does her inherited dealership) and that is invested with the additional symbolic value of wealth. Rabbit accesses the power, wealth, and comfort he enjoys in *Rabbit Is Rich* through Janice's "lettuce" (41). That Rabbit not only agrees to this arrangement but likes it is one secret at the heart of the Angstrom marriage: "He is rich because of her inheritance and this mutual knowledge rests adhesively between them like a form of sex, comfortable and sly" (36). Somewhat later, he thinks, "Nothing like the thought of fucking money. He doesn't fuck her enough, his poor dumb moneybags" (175). Updike picks up the association between women and money, that he introduced in *Rabbit, Run* and ties it in with the expanded economic metaphor here.²

That Rabbit must submit to the women in his life is made painfully clear in this novel and the next. He initially operates under the delusion that he owns part of Springer Motors through Janice and that he directs its operation. However, when Janice and her mother decide to fire Charlie Stavros in order to hire Nelson, they do so in the face of Rabbit's strenuous objections, demonstrating that he has no say in the matter. Ma Springer says, "As I understand Fred's will, he left the lot to me and Janice, and I think we're of a mind" (249). Rabbit is forced to play "dead doggie" (249). The seeming injustice of this situation continues to gall Rabbit in *Rabbit at Rest* where we learn that Ma Springer has left the business to Janice and Nelson exclusively.

It might seem, at first glance, that the women are in control here, but in fact they are not. Ma Springer says, "It isn't easy . . . being old, and a widow. In everything I do, after I pray about it, I try to ask myself, 'Now what would Fred want?' And I know with absolute certainty in this instance he would want little Nellie to come work on the lot if that's what the boy desired" (243–44). Fred Springer, a caricature of stereotypical masculinity and materialism (chasing clerks and making deals), controls them all from beyond the grave because mother and daughter have internalized the patriarchal will in the form of "an understanding of what Fred would want" (278). They operate not out of their own power or freedom but as extensions of a self-perpetuating system. Their condition is similar to Mary Angstrom's in *Rabbit, Run*. Mary, although a "mad captive" of an oppressive system, nevertheless conveys its ideology to her son. The men, first Rabbit and then Nelson, resent the women's inordinate power, without recognizing that the women themselves are victimized.

Selling Out

The patriarchal, capitalistic system to which Rabbit has sold out depends not only on the lure of the carrot, but on the acuteness of the rabbit's desire and on the rabbit's continued willingness to sell himself. I believe the carrot includes not only power, sex, and wealth but all of the tangibles and intangibles that might be included under the heading of domestic security. Rabbit thinks: "This is what he likes, domestic peace. Women circling with dutiful footsteps above him and the summer night like a lake lapping at the windows" (*Rich* 75). However, in a recent interview, Updike joked about a worldview centered on wanting and said, "We want sex, mostly, but then we seem to want to get good clothes so we can get the sex, and we want money so we can get clothes to get the sex" (Truehart F1). While hardly a revolutionary concept, this notion is interesting in relation to the vaguely Eastern philosophy espoused by Jill Pendleton in *Rabbit Redux* who understood those wants as "how they get you" into the system (*Redux* 273). Jill tries to reduce her wants in order to enhance her freedom, and Skeeter has to make Jill want heroin badly enough to enslave her again. Jill's response to the problem in *Rabbit Redux* is revived by Melanie, the first girl Nelson brings home in *Rabbit Is Rich*. As the novel progresses, Rabbit also discovers the truth in his own remark that the "freedom, that he always thought was outward motion, turns out to be this inner dwindling" (89). Freedom is in the reduction of wants, in the distinction between the necessary and the superfluous and in the distinction between what one can afford to sell or lose and what one dare not (Newman 77–78).[3]

Part of Rabbit's problem is that he resents, as he has from childhood, the terms of the social contract introduced by Mary Angstrom, and he lives in a state of chronic antagonism toward women or the demanding other represented by women. Both Rabbit and Nelson feel that "women . . . are holes you put one thing in after another and it's never enough, you stuff your entire life in there and they . . . are sorry you couldn't have done better" (*Rich* 336). In *Rabbit at Rest*, Janice, who attends women's groups, has an inkling of how difficult it is for men enculturated in this perspective to progress toward healthy relations with women. She thinks, "He called her stupid, it was true she was slower than he was, and slower to come into her own, but he was beginning to respect her, it was hard for him to respect any woman, his mother had done that to him, the hateful woman" (510).

Just as important as his resentment of the social contract and his antagonism toward women, however, is the fact that, in selling out, Rabbit has lost or suppressed important aspects of himself. Life, Updike says, is an "interim of gaining and losing" (*SC* 257), and to understand Rabbit's development, one needs to identify what aspects of himself Rabbit has sacrificed to success and what progress he makes toward recouping his losses. The novel pursues a reverse logic; Rabbit lost himself in pursuit of wealth, power, and position, and now he must lose (or spend, or surrender) what he has gained in order to reclaim himself (Newman 70–77).

First, Rabbit lost his spiritual sense. Nelson thinks Rabbit "believes there is a God he is the apple of the eye of" (*Rich* 303), but Rabbit himself now finds that "a stony truce seems to prevail between himself and God" (130). Under the influence of materialism, God has shrunk "to the size of a raisin lost under the car seat" (365), and Rabbit has consequently lost his sense of specialness. Updike says, "When we try in good faith to believe in materialism, in the exclusive reality of the physical, we are asking our selves to step aside; we are disavowing the very realm where we exist and where all things precious are kept—the realm of emotion and conscience, of memory and intention and sensation" (*SC* 250). Rabbit's liberating flight to the Caribbean reawakens his sense of God "everywhere like a radiant wind" (*Rich* 365), and his night with Thelma Harrison restores "his sense of miracle at being himself, himself instead of somebody else, and his old inkling, now fading in the energy crunch, that there was something that wanted him to find it, that he was here on earth on a kind of assignment" (392).

In addition to having abandoned his spiritual garden, Rabbit has also sacrificed much of his freedom and integrity, and Nelson despises him for it:

> Dad doesn't like to look bad anymore, that was one thing about him in the old days you could admire, that he didn't care much how he looked from the outside, what the neighbors thought when he brought Skeeter in for instance, he had this crazy dim faith in himself left over from basketball or growing up as everybody's pet or whatever so he could say Fuck You to people now and then. That spark is gone. (293)

Now Rabbit lives in his mother-in-law's home, has bought his father-in-law's and his society's version of success, and has agreed to all of the compromises involved. In selling his freedom, Rabbit has lost not only a sense of personal vision but even a sense of authentic preference. In the Poconos, where he and Janice vacation, Rabbit thinks, "There must be a good way to live" (128); and he begins to consider whether "life can be lived selectively, as one chooses from a menu, or picks a polished fruit from a bowl" (127). Each person's "specialness" is expressed through his or her freedom; thus, when Rabbit finally buys his own home, his preferences are reactivated. Rabbit thinks about gardening again and even considers the possibility of reading in his cozy den.

Finally, buying into the system has meant that Rabbit has had to suppress the feminine, a loss that is reflected both in his personal life and in his society. In Updike's mock interview with Henry Bech, published in *The New York Times Book Review*, the author comments:

> Well, this novel really has "Rural Rabbit" in it, since he keeps going out into the country to spy on this girl he thinks might be his daughter. Ever since his girl baby drowned in "Rabbit Run," Harry has been looking for a daughter. It's the theme that has been pressing forward, without my willing it or understanding it exactly, through these novels. ("Updike on Updike" 34)

Rabbit lost the feminine in Rebecca, whom he abandoned and whom he still mourns. By returning to his marriage in *Rabbit, Run*, he also sacrifices his child by Ruth; whether Ruth, in fact, had an abortion or determined to raise the child alone, that child is lost to him. In *Rabbit Redux*, Rabbit betrays the feminine again when he fails to love and support Jill, and this time his loss has broad social implications. In *Rabbit Is Rich*, we see that in pursuing his kingship, Rabbit has increasingly withdrawn into a masculine and materialistic world. His quest for his lost daughter reflects his wish to reclaim his lost youth as well as his continued quest for the ideal. However, as we shall see, Updike also suggests that Rabbit now needs to recover the lost feminine capacities within himself in order to resolve his current dilemma and go forward with his life. Part of what excites Rabbit about Annie, Ruth's daughter, who appears in this novel, and whom Rabbit, along with the reader, believes to be his, in spite of Ruth's vehement denials, is that it is "wonderful to think that he has been turned into cunt" (30). Furthermore, Rabbit needs to find the actual granddaughter who will link him spiritually and physically with the future. Like his spirituality, the lost feminine is left somewhat vague; however, a digression into the past will clarify its meaning in Rabbit's present.

In these novels, the self or "inner spark" of consciousness rises out of the material world, is delighted and nourished by the material world, and yet perceives itself, without salvation, as betrayed into annihilation by that same materiality. The self lives in dread of the death-bearing other. The limits that enrage Rabbit, and later Nelson, are traceable to their experience of this spirit-matter, self-other dichotomy. Beginning in *Rabbit, Run*, Updike conveys the problems of self and other in terms of Rabbit's hypersensitivity to any perceived diminishment or loss or negation of self in relation to significant others, whether those others be nature, death, God, women, children, or society. Even in the face of this fear, however, Updike believes that it is the self's responsibility "to achieve rapport" with the "cosmic other" (SC 357).

Nature, at least nature without God, seems to Rabbit an indifferent, even aggressive, agent of annihilation. This version of nature generates fear and even revulsion in Rabbit and in his technological society, whose increasingly successful efforts to dominate nature are chronicled in the four Rabbit novels. But in destroying nature, Rabbit (and his society) destroys what he loves and needs: "Harry loves Nature, though he can name almost nothing in it" (*Rich* 129). Updike's view is transcendental; when we suppress or destroy nature, we risk losing touch with our own spirituality. For example, when the beech tree at Ma Springer's is finally cut down in *Rabbit at Rest*, Rabbit realizes that he felt closest to God hearing the rain fall on the umbrella of that tree. However, not only does nature provide a spiritual link, it also provides a material link with the future in its cyclical and reproductive processes.

Rabbit associates women with nature as agents of the physical world; they give life but they also give death. According to Sherry Ortner, women are closely associated with nature in every known society (see "Is Female to Male").[4] Rabbit fears intimacy with all women who seem, like his mother, to have the capacity to overwhelm his sense of himself. He also fears their power to devalue the self with rejection and to limit the self with social demands (as agents of society). Because there is an important continuous link in the novels between nature and women, both of which Rabbit and society strive to dominate, reclaiming the lost feminine will involve reconciling old antagonisms and entering into a new relationship with both nature and women. In the Poconos, Rabbit "feels love for each phenomenon and not for the first time in his life seeks to bring himself into harmony with the intertwining simplicities that uphold him, that were woven into him at birth" (*Rich* 128).

Rabbit's fear of self-loss is further manifested in his paternity. In the earlier novels, Rabbit is unwilling to nurture and support his children because he sees them in a competitive context. Rebecca, Ruth's allegedly aborted child, and Jill are lost as a result, and Nelson is emotionally crippled. In *Rabbit, Run*, paternity is presented as a "thin tube upright in time in which our solitude is somewhat diluted," signifying the convergence of parent, child, and humanity, and past, present, and future (282). But even when Nelson was a toddler, Rabbit feared that the boy was the "Knell-son," signaling his father's death. In *Rabbit Redux*, Nelson not only witnesses his father's weaknesses and failures but also emerges as the sexual rival who might one day displace the dominant male. In *Rabbit Is Rich*, Rabbit feels that his paternity is like a "short steel bar" connecting him to Nelson (361). This image conveys both an unbreakable bond and an inflexibility that resists resolution. Reclaiming the lost feminine in relation to Nelson will involve Rabbit's surrendering his power and assuming a noncompetitive, nurturing role. Although Rabbit makes some moves in this direction, beginning to see similarities between Nelson and himself and offering sympathy to the boy, the process is never completed. Nelson runs away, and at the opening of *Rabbit at Rest*, their bitter relationship has festered. On the positive side, Rabbit does gradually progress from a jealous, murderous attitude toward his granddaughter, Judith, to a nurturing attitude, when he sacrifices his Caribbean pleasure for her welfare. He is rewarded for this development when the child, a physical replica of Rebecca, is placed in his arms.

Even in his quest for God, Rabbit has sought foremost to confirm his own importance and immortality. Several different and evolving versions of God appear in the Rabbit novels; often, however, Rabbit's God is no more than a projection of male power and aspiration as in *Rabbit Redux*, when Rabbit tells Jill that if "somebody came up to me and said, 'I'm God,' I'd say, 'Show me your badge'" (163). This comment not only reveals that Rabbit finds it difficult to sustain his belief but also that he conceives of a God at the top of the hierarchical ladder of force, outside rather than within his creation, who acts as an authoritarian enforcer. Rabbit blames this God for Rebecca's death, and now a "stony truce" characterizes their relationship (*Rich* 130). In questing for this masculine God, whom Updike describes elsewhere as the God of "No," Rabbit has missed the silent, encouraging God he once emulated in Horace Smith. In *Self-Consciousness*, Updike says:

> God is the God of the living, though. His priests and executors, to keep order and to force the world into a convenient mould, will always want to make Him the God of the dead, the God who chastises life and forbids and says No. What I felt, in that basement Sunday school of Grace Lutheran Church in Shillington, was a clumsy attempt to extend a Yes, a blessing, and I accepted that blessing. (231)

Far from an "insecure tyrant," the "Yes" God, according to Updike, is "a bottomless encouragement to our being"; he is "a dark sphere enclosing the pinpoint of ourselves, an adamant bubble enclosing us, protecting us, enabling us to let go, to ride the waves of what is" (*SC* 229). This God, womblike and nurturing, is so obviously, profoundly feminine that we might expect Rabbit to fear it more than he would Skeeter's wrathful God of justice. Nevertheless, in *Rabbit Is Rich*, he progresses tentatively toward the notion that "maybe God is in the universe the way salt is in the ocean, giving it a taste" (433). The idea of God permeating the world, including nature, death, women, and children, goes a long way toward resolving the dichotomies that imprison Rabbit.

Throughout the Rabbit novels, Updike has insisted that the various conflicts in Rabbit's life are interrelated, all arising from the same oppositional perspective. While each novel incorporates all of the conflicts introduced in *Rabbit, Run*, each one also focuses on a manifestation specific to Rabbit's gender and age. Thus, the conflict between self and other is most urgently felt in the young man's relations with women in *Rabbit, Run*. In *Rabbit Redux*, Updike shifts the focus to examine Rabbit's relations with adult males in society. In *Rabbit Is Rich*, he focuses on Rabbit's decline, his paternity, and the transfer of power to the rising generation of males. In *Rabbit at Rest*, the author focuses on Rabbit's long-dreaded confrontation with death.

Only for the briefest moments in his life does Rabbit glimpse the reconciliation he continually seeks. The foremost example of such a resolution occurs in *Rabbit, Run*, in the Smiths' Easter garden where the absent Horace, a type of the "Yes" God, offers Rabbit a model that reconciles the physical and spiritual worlds. By emulating Horace and assuming the role of a caretaker who cooperates with nature to create and sustain life, Rabbit is brought into a wholesome relation with the world. He begins to see nature as creative, death as part of the creative process, women as cooperative, and children (seeds) as life to be nurtured and surrendered.

In the past, Rabbit reduced women to silence, whether he actually let them die or not, maintaining his point of view at the expense of theirs. Now Updike places Rabbit in a situation in which he needs feminine perspective to lead him out of the maze of the problems he faces. He needs Horace's eyes, or perhaps Jill's, to see new possibilities. No matter how adamant he is, life now insists that Rabbit abdicate his power, and he needs feminine perspective in order to transform his surrender into a creative act that will enrich himself and others. In his relationships, Rabbit needs to move beyond competition with Ronnie, collusion with Webb, and exploitation with Cindy toward friendship and companionship with Stavros and Janice. He needs to focus less on superficial differences between himself and Nelson and focus more on the similarities that might lead to the empathy and affirmation Nelson desperately needs. Finally, Rabbit needs to rediscover his own specialness in his "rapture" (surrender), as Updike says, with "the giant, cosmic other" (*SC* 257).

Interestingly, Updike's insights into male midlife crisis are confirmed by psychologists in this fairly new field of study. Daniel Levinson suggests that because "no life structure can permit the living out of all aspects of the self," midlife development for men may involve a struggle to renegotiate gender-based polarities (200). Samuel Osherson agrees: "Men grow out of childhood and into adulthood not 'whole' but rather with the sense of self organized around personal achievement and self-action in the world. . . . the shift at midlife [is] to reclaim parts of the self left behind or devalued in the rush to become a man" (79). Furthermore, "the healthy growth of men's personalities in midlife and beyond is often described in terms that our society defines as *'feminine'*" (79; emphasis added). David Guttman expresses the transition as a focal shift away from agency and power toward receptivity and nurturance (see "Individual Adaptation in the Midlife Years").

Apparently, although specialists consider this transition to be the appropriate developmental task for men of Rabbit's age, studies reveal that only about one-third of the men involved actually make a successful transition (see Farrell and Rosenberg, *Men at Midlife*). Not only do some men resist the frightening loss of power, but the culture that molded their self-conception may undermine their efforts. Osherson claims it is a mistake "to underestimate . . . the powerful forces from work and family blocking change for men" (79). There is, on the negative side of *Rabbit Is Rich*, the pull represented by Webb Murkett, who advocates abandoning all ties with one's children and pursuing wealth and sex as the fountain of perpetual youth. More important, perhaps, is that the whole culture seems to disallow the image of masculinity that Rabbit must aspire to now, so there is no comfortable way for him to make the necessary transition.[5]

Osherson also notes that, as Updike's novel suggests, the transitional process may stimulate guilt and rage in other members of the family. Clearly, Nelson wants to destroy his father, and in *Rabbit at Rest*, one feels, especially as Janice prepares to sell the home Rabbit loves without his consent, that he has become the victim of everyone's liberation. In part, the rage underlying family behavior may be the result of so many years of accommodation:

> The family's rage toward the father lies in the years of accommodation that they may have colluded in creating. When children are growing up, father is seen as the patriarch. Family members relate to him by trying to placate or manipulate or cajole him so as to avoid direct clashes with his power. The father may be a hated and feared figure as well as a beloved one. As the family reorganizes

itself at midlife, the years of accommodation, having prevented everyone from finding safe ways to disagree with the father, may fuel the rage that the wife and children feel. In some families in therapy the wife and teenage children often act as serfs rising up against the powerful lord of the manor. (Osherson 80–81)

Thus, not only is Nelson, obnoxious as he is, Rabbit's creation, but the young man's anger may well be the by-product of the power and privilege held so long by Rabbit. A similar anger led Rabbit to his own attempted revolution against the Penn Parkers in *Rabbit Redux*.

Despite the difficulties, Rabbit seems to make real progress toward a successful transition, and this novel ends on a positive note. Unfortunately, in *Rabbit at Rest*, it becomes clear that Rabbit, still the representative American male, ultimately fails as badly as the majority of his compatriots to achieve an expanded identity.

Throughout all the novels and in many guises, the feminine has stood for the radically other. Rabbit's hunger for the feminine, in spite of his fear of contact, has nevertheless been a wholesome impulse that might enable the solipsistic self to reach beyond its boundaries. The feminine has also represented the additional perspective that makes reconciliation possible. In this novel, where Rabbit is so much concerned with his losses, his past, and his dead, by welcoming the feminine in the form of his granddaughter, Rabbit finds a way to recover some of what was lost as well as a way of connecting with the past, present, and future.

When Rabbit learns that Nelson has run off, abandoning his pregnant wife, and that Janice wants to leave the Caribbean, when he is expecting to finally sleep with Cindy that night, he balks, still hoping to have his "dream date" with Cindy (*Rich* 399). "I don't *want* to leave before tomorrow," he says, and then, "I still don't understand the rush. . . . Nobody's died" (398). Janice responds, "Not yet. . . . Is that what you need?" (398). This exchange recalls one years earlier when Rabbit left Janice prior to Rebecca's death; it was what *he wanted* and *felt* that was important to Rabbit at the time (*Run* 230). This time, Rabbit sacrifices the delights of the Murketts' hedonism and the quest for perpetual youth to protect and nurture the new baby granddaughter. This inconspicuous but sacrificial act is as close as Rabbit Angstrom comes to the kind of good father modeled by George Caldwell in *The Centaur* ("Now . . . Chiron accepted death" [222]). And when he returns home, Rabbit receives his reward—his lost daughter, his "fortune," and his garden are returned.

It is also interesting that, as Horace's garden of resolution in *Rab-*

bit, Run was an Easter garden, this reconciling granddaughter is a Christmas babe, or at least very nearly. The actual Christmas season, however, is described only in terms of its depressing materialism—the stars on the vault of Rabbit's bank, the carols in the background, the "lie told to children" (*Rich* 351). In terms of the equinox-solstice metaphor, which now coincides with events in Nelson's marriage, this season, dominated by the young man's self-interest, might well end in death. Because of Rabbit's (and Janice's) commitment, new life is possible, and Judith's birth is a belated but appropriate blessing and a reconciliation of the novel's dichotomies. Her birth also coincides closely with the 13 January anniversary of the birth of the mystic-philosopher, Gurdjieff.

Fiscal Alternatives

Robert Detweiler and, more recently, Judie Newman have analyzed the dominant economic metaphor in *Rabbit Is Rich*. The interpretation offered here is consistent with Newman's reading, which sees Rabbit as developing from a saver to a spender, a transition that involves recognition that his wealth is more of a burden than a blessing and that in accumulating money, he has become spiritually impoverished (Newman 63–78). I would add a few observations, however. First, the money-changing scenes function technically like the plurisignificant dream metaphor, providing a key to the images used throughout the novel, and thus clarify the interrelation between the areas of Rabbit's life.[6]

The exchange where Rabbit buys his gold and silver is appropriately named Fiscal Alternatives. Through the development of associated images and through exhaustive substitutions (similar to his use of overlapping circles in *Rabbit, Run*), Updike reveals the true nature of Rabbit's exchanges and further demonstrates the interrelatedness of the different areas of Rabbit's life. Rabbit's monetary and materialistic perspective transforms all—to Rabbit, Janice is "moneybags," his orgasm a "payoff," his son a "loser," his granddaughter "fortune's hostage" (175, 203, 427, 437). His mythological predecessor is King Midas, an example of folly, who "had very little profit" from his fleeting riches (Hamilton 278). Amusingly, Rabbit has inherited and passed on a slight crimp in the top of his ear—a vestige of Midas's donkey ears—and like Midas, seems unable to get a decent meal.

A second observation: Newman's interpretations can be profitably reconsidered within the context of masculinity developed here.

As noted earlier, Rabbit is not merely accumulating wealth in a transaction with a materialistic society; he is also doing so in a transaction with the absent patriarchs. He sells part of himself in exchange for the symbols of male power and self-esteem. When he spreads his coins out on the bed for Janice, he is again like Gatsby, displaying his shirts for Daisy, proving his worthiness or manhood and, in particular, proving his sexual potency in economic terms. Money-making is the competitive activity that supplants other games for adult males. Thus, Fred Springer knew that showing newspaper accounts of his son-in-law's basketball victories would boost sales, and likewise, Rabbit tries to get ahead by reading *Consumer Reports*. Furthermore, inextricably bound up with Tothero's ideology (patriarchy cum capitalism) is the objectification and denigration of women. Thus, Cindy is Webb's treasure, a possession for swapping and gloating over (in pornographic shots). As nature and women are associated, nature is also exploited nearly to the point of exhaustion. In the Poconos, Rabbit comes across a coal baron's castle, a symbol of the exploitation of nature for profit, and he himself plays with the pernicious notion that nature is something that can be possessed and "fenced off" for the exclusive pleasure of the wealthy (*Rich* 127). And, of course, when Rabbit fears that Nelson will steal his gold, his Krugerrands, he really deeply fears that the rebellious young man will steal his position of power and sexual dominance. All of these correspondences point to the essential fact that Rabbit's profit-and-loss mentality arises from his need to aggrandize a masculine self that is threatened by devaluation.

To briefly recount the money-changing subplot, Rabbit tries to avoid the losses threatening him in middle age by emulating Webb Murkett. Murkett copes with aging by accumulating money and practicing hedonism with a series of nubile brides. He also drives his older children away and affirms his masculinity by having new ones. (In *Rabbit at Rest*, Cindy has grown fat, and Webb has moved on to still another twenty-year-old wife.) Like Murkett, Rabbit now tries to pursue gold, have sex with Cindy, and displace Nelson with new children.

Acting on Murkett's information that the value of gold is rising, Rabbit goes to a seedy looking exchange called Fiscal Alternatives. The strange employees at the exchange represent materialism and corruption, an impression that is confirmed in *Rabbit at Rest*, where it is reported that the young blonde clerk has committed suicide and Lyle, her assistant, is dying of AIDS and is involved in Nelson's embezzlement scheme.

Rabbit buys thirty Krugerrands, which he will eventually trade for silver and then sell off to buy a home in Penn Park. The money is tied in with the novel's thematic concerns by a method of "accruing" or accumulating references that is staggering in its complexity. For example, the number thirty suggests betrayal, recalling not only Judas but Jill and Skeeter. Later, biblical allusions and additional references to Skeeter and South Africa will expand the suggestion of a betrayal of spiritual and social values in favor of materialism and will expand an association of wealth with class oppression and racism (a theme that Skeeter developed in *Rabbit Redux*).

The Krugerrands come in cylinders that have tops like "dollhouse toilet seats" and are stuffed with "toilet paper" (*Rich* 195–96). Updike continues to make connections between money and feces ("Money is shit" [157]), not only developing the idea that money is dirty but also developing the idea that accumulating and hoarding money reflects a fundamentally disordered personality (and society).[7] Money and feces will later also be tied in with the betrayal of spiritual values and with death, when in the next exchange scene at Christmas, Janice and Harry enact a paradoxical reverse nativity.

Updike makes use of the "perceived connection between faeces and money to illuminate flaws in Rabbit's system of values, and links between money and fantasy" (Newman 64). The representation of Rabbit as anal-retentive is amusing because of its aptness. The reader recalls accounts in the earlier novels of Rabbit as a child "that used to hate a mess" (*Run* 154), who "hated food that was mixed up" (*Redux* 376), who as an athlete "never fouled" or broke the rules (*Run* 63), and who achieved in order to win his mother's approval (*Redux* 89). Rabbit impregnated Ruth because of his desire for a "nice clean piece" (*Run* 139). Later, he hated printer's ink on his hands and changed into a white shirt after work to "cancel" the dirt (*Redux* 5). Janice thought he was "too fastidious, hates sex really" (*Redux* 57); he thought there was something revolting about women (*Run* 84). The man who withdrew from contact and withheld love and was obsessed with powerlessness and saw power struggles everywhere was obviously, all along, an anal-retentive protagonist. The characterization is so apt that one wonders if Updike had it in mind twenty years earlier when he began his portrait.

While Mary Angstrom was a sufficiently imposing mother to have made toilet training an ordeal, that is not the point here. Updike would be unlikely to see existential, theological, familial, and societal difficulties in terms of toilet training; but he does use Freudian-based theory to elaborate deep-rooted problems in Rabbit's character and in society (Newman 64). The aspect of Updike's psychological portrait that is not amusing, that is sadly serious, is that Rabbit has had trouble all of his life with surrendering; and his incapacity has caused a great deal of unhappiness for himself and everyone around him.[8] Now he has reached a point in life where he has little choice. He can continue to resist like Webb Murkett, but whether he cooperates or not, life will nevertheless begin to take everything from him. Once again, Rabbit's dilemma is similar to Lear's. If a man's value is linked by his culture to power (in Rabbit's case, masculinity, wealth, sexual dominance), then he had best hang on to the symbols of power for as long as he can, for if he gives up those, he will be at the mercy of dogs like Goneril and Nelson. But, of course, he *must* give them up, for even beyond the revolutionary connivings of the new generation, the real thief is death. One way that people deal with this problem is by investing in the future, which is why the issue of paternity, which is considered in greater depth in the next chapter, is critical in *Rabbit Is Rich*. With Nelson a seeming traitor, Rabbit, like Lear, must reclaim his rejected daughter.

To return to Rabbit's financial investment, he brings his Krugerrands home and waits for an opportunity to display them to Janice. In the meantime, he hides them in the same drawer where, he recalls, he had kept his condoms in earlier years; also, he remembers once having suspected Nelson of stealing some. Updike makes the important connection between Rabbit's money and his masculinity, i.e., sexual vigor and potency. The memory of the missing condoms triggers some memories of Nelson as an adolescent, and it becomes clear that "Harry wanted out of fatherhood" as soon as Nelson became sexually mature (197). Not only does Rabbit fear that Nelson will displace him at the lot, steal his gold, and later steal his silver, he is afraid that Nelson will displace him sexually as the dominant male.

When Janice comes from her shower, Rabbit spills the coins onto the bedspread. He then lies down and places coins on his eyes, establishing the connection between gold and death. Newman suggests these coins are for the ferryman, Charon (71). Indeed, Rabbit is haunted by his dead relatives throughout this novel. His gold comes to him from old man Springer just as his physical inheritance comes from his own parents (i.e., death is a legacy).

Displaying his gold and savoring Janice's reaction stimulate Rabbit sexually, and when Janice asks where he will put his gold he replies, "In your great big cunt" (*Rich* 202). He then covers her body with coins and holds up the last one "as if to insert it" (202). "Interest compounds" until his "payoff" (202, 203). When he and Janice finish having intercourse, Rabbit discovers that in his preoccupation, he has lost one coin for which he searches frantically. This coin, called "the precious thirteenth" (203), is interesting for several reasons. It recalls the lost thirteenth disciple, Judas, who like Skeeter was given thirty pieces. The coin also alludes to the parable of the woman who lost one coin and valuing it above those she retained, searched until she found it (Luke 15.8–10; Detweiler, *John Updike* 176). Like the parable of the lost sheep, this one represents God as a good parent who searches for his lost child. Evidently, Rabbit once did put his precious gold into Janice and subsequently lost one of his coins, his daughter, Rebecca. Unlike the Krugerrands, the lost child is his true fortune for which he also searches (in Jill and Annie) until he is given his grandchild, Judith. Rabbit also values the lost child above Nelson whom he has retained. Thus, Updike integrates notions of profit and loss, not only with Rabbit's sexuality, but with his paternity.

Again on Webb Murkett's advice, and increasingly fearful of potential losses, Rabbit decides to exchange his Krugerrands for silver. He and Janice meet downtown, remove the gold from their safety deposit box and walk to Fiscal Alternatives through an impoverished neighborhood, where they draw "bitter" glances (*Rich* 341). In these scenes, the corrupt, perverse aspect of the well-heeled success of the money-changers is hinted at; the "sacred metal" becomes "crap"; the benefit becomes burdensome; the "ultimate security" becomes the source of jealousy and possible theft; and the treasure vault becomes a "stifling" crypt (196, 350, 343, 349).

On the way to the bank, Rabbit tells Janice, who is struggling to carry the silver, to pretend that she is pregnant. When they arrive, Christmas carols peal through the blue, vaulted, groined ceiling of the Brewer Trust. In this cathedral of materialism, a weird "nativity" of death (or nativity/defecation) is enacted. Janice and Rabbit "push and tug" like "surgeons working on a hopeless case" (349), but despite their efforts, "the coins keep escaping the mouth of the sack" (349). Janice sweats from her "exertion," but even "when they have pressed the absolute maximum," three hundred coins remain (349). Finally, the couple put their treasure/"crap" into a manger/ coffin, "a long slender . . . [safe-deposit] box" (349, 350). Rabbit puts the overflow into his pockets, and they take the box into the vault where Rabbit slides his "long box into the empty rectangle" and thinks, "R.I.P." (*Rich* 350; Detweiler, *John Updike* 172–78). As they leave, Rabbit apologizes to the bank attendant, "Sorry we loaded it up with crap" (*Rich* 350).

This perverse nativity scene occurs on or near the winter solstice (on 22 December), a period of disharmony and death that the celebration of Christmas is intended to counter. But no baby, no regaining of the lost feminine, no spiritual rebirth is possible in so corrupted an environment. So the Christmas event—the arrival of new life symbolizing spiritual renewal—is delayed until 13 January when Judith ("the precious thirteenth") is born. Updike implies that a rejection of materialistic values is necessary for spiritual renewal, and Janice and Rabbit's unselfish sacrifice of the hedonistic pleasures of the Caribbean is a figuratively saving act.

Later, Rabbit and Janice return to Fiscal Alternatives a third time exchange their silver for the cash they need to buy a home of their own. We now learn that, despite his earlier complaints, Rabbit had stayed with the Springers following the fire of *Rabbit Redux* because the arrangement provided him with an easy way out of his marriage should he want one. So Rabbit's purchase of a new home now represents not only a reclamation of his freedom (made partly in response to Stavros's remark that Rabbit has freedom he hasn't used) but also a new commitment to his marriage. On the other hand, a new home for the parents will leave Nelson an open field, and in view of the toxic relationship between father and son, that is perhaps the best that can be hoped for. The following day, Rabbit spends his profit and even incurs a debt (this "debt is a good thing" [*Rich* 366]) to purchase back some of his freedom, preference, and integrity—to purchase a home that, fittingly, is "a little stone house, once a *gardener's cottage*" (366; emphasis added).[9]

NINE

Laius and Oedipus

DEFINING MASCULINITY in terms of achievement and competition not only leads to distorted values, as revealed in *Rabbit Is Rich*, but also "poisons" the relationships between Rabbit and Nelson (*Rest* 418). Father/son relationships have recently become the focus of attention in several fields, and although findings are still tentative and fragmented, work that has been done in this area suggests dynamics extremely complex and replete with ambivalence, as are, in fact, the dynamics of the relationship between Rabbit and Nelson. For example, Rabbit complains that Nelson won't grow up, stand on his own, and be a man; yet when Janice questions why his heart is hardened against the boy, Rabbit realizes it is "because Nelson has swallowed up the boy that was and substituted one more pushy man in the world, hairy wrists, big prick" (*Rich* 209). But Rabbit himself is such a man, and his hatred for his son reflects his hatred for himself, a self-hatred that expresses itself in rejection of Nelson and is thereby passed on to Nelson. Janice says, "He . . . *hates* himself, Harry" (399). Yet in a strange way, Nelson and Rabbit continue to love one another. As psychologist Samuel Osherson demonstrates, the very nature of masculinity is ambivalence (15–43). Under these conditions, tidy, linear argumentation is neither possible nor desirable.

In *Rabbit Is Rich*, Nelson has now grown into adulthood and is ready to wage his own revolution against the tyrannical patriarch. Although Nelson is engaged in an oedipal conflict, Janice is not the presently contested prize. He has already won her allegiance, as well as

Bessie's, against Rabbit, who is "not a Springer" (*Rich* 116). What Nelson wants is to grow up, to take the old king's place in the world by assuming the wealth, power, and sexual dominance (which is what the possession of Jocasta represents) that are the mantle of adult masculinity. He also wants revenge for the terrible wrongs done to him.

Osherson reminds us that two such wrongs committed by Laius are at the heart of the Oedipus story. Having learned that he will die by the hand of his own son, Laius sets out to destroy his child in order to perpetuate his own life. This initial rejection and betrayal is similar to Nelson's experience of his father. When Rabbit runs away in *Rabbit, Run*, he sacrifices his children to his self-interest. Later, in *Rabbit Redux*, Rabbit fails to nurture either Nelson's self-esteem or Nelson's masculinity, and he betrays the boy again by failing to protect Jill. Nelson, in fact, locates the source of his rage against limits in his father's power and in his own helpless inability to save his loved ones (*Rich* 138).

The story of Oedipus contains a second wrong not generally identified; Laius arrogantly refuses to step aside for Oedipus on the road (Osherson 36–37). Rabbit similarly refuses to step aside for Nelson, and the two have been locked in virtual mortal combat since Nelson reached puberty. The conflict continues in *Rabbit Is Rich*. Nelson leaves college and comes home, sullen, obviously disturbed by something, and pressures his father for a job at the car lot. Rabbit resists, and there is clearly more to his objections than his proffered interest in Nelson's future. He does not want to move aside for Nelson.

Unfortunately, Nelson, although too thwarted by Rabbit's competitive stance to move beyond a stunted, infantile attitude, is nonetheless old enough now to have adult problems. He has, it turns out, impregnated a girl. He marries her and is given, against Rabbit's will, a job at the lot by his mother and grandmother. He begins to fight with Rabbit at work and regularly smashes Rabbit's cars. He later expresses his rage and resentment toward his marriage by pushing his pregnant wife down the stairs, and, finally, by running away before the baby is born. This is the fruit of Rabbit's oppositional relationship with his son.

A large part of the problem between Rabbit and Nelson is that both, but more importantly Rabbit, have been culturally deprived of successful noncompetitive models of relationship and conflict resolution. Rabbit remembers being raised in an "embattled" household. Not only was the Angstrom marriage contentious, but both Mary and Earl modeled suspicious, competitive attitudes toward all outsiders.

> Living embattled, Mom feuding with the neighbors, Pop and his union hating the men who owned the printing plant where he worked his life away, both of them scorning the few kin that tried to keep in touch, the four of them, Pop and Mom and Hassy and Mim, against the world and a certain guilt attached to any reaching up and outside for a friend. *Don't trust anybody: Andy Mellon doesn't, and I don't.* (Rich 63)

Interestingly, Updike associates these negative attitudes, which were further cultivated by Tothero through competitive athletics, with the needs of capitalism.

Once again, Updike seems to be in the psychological avant-garde. Writing in 1986, Osherson comments on the neglected (I believe, suppressed) aspect of the oedipal relationship, that is, the father's antagonism toward the son. He says:

> Our fathers perhaps secretly feared us [sons] too. The ambivalent love between fathers and sons is underestimated. It is the dark side of the big value boys are given in our society. Since so much of male identity is based on performance, sons will some day outdistance Dad. We become ambivalent objects, loved and feared by our fathers. Indeed, as we are learning more about fathers and children, researchers have proposed the phrase "Laius complex" to refer to the father's feeling of threat from his son and need to put him down. . . .
>
> A son may represent a father's mortality in very uncomfortable ways. As the son becomes a man, the father must recognize his own aging. . . . Fathers and sons may find it much easier to display anger and hostility to each other than caring and affection, given the son's conflicting pull to mother, the father's sense of being displaced and jealousy of his son, and the limited opportunities for men in the family to express a range of feelings to each other. (36–37)

This description precisely fits Rabbit. But if Rabbit has a Laius complex, both he and Nelson also carry within themselves what is now called a "wounded father." The "wounded father" is defined as "a conflicted inner sense of masculinity rooted in men's experience of their fathers as rejecting, incompetent or absent" (Osherson 22–23). This conflicted inner sense may arise either from an accurate perception of the father, as in Nelson's case where Rabbit is actually hostile and rejecting, or it may arise from the son's mistaken projections. For example, where the father is absent, the son may merely imagine him as rejecting, authoritarian, vulnerable, and so on.[1]

In understanding this theory, it may be helpful to recall Fetterley's remarks on Sherwood Anderson's "I Want to Know Why." The boy in that story is left unsure of how to identify with a male world that he perceives as treacherous and exploitive. How the boy resolves the problem of identification will shape his adult interactions with men, women, and children. The "conflicted inner sense" amounts to a psychological obstacle arising from the son's perception and experience of his father, which in turn affects the son's image of himself and inhibits him from comfortably assuming his gender identity. Rabbit sees his own father as both long-suffering and weak, and while he rejected Earl's model of masculinity, he nevertheless incorporated the fear that "suffering and entrapment are the male fate" (Osherson 27). According to Osherson, the sons of fathers who are perceived as weak or incompetent at home may withdraw to the world of work (and in Rabbit's case, games) in an effort to avoid the same fate. Such men may also have a special need to reject and control threatening women, because in the absence of a strong father, they can only establish their masculinity in opposition to the feminine. For these males, the unresolved conflicted inner sense, however, will continue to plague their relationships and reappear with special force when their own sons reach the same critical stage of development.

Michael Farrell and Stanley Rosenberg say that "adolescent children and their middle-aged fathers confront similar identity issues. Their simultaneous attempts to confront these issues may exacerbate the difficulties of both, while also creating the possibility of mutual support" (142). A. Siskind, however, adds that "conflicts and crises in the father reactivated by those of the son have a tendency to make the father act unhelpfully or even destructively towards the son. Only by coping with his own conflicts and controlling his response can the father counteract this tendency and help the son accomplish his adolescent task" (qtd. in Esman 268). While Rabbit initially rejects the notion that Nelson is anything like him, he is extremely distressed that the boy seems to be reliving his own experience of entrapment. This is, in fact, exactly what Nelson is doing, but we are left to question whether he is entrapped by society; by Pru; by nature; by personal history and temperamental inclination; or by some, and if so by what, combination of the above. Recent theories suggest that Nelson's conflicted inner sense is passed on to him by his absent, wounding father and causes him to relive the father's crisis. In other words, Nelson's problem, his solution, and his temperament are all part of his wounded masculine inheritance.

Nelson not only perceives Rabbit as "secretly weak and incompetent," but more important, he experiences Rabbit as a "wounding" father and perpetually suffers from "the loss and needy feelings . . . experienced in having been rejected or having disappointed the father" (Osherson 23). Nelson is locked in his whining boyhood because he cannot identify with Rabbit nor win his approval nor abandon the effort—and this last is very important because although their relationship is clearly destructive, both Rabbit and Nelson cling to it, feeding and perpetuating it, which suggests that their need for some mutual relationship outweighs the pain they inflict on each other.

In addition to their competitive context, father and son have been further distanced by their cultural segregation. As Rabbit has withdrawn from the messy emotions of family life into the world of business, Nelson has had difficulty identifying with an absent father. In *Rabbit Redux*, Rabbit had already grown so ignorant of his son that he could no longer recognize or provide for his needs. Their problem is further exacerbated by the prohibition the masculine world tends to impose on men against expressing the tender emotions that might heal or mitigate wounds on both sides. Nelson must literally smash cars and Rabbit needs to "break out" in order to overcome their inhibitions against the simplest loving embrace (*Rich* 262). All of these problems are specifically masculine in origin even though they may also reflect the universal experiences of loss and limitation. Janice, for example, has no such problem and has remained close to Nelson over the years despite the fact that she too wronged the boy and suffers remorse. Rabbit envies her relationship with Nelson thinking, "Typical of the way things have gone, that the kid's growing up should seem a threat and a tragedy to him and to her an excuse to steal a T-shirt" (*Rich* 128).

Osherson's work suggests that by stressing competition, our culture has focused on the oedipal aspect of the father-son relationship while failing to sufficiently emphasize models of reconciliation, like the one contained in the Odysseus myth. The reunion between Odysseus and Telemachus "points to a deep yearning for each other in both father and son, and it contains a lesson for our time" (Osherson 42). The relationship between Rabbit and Nelson is, in fact, extremely intense, intimate, and in some ways, exclusive. No one but these two understands what is going on between them; only they can read each other's motivations and intentions accurately. Rabbit says, "For all that is wrong between them there are moments when his heart and Nelson's might be opposite ends of a short steel bar, he knows so exactly what the kid is feeling" (*Rich* 361–62). Nelson feels that "if he could *just once* make him [Rabbit] see himself for the shit he is, I maybe could let it go" (296). But he doesn't let it go. And whatever other motives may be at work, it is certainly true that the conflict between father and son over Jill in the previous novel, for example, and over Pru in the next have the effect of placing the two men in an intense if unsatisfying relationship.

To return to the Odysseus myth, when Odysseus returns, father and son throw themselves into a healing embrace and weep over their sense of loss. Telemachus is on the brink of manhood, "hardly knowing how to protect his mother, until "the miraculous return of the father . . . propels Telemachus into a confident and strong sense of manhood" (Osherson 42). Together, father and son overwhelm the usurpers. According to Osherson, this model of reconciliation works if the son identifies with something positive in the father and the father, on his side, affirms his son's masculinity and defines "masculine strength in a changing world" (42). Osherson also suggests that the fact that Odysseus introduces his son to manhood through conquest is unimportant (42). However, the competitive, hierarchical context of the affirmation of the son's manhood may be the critical and self-defeating element in the myth; that is, so long as the structure within which the men operate is based on performance and competition, the masculine identity passed from father to son will break down whenever the son's needs or abilities do not match those required by the father's need for an ally, an expansion, that is, or aggrandizement of himself. It is interesting to speculate on how Odysseus might have reacted if Telemachus had felt, say, a moral need to fight alongside the Trojans or if he had been a better warrior than Odysseus or in a modern context, if he had been unathletic or homosexual or more educated or had in any other way threatened either his father's dominance or status among other men. In other words, once the context of competition and achievement is established, the father will only be able to initiate the Odysseus/Telemachus confirmation with the "right" son, the one that in no way diminishes him. A cultural model other than that of a warrior is perhaps needed. (Updike, with his usual perceptiveness, provides a very interesting one—a gardener. Gardening is, in fact, one of the few acceptable "male occupations" that employs and fosters the more feminine qualities of nonexploitative, noncompetitive empathy and nurturing. Gardening is also involved with a cycle of death and regeneration, rather than endless exploitation.) At any rate, it is certainly not surprising within the context of the "right" son that Rabbit and Nelson never achieve the reconciliation that would answer both of their needs, although the fear of diminishment is so pervasive in Rabbit's case that it is doubtful that his relationship with Nelson would have been positive even if Nelson had been a few inches taller, more athletic, and physically more like an Angstrom.

Nelson and Rabbit are very much alike, however, in their masculinity. Each identifies masculinity with wielding power over others. Each is plagued by the need to perform and receive approval. Each is suspicious and jealous of the other's sex life. Each feels entrapped by social demands and resents the wife, who signifies responsibility. Each resents the life of his own child. It would appear that, at least in the Angstrom family, the conflicted inner sense is not only the effect of an unresolved conflict between generations, it is a legacy passed on from one generation to the next.

The complexities of the relationship between Rabbit and Nelson are clearly labyrinthian. Updike, because of the accuracy of his chronicle, is able to tap into the emotional power of this culturally suppressed flip side of the oedipal conflict without totally unveiling it (much as he did with his portrait of Mary Angstrom). Updike's characters are once more sufficiently unique to protect the reader (and again, I suspect, the author) from unpleasant associations. Nevertheless, the relationship between Rabbit and Nelson resonates because it touches on a psychological reality hinted at, but usually denied, by our culture, as for example, in the stories of Thyestes who ate his children (but not intentionally), Abraham who would have sacrificed his son (but was prevented), or Herod who slew the innocents (but they were not his own). In the course of the Rabbit novels, Rabbit destroys Nelson, and Updike also hides or mitigates this fact by drawing Nelson as such an obnoxious character that he seems to deserve his fate, when in fact the boy is Rabbit's creation. Perhaps here again is the ambivalence of the male author who examines masculinity and discovers truths too disturbing to name openly.[2]

In *Rabbit Is Rich*, Rabbit unconsciously fears that Nelson will steal four things: his life, his self-esteem, his money, and his women— the last two, especially, signifying masculine power. In *Rabbit, Run*, Rabbit not only resists the progress of his own life but feels squeezed out and threatened by the younger generation. Now in *Rabbit Is Rich*, as his life crests and begins to wane, Rabbit is acutely aware of both its sweetness and its ebbing. He hears "rumors of universal death" and is frightened by the growing number of dead who whisper and beckon to him from the caverns beneath the grass (67, 165, 7). Still, "happy . . . simply to be alive," he resists the call (7). Rabbit's problem is how to extend his life, whether by resistance, which is ultimately futile, of course, or by emotional, spiritual, or physical investment in the future through identification with his progeny. Initially, Rabbit chooses the path of maximum resistance, rejecting his son and clinging to his position as tenaciously as an old king hoarding his treasure. When Rabbit hides his gold, the narrator reveals that

> two glimpses mark the limits of his comfort in this matter of men descending from men. When he was about twelve or thirteen he walked into his parents' bedroom . . . and the old man was standing in front of his bureau in just socks and an undershirt, innocently fishing in a drawer for his undershorts, that boxer style that always looked sad and dreary to Harry anyway, and here was his father's bare behind, such white buttocks, limp and hairless, mute and helpless flesh that squeezed out shit once a day and otherwise hung there in the world like linen that hadn't been ironed; and then when Nelson was about the same age . . . Harry had wandered into the bathroom and had seen the child frontally: he had pubic hair and, though his body was still slim and pint-sized, a man-sized prick, heavy and oval, unlike Rabbit's circumcised and perhaps because of this looking brutal, and big. Big. (*Rich* 197)

Somewhat earlier, Rabbit remembered seeing Earl in the bathhouse at the beach: "His father's skin where the workclothes always covered it seemed so tenderly white. He loved his father for having such whiteness upon him, secretly, a kind of treasure . . . he and Pop changed together rapidly, not looking at one another" (*Rich* 126). In *Rabbit, Run*, whiteness is negatively associated with the feminine and with death; in *Rabbit Redux*, it also signifies spiritual enervation. Here, however, Earl's whiteness conveys mildness and vulnerability (the repressed feminine?) and seems to the son like a treasure, albeit an embarrassing treasure to be quickly and shyly hidden. In his youth, Rabbit rejected Earl as a model of masculinity because he lacked the culturally valued "force," or masculine presence (*Run* 21). Earl's old-womanliness has been troubling for Rabbit, but in this instance, the father's mildness is a blessing and a bond. It signifies that this Laius has no will to impede the rising male's progress; Earl not only steps aside for and befriends his son in *Rabbit Redux*, he also nurtures his development. Interestingly, dead Rabbit now hears his mother "hissing" at him in the night, but when he does well, he thinks his father would be proud (*Rich* 178). Rabbit also recalls Fred Springer's unintentional generosity in making space. After negotiating his bargain, Fred had "the kindness to die," leaving Rabbit as "the king of the lot" (*Run* 252; *Rich* 2).

At the opposite limit of Rabbit's comfort in the matter of "men descending from men" stands Nelson, "looking brutal, and big."

Nelson's sexual maturity is threatening to Rabbit for a variety of reasons, and Rabbit responds, as the language suggests, defensively. He does not want to step aside for Nelson. On the contrary, he undermines Nelson's confidence in order to stay on top, displaying the same purpose, persistence, and cruelty he showed in his earlier efforts to undermine Janice's confidence. Now, of course, "Janice is harder to put down than formerly" (*Rich* 115). Again, it is intriguing that Updike disguises the situation exactly as he did with Janice by making the victim so unappealing that it is easier to identify with the abuser.

Rabbit and Nelson battle over self-esteem. Because Rabbit has been culturally geared toward performance, he needs constant recognition and approval. Now, though he has lost the "witness" that family and fans once provided ("What you lose as you age is witnesses, the ones that watched from early on and cared, like your own little grandstand" [433]), he makes do with the approval of the Rotarians and the acceptance of the gang at the Flying Eagle Country Club. Nelson, however, remembers his father's earlier indiscretions and betrayals and thus threatens Rabbit's respectable reputation or, more precisely, threatens Rabbit's sense of deserving his reputation: "No witness but Nelson stands in the universe to proclaim that his father is guilty, a cheat and coward and murderer, and when he tries to proclaim it nothing comes out, the world laughs as he stands there with open mouth silent" (338). Like the women in *Rabbit, Run* who have the power to devalue Rabbit by their rejection, Nelson has the power to diminish Rabbit's self-esteem by his witness and his memory of his father's failures. Rabbit tells Thelma, "I think one of the troubles between me and the kid is every time I had a little, you know, slip-up, he was there to see it. That's one of the reasons I don't like to have him around. The little twerp knows it too" (161).

The comment reveals Rabbit's continued reluctance to accept responsibility; it also reveals his resentment of a power only he and Nelson seem to recognize. As a result, Rabbit tries to keep his son down by undermining his self-esteem. Updike suggests that Rabbit's opinion of Nelson represents a somewhat distorted reality, as no one else shares it entirely and as Nelson's ideas on improving the business turn out to be successful. It becomes apparent in *Rabbit at Rest* just how willing Rabbit is to completely destroy Nelson's self-esteem when he [Rabbit] steals his son's wife (a variation on the Oedipus story).

Rabbit senses that Nelson, in joining the business, is making a move to usurp everything that his father's wealth symbolizes, including his life, his self-esteem, his power, and his sexual dominance. Rabbit feels "loss after loss" as he stands by helplessly while Nelson smashes car after car.³ Newman points out that while Rabbit is a saver, Nelson is a wastrel (70), which is true, but Nelson also recognizes Rabbit's materialism as the chink in his father's armor. Nelson not only exercises power by exasperating Rabbit, thus demonstrating his weakness, but he also uses these attacks as way of reaching the father he still somehow loves. Rabbit also senses this when he remembers that "he hasn't felt so close to breaking out of his rut since Nelson smashed those convertibles" and the two men embraced (*Rich* 262). Nelson's pursuit of violence is similar to Rabbit's in *Rabbit Redux* in that direct action seems to him like a way out.

Finally, sexual dominance is an important aspect of Rabbit's relationship with Nelson. The scene in *Rabbit Is Rich* that focuses on "whiteness" suggests that Rabbit has long felt threatened by Nelson's sexuality. Nelson is thirteen years old in *Rabbit Redux*, and Rabbit's memory that his son "had come to love her [Jill] like a sister. At least like a sister" suggests that Jill may not only have been Nelson's first love but also his first sexual partner (*Rich* 67). Certainly, he loves her enough to pursue her ghost in other women. Melanie and Pru both resemble Jill, although in different ways. When Rabbit and Skeeter treat Jill as a possession they can exploit and destroy, and Jill colludes with them, Nelson, entirely innocent and touchingly courageous, tries to save her. Without his father's help, however, he is unable to do so and consequently becomes a bitter, resentful man. But Rabbit remembers events quite differently. When Janice asks why he is so hard on Nelson, what springs immediately into his mind is: "Fucking kid not thirteen years old and tried to steal Jill from him, back in Penn Villas" (*Rich* 331). The sexual rivalry initiated in *Rabbit Redux* is in full swing now and continues in *Rabbit at Rest*, where Rabbit takes yet a third beloved woman away from his son.

Webb Murkett acts as model for handling physical decline by his continual pursuit and impregnation of nubile women. Rabbit follows his lead by becoming obsessed with young Cindy. Meanwhile, Rabbit is also jealous of Nelson's having two young women. He particularly wants Pru, whose "rangy bearing" reminds him of Mary Angstrom. The moment he sees her "he feels kinship with this girl, is touched by her, turned on: *he* wants to be giving her this baby" (*Rich* 171). When he voices his desire, even liberal-minded Stavros is alarmed, saying "I don't even want to hear about it . . . They're about to get married, for Chrissake" (208).

Not only is Rabbit jealous of Nelson's claim on Pru, he is also jealous of his son's reproductive power (Rabbit's own wife is now sterile). He wants Pru to have an abortion, partly to free Nelson, but also, as Nelson recognizes, out of envy: "It's as if you want to deny her to me, as if you're jealous of something. The way you keep mentioning her baby" (192).

Worst of all is that Rabbit's desire for Pru is tied to his wish to destroy Nelson: "He wants to hear that Pru hates Nelson, that she is sorry she has married him, that the father has made the son look sick" (367). Earlier, in regard to Mary Angstrom's decline, I suggested that Rabbit's wish for her death was "magically" realized. In *Rabbit at Rest*, Rabbit does sleep with Pru, and although their sexual encounter is presented as accidental and almost innocent, one cannot help but feel that Rabbit's behavior is intentional on some level, especially as he later wrests the acknowledgment from Pru that she was always attracted to him (446). "The one sex scene in *Rabbit at Rest* was meant to be possibly offensive to some," Updike says, but he admits that "it is hard to keep being sensational" (qtd. in Kaplan 112). Indeed, what is shocking is not the "quasi-incest" at all but the father's willingness to destroy his son (Kaplan 116). On the other hand, one wonders if Nelson could have chosen and then brought home a girl who physically resembled Rabbit's mother, without on some level realizing her value in terms of his father. As already noted, Nelson's masculinity is his legacy from Rabbit, and it contains much ambivalence.

Nelson is now an almost entirely obnoxious person. But Ma Springer remembers him as a "very hopeful little boy" (*Rich* 73), and Janice tells Rabbit, "There's a lot of sweetness in Nelson" (114). In *Rabbit Redux*, Nelson is the only pure light in a dark world. One of the great strengths of Updike's work is a scrupulous honesty that requires that "all our bad checks" be cashed (*Redux* 348), which is to say that in *Rabbit Is Rich* especially, the author makes his characters live the consequences of their actions. Nelson's grievance and his store of painful memories clarify the limitations of his character. Except for a brief idyll in each of the previous novels and one embrace and one brief conversation in this novel, Nelson has lived with almost total rejection by his father who finds him not tall enough, not athletic enough, not masculine enough, not responsible enough, not Angstrom enough. Interestingly, Nelson is like Skeeter in the sense that, although he too comes from a different place, so to speak, he is nevertheless a product of a patriarchal system and ends up harboring the same destructive attitudes and acting out the same destructive behaviors. He even lives more or less the same life as his father. But Nelson is worse off than Rabbit; he has no sense of specialness except as a victim, and he has no faith at all ("When you're dead, you're dead" [*Rich* 183]). Just as Updike is unwilling to idealize oppressed women and blacks, he does not idealize Nelson as a victim. If children are abused, they are less likely to turn into appealingly helpless victims than into power-hungry, destructive individuals like Nelson. Nelson is his father's creation, the product of Rabbit's failure to resolve the essential dichotomies of his own life.

One way that people try to deal with the sense of declining life is by investing emotionally and spiritually, as well as genetically, in their children. Dissatisfied with his own male child, Rabbit idealizes the lost daughter and begins to search for her in Annie Byer. When he goes to Ruth's home, she closes the door on that dream, and Rabbit is forced back to Nelson. As Stavros tells him earlier, "Don't give up on the kid. He's all you've got" (*Rich* 24). Rabbit has already made some small moves toward reconciliation—his embrace, his identification at the wedding, his resignation to Nelson's working at the lot. Also, when Nelson admits that he might have pushed Pru down the stairs, Rabbit identifies with the boy: "We're not crazy, either of us. Just frustrated sometimes" (*Rich* 355). Nelson disappears while Rabbit is in the Caribbean so that a complete reconciliation is never achieved, but in returning home, Rabbit sacrifices his pleasure to save Nelson's child and thus makes a real move toward the other.

Stavros, Thelma, and Melanie

In his attempt to resolve his middle-age crisis, Rabbit is, on the one hand, lured by Webb and Cindy toward materialism and hedonism. On the other hand, he is counseled by three guides, Stavros, Thelma, and Melanie, who all offer the same advice: accept loss, nurture life. In terms of the interpretations offered for the other novels, the message can also read: surrender, unite. Both Stavros and Thelma suffer from fatal illnesses; because they accept death as inherent, they are able to establish positive relationships; that is, having internalized death, they are freed from the oppositional framework. Both of these characters urge Rabbit to be patient with Nelson and point out similarities between father and son that might lead Rabbit into sympathy and identification. At the car lot, Stavros offers to "take Nelson under his wing" (*Rich* 119), and he eventually gives up his own position without rancor. He models an acceptance of change: "Charlie's not like you, Harry . . . He's not scared of change" (247). Stavros has already been discussed in detail, but to reiterate briefly, in the context of a guide, he not only offers Rabbit a model for friendship and for nurturing, but he has come to terms with the death he recognizes as part of himself rather than as a threatening other.

The second guide, Thelma, restores Rabbit's sense of specialness, of being valued for his unique self. During their night together, she reveals that she loves him, and why; she asks nothing in return and she puts her body at his full disposal. The fact that—while they indulge in oral, manual, and anal sex, and end by urinating on each other—there is no vaginal penetration emphasizes that the core of this scene is something other than sexual. When Rabbit enters her rectum, he experiences "a void, a pure black box, a casket of perfect nothingness. He is in that void" (*Rich* 391). Rabbit's anal intercourse with Thelma has been interpreted "as deeply nihilistic" by critic Ralph Wood (225), but what may be happening is that Rabbit, supported and given courage by Thelma's unconditional love, experiences the void he finds within Thelma in a manner that neutralizes his terror of death as well as his associations of women and sex with death, freeing him to get on with this phase of his life. Their urinating on each other suggests a regression to the infantilism Rabbit has not been able to get past, which for this reason could be where healing might best be initiated. Afterwards, Thelma and Rabbit have a conversation in which "he talks to her as he has talked to none other" (392). She counsels him, explaining that he and Nelson are more alike than he thinks and why sleeping with young women like Cindy devalues him. Although Thelma has opened a door for Rabbit, he only manages to peek at what lies on the other side. He takes the love and advice and comfort Thelma offers him, but gives her little in return. And while he gains a renewed sense of himself, greater freedom, and ultimately a release of his capacity to love his new granddaughter, the decidedly unsatisfying tone of the scene between Rabbit and Thelma presages what is revealed in *Rabbit at Rest*, that in the exchange between Rabbit and Thelma, the gain has been all Rabbit's.

Rabbit's third and most intriguing guide is Melanie. When Melanie arrives, Rabbit takes an immediate inexplicable dislike to her. Although his reaction is instinctive, his dislike is also consistent. She is like Jill Pendleton, whom Rabbit was also unable to love. At one point, Melanie speaks about "plural identities," which are a common enough phenomenon in this novel. Not only are the characters like their parents and grandparents, they are somewhat like mythical figures and even like characters in another novel (*Babbitt*). Melanie suggests two other identities, Jill and mystic G. I. Gurdjieff.

Melanie apparently comes from a wealthy background. Unlike Pru, she has had orthodonture, and her brother played polo, but like Jill, Melanie has rejected materialism. She abandons her expensive bike at Rabbit's house because, she says, if she brings it to Kent, someone will only steal it. Rabbit resents women with independent wealth, and he resents in Melanie the same contemptuous attitude toward possessions that he recognized in Jill, who neglected her Porsche. Melanie, like Jill, has a certain contempt for the body as well; she says sleeping is "giving in to the body." When she has sex with Nelson, she doesn't expect to have an orgasm but, like Jill, expects "to service the baby male" (*Rich* 125); her detachment annoys Nelson, as Jill's did Rabbit, perhaps because it means she is less susceptible to sexual manipulation. Like Jill, Melanie changes the family's eating habits and seems to bring new vitality into the house. Melanie has come east to avoid further entanglement with a man who was both a drug dealer and father figure. However, she seems to understand her vulnerability and to protect herself better than Jill did. Her name in Greek means "dark," so like Jill, she represents the other and is paired with Charlie Stavros (De Bellis 37). Stavros believes that "she is one of those women who see it all so clearly that they won't let themselves go" (*Rich* 117).

Melanie's vision is important. One of the things Rabbit dislikes about her is that she seems to him to "make his world seem small," just as Jill did. Melanie reads philosophy and mysticism and withdraws "to mental realms" that Nelson cannot reach (*Rich* 138). She is more intelligent than either Rabbit or Nelson, and Rabbit has never found intelligence interesting in a woman (51). Updike pointedly mentions that Melanie studies the works of the Greek-Armenian mystic-philosopher G. I. Gurdjieff. Nelson ridicules her interest, but she recommends that he also read Gurdjieff instead of going out, and in fact, the reading might do him good because the philosopher discusses a man with all of Nelson's negative attitudes. Updike repeats the philosopher's name three times in this exchange (138–39).

There are several parallels between Melanie and the philosopher. For one thing, Gurdjieff was an "expert hypnotist" "interested in suggestion" (Speeth 8), and what Rabbit "thinks he dislikes about this girl was that she was always trying to hypnotize him" (*Rich* 90). Another parallel is this: Gurdjieff traveled all over the world but often turned up in places where revolution and civil unrest were imminent (Speeth 9). Melanie (and Jill before her) has traveled to Rabbit's house, where a revolution is fermenting. When Gurdjieff traveled, he also picked up odd jobs along the way but, interestingly, seems to have had a sideline as a spy (9). Melanie works as a waitress but has been sent by Pru to keep an eye on Nelson.

Gurdjieff's philosophy is extremely complicated; however, a few of his ideas seem particularly relevant. The man was a seeker and a spiritual awakener committed to developing a methodology for establishing harmony between the mind, spirit, and body and for developing higher consciousness (Speeth 3–17). Gurdjieff envisions four states of consciousness but describes the ordinary person as living in a condition of waking sleep. Kathleen Riordan Speeth explains that the child loses its authentic self in the process of socialization and acquires "sets of habits, roles, tastes, preferences, preconceptions, prejudices, desires and felt needs, all of which reflect family and cultural milieu and not necessarily innate tendencies and predispositions. These make up personality" (47). The ordinary person has no sense of separate awareness but lives like a prisoner of ignorance and conditioning. To move onto a higher plane of consciousness, the prisoner must be awakened. What Gurdjieff describes has obvious relevance to the situation that unfolds in both *Babbitt* and *Rabbit Is Rich*. The process of awakening and discovering oneself to be a prisoner produces a great desire for freedom and higher consciousness. But the prisoner is unlikely to find the way alone and needs guides. Thus, Gurdjieff developed his detailed methodology, and Updike provides Rabbit with his gurus. Melanie gives Rabbit the crucial piece of information he needs when he asks for her opinion on the energy crisis, the metaphor for Rabbit's declining middle years:

> The luminous orbs of Melanie's eyes scout their faces in a sweep that ends in an upward roll such as you see in the images of saints. "I believe the things we're running out of we can learn to do without. I don't need electric carving knives and all that. I'm more upset about the snail darters and the whales than about iron ore and oil." She lingers on this last word . . . and stares at Harry. As if he's especially into oil. He decides what he resents about her is she seems always to be trying to hypnotize him. "I mean," she goes on, "as long as there are growing things, there is still a world with endless possibilities." (*Rich* 90)

Surrender; nurture life.

Incidentally, although Melanie does not appear in *Rabbit at Rest*, what we learn of her progress supports the interpretation offered here. In *Rabbit Is Rich*, Rabbit begins to understand Tothero's insatiable appetite and recalls the old coach saying, "You eat and eat and it's never the right food" (117). Rabbit has already begun the munching habit that eventually destroys his arteries. He is not only spiritually starving in a materialistic culture, but as his vitality declines, he hungers for more and more life. Melanie, like Jill, understands the destructive effect of dealing with needs and desires on a superficial level, and in *Rabbit Is Rich*, she warns the Angstroms that "we all eat too much sugar and sodium" (86). In *Rabbit at Rest*, in fact, we find that Melanie, with the encouragement and support of Charlie Stavros, has become a gastroenterologist, treating those who suffer from disorders of the alimentary and intestinal tracts, while Rabbit, gorging on sugar and salt in an effort to experience more life, is in effect eating himself to death. Rabbit has not identified the real objects of his craving, but Updike gives the reader a broad hint with the suggestion that "maybe God is in the world like *salt* is in the ocean, giving it a taste" and that "there's a lot of *sweetness* in Nelson" (*Rich* 433, 115; emphasis added).

Judith

The wasteland society in which Rabbit lives and the wasteland he discovers in his personal life have resulted from the triumph of hierarchical masculine values and the suppression of nurturing feminine values. In order to renew himself and resolve the dilemma presented by his diminishing life, Rabbit begins his search for his lost daughter. In the course of his search, he seems to surrender the symbols of both his materialism and his male power. As Melanie suggested, he can probably "do without" the money and his control over the lot; he can do without Cindy; and he can adjust to his diminished sexual horizon. On the positive side, he regains some of his freedom, his specialness, and his garden. Most important, by returning from his vacation, Rabbit makes a sacrifice that affirms the value of life. In his limited way, he progresses from one who asserts and controls to one who surrenders and nurtures. Thus, he recovers the lost feminine which is symbolized by the child Judith, who links him to the "world of endless possibilities" (*Rich* 90).

Of the first three Rabbit novels, this one seems to have the happiest ending. As Rabbit observes the annual masculine rite of Superbowl Sunday, Pru brings in the baby (De Bellis 34). Rabbit then holds his granddaughter on his lap. He loves her; all is well. Once again, however, Updike strikes a muted but discordant final note. Throughout *Rabbit Is Rich*, Rabbit hears the sound of his lesbian neighbor's hammering in the background as they extend their home. The sound, reminiscent of the hammering in Faulkner's *As I Lay Dying* (1930), is associated with death because Rabbit hears it when he remembers the night Jill died. On Nelson's wedding day, Rabbit is puzzled that the distant sound has "the power to hurt him, to make him feel excluded" (230). And later, Updike links this troubling portent to Rabbit's new granddaughter who is described as "another nail in [Rabbit's] coffin" (437). The references not only mark Rabbit's decline but seem to relate it to the arrival or ascendance of the new woman.

More ominous still is the child's name. Critic Jack De Bellis demonstrates the meticulous care with which Updike chooses the characters' names in these novels, and here the name of the lost Rebecca is specifically rejected in favor of Judith. In the Apocrypha, Judith is the courageous, sly, aggressive savior of her people. She wins her victory by ingratiating herself with the tyrant Holofernes and decapitating him in his sleep (Jth. 14). Judith represents the ascendance of female power. In *Rabbit at Rest*, Rabbit takes the eight-year-old granddaughter he adores out sailing, and their boat overturns. He fears she will drown like Rebecca, and searching for Judith initiates the heart attack that eventually leads to his death. Following the incident, the child and her mother both suggest that Judith hid deliberately to tease Rabbit. Thus, the "happy ending" of *Rabbit Is Rich* is a fragile "island of truce" (*SC* 131).

Once again, a compromised or uncertain closure invites the reader to consider several unpleasant possibilities. While Rabbit seems to have made some progress toward transcending the oppositional framework of the stereotypical model of masculinity provided by his culture, the text also suggests that the movement toward the feminine within him will precipitate his destruction as well as signal the general disempowerment of men in society at large. In other words, the text suggests that the ascendance of female power causes (or results in) the death of the masculine. In addition, given the fact that Judith is clearly a new Rebecca and given the significance of her name, there is also a suggestion of vengeance in this reversal. Power has shifted from the male to the female, but the oppositional framework still holds. We do not see the emergence of a new and more constructive male or the ascendance of feminine empathy and nurturing. In *Rabbit at Rest*, Rabbit continues to resist change through passivity and self-destructiveness. While the new marital arrangement is an obvious improvement over the previous relationship when Janice was a passive victim and Rabbit a selfish tyrant, there is little joy in moving forward to a time when powerful women will become murderous (as in *The Witches of Eastwick*). This vision may indicate the limitations that the male author, trapped within his own oppositional thought patterns, encounters when he examines the problems of masculinity. As Tolson observes, "Men hang on to this institution, not simply for chauvinist motives, or because they do not possess the personal courage to change, but because they cannot foresee a future beyond its determinations" (118). At any rate, as we shall see in a moment, Updike incorporates into the structure of the novel this conflict between the possibilities of personal transcendence and social progress and the pressure exerted by the cyclical nature of life and the tendency of cultural systems to perpetuate themselves.

Perspective, Structure, and Vision

In *The Fiction of Philip Roth and John Updike*, George Searles observes the complexity of the narrative perspective in the Rabbit novels. He notes "a very deliberate and remarkably well-controlled interweaving of voices" that allows Updike to "exploit the advantages of both first and third person narration" (114). Although the events are presented in the third person, "the implied value judgments are clearly Rabbit's own as is much of the diction," and through the balancing of these voices, "Updike is able to reveal character by giving Harry his say, while still maintaining a polished effect" (115). The narrative technique Searles observes is discussed earlier in relation to *Rabbit, Run*, where Updike uses the third-person narration and yet manages to limit the novel almost entirely to Rabbit's perspective. In *Rabbit, Run*, Rabbit's control of perspective amounts to a tyranny of the imagination by means of which he exercises the male prerogatives of naming, defining, assigning, limiting, and so on. In that novel, Rabbit's "say" equals power, and characters with competing perspectives are reduced to silence or confined to interior monologues. Rabbit's perspective represents a form of domination or control. However, unlike Searles, I see an evolution in the narrative technique in succeeding novels, which reflects thematic differences.

Because *Rabbit Redux* is about challenges to the dominant perspective, the narrator is more intrusive, more likely to interpret and comment on Rabbit's behavior. In addition, other characters are allowed to express themselves. And in *Rabbit Is Rich*, Updike returns to the narrative strategy of *Rabbit, Run* but with a very different purpose and effect. The narrator is once again nearly invisible, and Rabbit's perspective dominates entirely except, and this exception is important, in the two sections where Nelson is given an equally exclusive view. Although the technique is similar, in *Rabbit Is Rich*, the masculine perspective equals limitation rather than power. The problem now for Rabbit and Nelson is not so much that they impose their view on the others (Janice and Pru are not so easy to bully) as that they are imprisoned within their demonstrably skewed perspective. They cannot see what is obvious to those around them. More important, they are blind to each other. Judie Newman observes that although Rabbit is "obsessed with inside financial information" and "treasures financial and other secrets," he is nevertheless the last to know that Pru is pregnant, that Nelson wants a salesman's job, that Stavros has been ousted, and even that Thelma loves him (65). Newman also points out that Updike places the reader in the same position as Rabbit so that "in the experience of reading, hero and reader advance towards knowledge at the same pace, establishing a strong empathetic relationship which creates a degree of sympathy for Harry" (67). This strategy actively involves the reader in a reassessment of society. In addition, however, when surprised by events due to lack of information, the reader recognizes that he or she is trapped within an inadequate perspective (Newman 65–67). The problem of self-deception aside, Rabbit is a fallible witness because he is myopic.

Worse, he and Nelson also lack the inward vision that might lead to self-understanding. In his essay "The Masculine Mode," Peter Schwenger makes the following observation, which applies to the perspective in the first three Rabbit novels. He says that

> one of the most powerful archetypes of manhood is the idea that the real man is the one who acts, rather than the one who contemplates. The real man thinks of practical matters rather than abstract ones and certainly does not brood upon himself or the nature of his sexuality. To think about himself would be to split and turn inward the confident wholeness which is the badge of masculinity. And to consider his own sexuality at any length would be to admit that his maleness can be questioned, can be revised, and to a large degree, has been created rather than existing naturally and irresistibly as real virility is supposed to.... Self-consciousness is a crack in the wholeness of his nature. (110)

The narrative perspective of the Rabbit novels conveys the outer-directed quality of stereotypical masculinity. Critics who initially complained of Rabbit's lack of intelligence and inarticulateness may have been registering his lack of introspection and self-consciousness, but the stereotypical "real man" projects his fears onto the others he meets in the world and fixes his gaze steadily outward so as never to see the really terrifying other within.

Not only is Rabbit limited by faulty perspective in *Rabbit Is Rich*, he is also limited by the natural cycles of life. When Rabbit overturns his sailboat during his Caribbean vacation, he wonders aloud about the danger of sharks. Cindy asks if he has seen *Jaws II*, and Rabbit responds by asking, "D'you ever get the feeling everything these days is sequels . . . Like people are running out of ideas" (377). His query is amusing as he is himself the protagonist in a sequel, but it is also intriguing because this novel is so full of repetitions, many of which are dangerous or unpleasant (Newman 67). *Rabbit Is Rich*, in fact, is formally structured in such a way that patterns of repetition and divergence from those patterns convey important information about the nature of human life.

Some of the repetitive elements include the following. Of the five chapters, the first chapter opens at the summer solstice and the last closes near the winter solstice. According to the metaphor carried forward from the earlier novels, both are seasons of imbalance and danger. During these periods Nelson, like his father before him, flees from the responsibilities of marriage and family. Chapter 3, the center of the novel, includes a moment of precarious balance and harmony on 22 September, the day of the autumnal equinox, and features Nelson's and Pru's wedding as well as Rabbit's compassionate identification with his son. Although the novel focuses on Rabbit's as the others, the application of the seasonal elliptic metaphor to Nelson's marriage rather than Rabbit's is an indication of Rabbit's increasing irrelevance in the procreative physical world. In *Rabbit at Rest*, Updike confirms this shift when Rabbit observes that: "Brawling. Fucking. . . . Young couples give off this heat; they're still at the heart of the world's business, making babies" (101). It is, of course, the trauma of being pushed slightly aside from the hot center of life that Rabbit faces in middle age, so he particularly resents and resists Nelson's sexual dominance.

Each of the first four chapters includes a scene at work, at home, in bed, with the Angstroms' friends, and with a glimpse of Annie Byer. The obvious patterns of interruptions and smashed cars draw further attention to a cyclical or spiral structure. Not only does Updike repeat a number of elements within this novel, he also repeats many of the elements introduced in the earlier novels.

For example, in addition to the equinox-solstice metaphor and the flight of the husband-father, Updike repeats an unplanned pregnancy, a quest for lost youth in sex, and a quest for Rabbit's lost daughter. He updates his portrait of America and expands the correspondence between Rabbit and the nation. He repeats Rabbit's nostalgic rides through Brewer and continues to draw on current events and the media. The author also returns to the imagery of cars, flight, water, ghosts, and gardens. Even Rabbit's problems are repetitive in the sense that his unresolved conflicts manifest themselves in new circumstances and in the sense that the reader can witness the consequences of Rabbit's earlier actions. All of the dead from the earlier novels return in Rabbit's reveries and seem to have a hold over the living. Furthermore, several characters have "plural identities" (*Rich* 139); Jill Pendleton and Mary Angstrom seem to reappear in Melanie and Pru. Mim says Rabbit seems like his father to her, and Nelson seems to be reliving Rabbit's life.

These repetitions contribute to the impression of continuity in Rabbit's life, but at the same time, they generate tension because the reader begins to anticipate that tragic events will reoccur. These two elements, continuity and limitation, are essential to the meaning of the novel. Updike emphasizes cosmic, natural, cultural, national and filial cycles, and repetitions throughout the novel, suggesting that Rabbit, Nelson, and all of us are subject to powerful forces beyond our control. Rabbit expresses this notion in regard to the physical world in *Rabbit at Rest* when he thinks, "It's hell to be a creature. You are trapped in yourself, the genetic instructions, more strictly than in a cage" (105).

Nevertheless, while the physical world is the source of limitations, the ultimate limitation being death, its fecundity is the source of new life, and, therefore, as Melanie instructs Rabbit, of infinite possibilities, including the possibilities represented by Rabbit's granddaughter, Judith. The limitations imposed by the cycles of the physical world may seem like a curse, but the infinite possibilities are a source of unexpected and undeserved blessings. As John Neary suggests, these repetitions come "from beyond him," "take him by surprise," and "move his narrative forward" (76). Like the poet who disturbs the meter of one line or suddenly breaks the rhyme, Updike suggests that human individuality and freedom are expressed against the background of limitation. It is possible for Rabbit to exercise what freedom he has, learn from the past, and take positive action.

Whereas heredity provides one example of the limiting and repetitious nature of the physical world, it is also important to recognize that while the limitations imposed on the spirit by matter have been a critical problem throughout these novels, in *Rabbit Is Rich*, Updike focuses on other determining forces as well. Cultural repetitions and limitations are suggested in the notion of plural identities, in the appearance of mythological types, and even in the recurrence of literary types. Both cultural and familial repetitions are suggested by the lingering influence of the dead, by Updike's emphasis on Freudian psychology, and by the transmission of conflicted masculinity from father to son.

Heredity is particularly emphasized as an example of the cyclical and therefore limiting nature of the physical world. Rabbit is fascinated by the precision of a genetic code that can reproduce the crimp in Nelson's ear. Staring at Annie Byer's photograph, he looks for that crimp as the indisputable evidence of her origin. The long-standing clannish antagonism between the Angstrom and Springer families, a manifestation of the problem of self and other, is expressed in terms of heredity. Rabbit's strong preference for his own genetic pool is confirmed in *Rabbit at Rest* as a "limitation within him really, a failure or refusal to love any substance but his own" (328). He likes women like Pru with the lanky look and large hands of Mary Angstrom, and he has a special love for Mim, who seems like "himself, with the combination jiggled" (*Redux* 361). On the contrary, he dislikes the Springers, who embody a very different physical type and whose reproductive capacity was the instrument of his entrapment (Janice's pregnancy with Nelson). He dislikes his son partly because of the evidence of the Springers' influence in his dark coloring, small stature, clumsiness, and "little Springer hands" (*Run* 211). Of course, where Rabbit sees only genetic difference between himself and Nelson, others see similarities. Stavros and Thelma both see Nelson as temperamentally very much like his father. In fact, Nelson's angry energy and deflating honesty are similar to his father's. The point here is that Rabbit resists the other, but necessary, half of Nelson's genetic inheritance, finding his son unacceptable because of it. Ironically, it is Nelson, who is a union of Angstrom and other, who holds Rabbit's only hope for regaining the "endless possibilities" symbolized by Judith. What is conveyed, once again, is the kind of limitations any human life must operate within, including not only death but cyclical and self-perpetuating cultural and genetic inheritance as well as a personal history that also has strong inclinations toward the cyclical. Transcendence of these limitations is possible, as in the case of Rabbit's love for his granddaughter, but only within these limitations. Rabbit's granddaughter is part Nelson, that is, part Springer. Rabbit sees Nelson as failed and unacceptable because of his genetic inheritance, but it is precisely Nelson's physical inheritance, which so repulses, that is Rabbit's only hope of touching the infinite possibilities symbolized in Judith.

In *Rabbit Is Rich*, Rabbit begins to adjust to middle age. With the help of his guides, he reclaims some of his specialness and some of his freedom. He reaffirms his marriage and takes up gardening. Most importantly, he is able to affirm his connection with the future through his granddaughter. He does far less well with his troubled son Nelson, and in *Rabbit at Rest*, Updike resumes his exploration of the ambivalent relationships between adult males.

TEN

Rabbit at Rest
More Mail from Tunis

Rabbit at Rest opens with Harry Angstrom, who is wintering in a Florida retirement condo, waiting gloomily at the airport with Janice for Nelson and his family to arrive for a post-Christmas vacation. Harry is now fifty-five. He is overweight, out of breath, and mentally scattered. In short, he suffers from all of the discomforts associated with an incipient heart attack. During the week-long visit, father and son resume their old rivalries. Nelson is irritable and erratic; Pru and the children, eight-year-old Judy and four-year-old Roy, seem unhappy and anxious. When Rabbit takes Judy sailing, their boat overturns, and he suffers his first heart attack trying to save the child. Meanwhile, Janice confronts Nelson who admits to using cocaine. This section, "FL," ends with Rabbit recovering in the hospital and saying goodbye to Nelson's family on New Year's Eve of 1989.

In "PA," Rabbit and Janice have returned to their Penn Park cottage in the spring. The extent of Nelson's addiction unfolds, including the fact that he has embezzled money from the dealership to support his habit. Rabbit reenters the hospital for an angioplasty, which his doctor warns is only a temporary measure as Rabbit needs bypass surgery. He is cared for by Ruth's daughter Annie, who is now a nurse. Rabbit returns from the hospital on the same day that Nelson, forced by his mother, leaves for a drug rehabilitation center. That night, while Janice attends a real estate licensing class, Rabbit and Pru console each other by sleeping together.

Rabbit runs Springer Motors in Nelson's absence. The Toyota representative agrees not to prosecute Nelson if the embezzled money is repaid, but the Angstroms lose their franchise and are left heavily indebted. Nelson returns rehabilitated and self-righteous, and tensions between father and son rise again. Janice hopes to pay off Nelson's debts and retain the lot by selling the Penn Park home that Rabbit loves and moving back into Ma Springer's old house with the younger Angstroms. She goes to Nelson's to discuss her plan, but Pru subverts it by revealing the incident with Rabbit. Janice calls Rabbit, demanding that he come and "help undo some of the damage you've done for once in your life" (*Rest* 435). Instead, Rabbit heads south as he did in *Rabbit, Run*. The remainder of the novel charts his flight toward death, both on the highway and in the progressive symptoms of his approaching myocardial infarction, or MI (Raban 1). Rabbit, who has been eating himself to death throughout the novel, turns gluttony into an "athletic feat" (84). He stays at the condo and waits anxiously for Janice, who does not come. He finally collapses while shooting baskets with a black teenager he calls Tiger. Janice and Nelson visit him in the hospital where he is dying.

Updike says that "the last book deliberately curves around the first" (Trueheart F4). This curving involves the repetition or reversal of a number of elements in *Rabbit, Run* and serves a variety of structural and thematic purposes. For example, some repetitions highlight the continuity of Rabbit's personality, the persistence of the self beneath change. We met Rabbit thirty years earlier as a young man playing pick-up basketball in a back alley of Brewer; we now see him at fifty-six on the streets of Deleon, still looking for answers and open games. Despite radical changes in his life and a modest degree of maturation, Rabbit still has his own starting place, his basic approach, and his particular style. Other repetitions suggest that the God of Ecclesiastes continues to work quietly in Rabbit's life (*Rest* 306). Rabbit is forced back again into those crucial situations that provide him with an opportunity to work on what Updike considers the fundamental task of life—coming to terms with the "cosmic other" (see Neary 43–84; *SC* 257). And, of course, "the well-worn wheels of nature" now return for Rabbit who has always had "a superstitious interest in astronomy" (*Rest* 170). The novel opens following the winter solstice, a period of dangerous imbalance when Nelson's marriage and Rabbit's health are precarious, and when a sailboat carrying Rabbit and Judith easily tips over into disaster. It progresses toward the autumnal equinox which, as in *Rabbit Redux*, combines the season of death with the restoration of balance.

As in *Rabbit Is Rich*, some repetitive elements suggest Rabbit's participation, not always conscious or willing, in the continuity of human life—in the whole design of convergence suggested by the linear tube of fatherhood in *Rabbit, Run*. Now, in *Rabbit at Rest*, Rabbit is disappointed that his physical life has produced nothing more than an unsatisfactory son: "It's a depressing thought . . . that the whole point of his earthly existence has been to produce little Nellie Angstrom, so he in turn could produce Judy and Roy, and so on until the sun burns out" (48). Nevertheless it *is* Rabbit's turn to play the outraged father to Nelson's irresponsible youth, and eventually, like Fred and Earl before him, to smooth the way for the young man's return. In fact, while he is dying, Rabbit is aware of doing Nelson a favor by making room as the older men did (233).

Updike also uses repetition as a structural device somewhat like a curtain call to provide closure for the tetralogy. As Rabbit revisits his old haunts and remembers the people from his past, each one comes forward, is given full attention, and takes a bow (Miller E6). So much of the novel's pleasure derives from discovering the extent to which we now share Rabbit's memories that it is difficult to imagine how readers unfamiliar with the earlier novels would respond to *Rabbit at Rest*. Closure is also produced by repetitions that suggest having come full circle. The tetralogy is obviously framed by two street games and two flights south. And, as Joyce Carol Oates suggests, the young man dubbed "Mr. Death" in the first novel now ironically fulfills his destiny ("So Young!" 43).

Other reverberations connect *Rabbit at Rest* with *Rabbit, Run*. The questions of freedom versus responsibility and of the possibility of conflicting moralities continue to be raised. The problem of human "wants," of questing after "instant happiness" in sex, alcohol, cocaine, and junk food continues to plague the Angstrom family (*Rest* 58). Familiar metaphors and images also recur. The beckoning mermaids and the drowned infant, Rebecca, reappear in Judith, who lures her grandfather underwater. The imagery of gardens, of falling, and of converging recurs; the hospital scenes, the fights with Ronnie Harrison, the funeral service, and the foolish minister all have counterparts in the earlier novel.

In addition, Updike again emphasizes the "twoness." Doubles, pairs, and dichotomies abound once more: Rabbit lives in two states; he has two grandchildren of opposite sexes; he has two lovers; he visits two gardens; he chooses between two paths; he works in his garden twice; he thinks Ronnie Harrison may be his double; and he suffers two massive heart attacks. This twoness signals that Rabbit's world is falling back into its original dualistic configuration—spirit and matter, self and other. The busy midlife years distracted Rabbit somewhat from the horror of his epiphany, but now, as a dying man, he is again directly confronted by the possibility that human consciousness, the spark of recognition "struck in the collision of two opposed realms," may be vulnerable to extinction (*Run* 275). On the one hand, Rabbit wants to believe that he is "a God-made one-of-kind. . . . apprentice angel," but he is deeply afraid that "we're all trash" and "disposable meat" (*Rest* 344, 82).

In *Rabbit, Run*, Rabbit's philosophical and spiritual problems were manifested primarily in terms of his sexual relationships. Now, however, due to his age, poor health, and the side effects of medication, Rabbit is less sexually driven and consequently less preoccupied with the "nullity of fusion" with sexual partners (Woodcock 21). Nevertheless, Rabbit's masculinity continues to shape many of his responses. On the one hand, Rabbit moves in the direction of union with the other represented by the women—this progress leads him to risk his life to save Judith. On the other hand, he also begins withdrawing from family and friends. More important, his mounting conflict with Nelson and his almost Manichean contempt for his body suggest that Rabbit's failure to reconcile his nature (i.e., his alignment of himself with pure spirit) is blossoming into self-hatred. He now vents his hostility not against the women but against his own body, against Nelson and Roy, and against Ronnie Harrison, all of whom remind him of the death-bearing other within.

More Gardens

The reader is by now familiar with Rabbit's twofold dilemma. First, if he is an "apprentice angel," a spiritual being imprisoned in flesh, then Rabbit is at odds with the whole threatening material world (*Rest* 237). And as long as he fails to reconcile his own nature, Rabbit will continue to vacillate between his need and contempt for the other wherever he identifies or projects it. Second, if Rabbit must succumb to the force of nature, the spiritual fate he anticipates depends on the kind of nature he envisions. In *Rabbit, Run*, Horace Smith's garden stands against the possibility of annihilation revealed in the pine forest. The two gardens in *Rabbit at Rest* represent a similar dichotomy, although they are more complex than the originals.

When Rabbit's grandchildren visit him in Florida, he and Janice take Judy and Roy for an outing that includes "the Thomas Alva Edison Winter Home, which nearly does them in" (*Rest* 93), and Jungle Gardens, which "works out better than anyone dared hope" (103). The Edison home is a well-groomed, commercial success, but the children are bored and unpleasant as they tour its gardens, led by a tedious guide with a set monologue. The guide points out "funny" trees with long Latin names and "cute" nicknames like "the sausage tree," "the fried egg tree," and "the dynamite tree" (93–94). One of these hideous specimens has seed pods resembling human ears. The Edison garden represents nature (or matter) as indifferent to humans. Two possibilities emerge. The Edison garden is a purely scientific, Darwinian sort of garden where diversity is either accidental or directed toward some goal unknown or unrelated to humankind. Edison brought the trees to Florida as part of a "heavily financed search for a substitute rubber" (the backing of industrial magnates suggesting a connection between capitalism and materialism) (95). In this context, the specimens' specialness becomes utilitarian, merely eccentric, or at worst, monstrous and meaningless. On the other hand, if there is a God in this garden at all, Rabbit conceives of him as a slightly daft scientist preoccupied with independent projects: "*Why did God bother*, Harry wonders, *to do all these tricks, off by Himself in the Amazon jungle?*" (94).

During the tour, little Roy announces that he has to "pee," and his grandfather, who dislikes the boy, responds nastily, "Yeah well, your need to pee isn't the exact fucking center of the universe" (96).[1] This brutal point, that the individual is not the center of universe, is reinforced later when Rabbit says that in the laboratory, he was most interested in the "nine *thous*and [failed] experiments" leading to Edison's invention of the storage battery (98). It is worth noting that in the Trueheart interview, Updike comments on the same baffling multiplicity of nature in terms of human sexuality. He says, "There is an excess about sexuality, especially from the male standpoint, in that we put out a lot more than we strictly need to make a baby or two. As trees drop many more acorns than they need to make more oaks. So there is this terrific excess. But then in a way it's excessive to be alive at all. It's sort of ex*trav*agant, isn't it?" (F4).

The four Angstroms leave the Edison winter home discouraged and continue on to Jungle Gardens, which represents nature either redeemed or inhabited by God, or at least, invested by man with value and meaning in the existentialist manner. This "spiritual garden" has a ragged, neglected appearance, suggesting that the view of life it conveys is no longer practical, profitable, or well-cultivated. It is reminiscent of the overgrown gardens in *Rabbit, Run* that reflect a neglect of spiritual concerns. As the Angstroms enter the gardens, they choose between two paths. The path leading to the "Reptile Show and the Gardens of Christ" (*Rest* 103) stands for the traditional Christian view of nature and humanity as fallen into sin and redeemed by Christ. While this view affirms the importance of the individual and offers the hope of immortality, Rabbit has rejected institutionalized Christianity in the earlier novels, as he will again at Thelma Harrison's funeral where he finds the minister to be foolish and irrelevant.

The second path leads to an area known as the Bird Show, which Rabbit's golf friend Bernie Drechsel had recommended to entertain the visiting grandchildren. The Bird Show introduces an Emersonian view of nature. In the Trueheart interview, Updike distinguishes his own religious perspective from his character's, saying that Rabbit's theism is "instinctive": "He is much less structured, much less interested in theology. . . . You might even say that he's kind of an Emersonian: . . . the self is enough to prove that everything is all right" (F4). Significantly, as the Angstroms travel down the second path toward their goal, Flamingo Lagoon, Rabbit ponders the fate of the Dalai Lama, a recurring figure in the Rabbit novels. The Dalai Lama was born around the same time as Rabbit, who "identified with him" and takes a continuing interest in his exile (*Rest* 206). Here Rabbit wonders, "Do you still believe in God, if people keep telling you *are* God?" (103). Later in the novel, the narrator says, "The Dalai Lama can no more give up godhood than Harry can resign selfhood" (294). As Updike's remark suggests, Rabbit, like Emerson, links the existence and specialness of the self to divinity:

> Harry is a kind of religious fellow who clings to the notion that his inner promptings are somehow worthwhile . . . That we're not just mechanisms planted here to create more mechanisms. That somehow our feelings, especially our feelings of joy, have value. . . . This is an indefensible position, rationally . . . But Harry never quite gets it. He never believes that that's all there is. He believes there must be more, that God in some way exists—is what it really comes down to. (Trueheart F4)

Emerson's unitary view, that man, nature, and the Over-Soul participate in the same spiritual essence, not only affirms human significance but represents nature as beneficent, invested with transcendental meaning, and speaking eternal truths to those who will listen. When Rabbit reaches Mirror Lake and sees the flamingos, nature speaks to him.

> Flocks of flamingos, colored that unreal orange-pink color, sleep while standing up, like big feathery lollypops, each body a ball ... balanced on one pencil-thin leg and wide weird leathern foot. Others, almost as marvellous, are awake and stirring, tenderly treading. "Look how they drink," Harry tells his grandchildren, lowering his voice as if in the presence of something sacred. "Upside down. Their bills are scoops that work upside down." And they stand marveling, the four human beings, as if the space between farflung planets has been abolished, so different do these living things loom from themselves. The earth is many planets, that intersect only at moments. (*Rest* 103)

Nature continues to speak eloquently to Rabbit throughout the novel.

Nevertheless, even if traditional Christianity and Emersonian theism secure human dignity and preserve the soul, they do not spare Rabbit the necessity of death. At this point in the outing, Rabbit makes the "historic blunder" of eating parrot food, an action that symbolizes his participation in the material world (104). Immediately, he hears the "anguished crying" of the peacocks at his back (105). The flamingos affirm the self's specialness, its unique spiritual aspect, but the peacocks speak of inevitable death. Rabbit is doomed and knows it and thinks, "It's hell to be a creature" (105). Convinced of his mortality, he is susceptible to his first heart attack, which occurs on the following day. As Rabbit lies on the beach waiting for the ambulance, he tries to minimize his distress to Judith by joking that "it must have been that birdfood I ate" (142).

Toward Union

The richness and complexity of Updike's representation of Rabbit's self in *Rabbit at Rest* are consistent with observations he makes in the last two chapters of *Self-Consciousness*. In his own self-portrait, Updike includes all of the physical peculiarities of his body, the tendencies and habits of his mind, the visible and invisible signs of his encounters with the world, and all of the information he has learned or inadequately learned. He says, "Such embedded data compose my most intimate self—the bedrock, as it were, beneath my more or less acceptable social, sexual, professional performance" (214). He also speaks of a developing self, one that initially emerges from a unitary relationship with the mother and is "flavored" by early subconscious impressions (*SC* 220); of a self entrusted to the subconscious realm of dreams; and of a self influenced and shaped by culture. He speaks of the conditional nature of selves and observes that some selves die. He links the self to its ancestors ("they participate in our being" [211]) and its descendants and to the thread that Emerson says runs through all things.

What strikes Updike as the miracle of the self is its specificity, "the oddity of consciousness being placed in one body rather than another, in one place and not somewhere else, in one handful of decades rather than in ancient Egypt" (SC 40). He also sees consciousness of self as problematic, however, and he quotes Unamuno as saying that "consciousness is a disease" for which religion, construed broadly, is the cure; or put another way, "The self is the focus of anxiety; attention to others, self-forgetfulness, and living like the lilies are urged, to relieve the anxiety. Insomnia offers a paradigm: the mind cannot fall asleep as long as it watches itself" (226, 232). What is relevant to this discussion of *Rabbit at Rest* is Updike's perception of the richness of the self and the distinction he draws between the self, which, as we have seen in Rabbit's case, suffers from fundamental anxieties that have been exacerbated and shaped by society into defensive behaviors, and on the other side, a "self-forgetful" self, which some of Rabbit's critics have, for example, interpreted as behaving according to its wholesome natural instincts or even its inner light.[2]

In the course of the novel, different aspects of Rabbit's self seem to move toward and away from union with the other, and Rabbit himself is not always aware of these motions. His "self-forgetful" capacity leads him toward union while the "anxious" self continues to react defensively. Furthermore, while this dynamic plays itself out, forces "totally other" and independent of Rabbit seem to arrange for his redemption. Thus, in this novel, we see Rabbit behave as well and as badly as he ever has yet be saved, as it were, without much awareness on his part, as, for example, when he lies in the hospital and "his consciousness comes and goes, and he marvels that in its gaps the world is being tended to, just as it was in the centuries before he was born" (*Rest* 511).

Two of the self-forgetful ways that Rabbit approaches union in *Rabbit at Rest* are through his attention and memory. For example, following his first heart attack and hospitalization, Rabbit and Janice return to Pennsylvania in the spring of 1989. As Rabbit drives through his old neighborhood, he is stunned by the beauty of Brewer's flowering pears:

> Rabbit is suddenly driving in a white tunnel, trees on both sides of the street in white blossoms, the trees young and oval in shape

and blending one into the other like clouds, the sky's high blue above tingeing the topmost blossoms as it does the daytime moon. And up top where there is most light the leaves are beginning to unfold, shiny and small and heart-shaped, as he knows because he is moved enough to pull the Celica to the curb and park and get out and pull off a single leaf to study, as if it will be a clue to all this glory. Along the sidewalk in this radiant long grove shadowy people push baby carriages and stand chatting by their steps as if oblivious of the wonder suspended above them, enclosing them, already shedding a confetti of petals: they are in Heaven. (187–88)

The quality and tone of the writing in this passage, noted by several reviewers, again suggests a state of unitive consciousness. Later at home, Rabbit asks Janice why he has never seen these trees before, and she tells him, "You've seen, it's just you see differently now" (188). The self-forgetful, rapt witness experiences "an utterly unconscious unity of self with other" (Neary 48). Updike associates this kind of rapt witnessing with a deep cosmic joy (SC 34–35). As in Horace Smith's garden, Rabbit is again reconciled with nature and by extension, with women. He later hopes to meet Ruth some time "under the pear trees of Paradise" (*Rest* 293), and he experiences Pru's "wide-hipped nakedness . . . much as those pear trees in blossom . . . a piece of Paradise blundered upon, incredible" (346).

Rabbit also reconciles with humankind—with all of those whose lives touched his own. Like his vision, his memory is intensified by the approach of death, and the quality of his remembering is similar to his attentiveness. People, places, and even objects (the plastic clown under the stairs in Mt. Judge) are renewed and cherished in Rabbit's memory. Updike seems to be experimenting with the limits of consciousness; Rabbit's memory incorporates the people, places, and things he has known, and his memories are now also the reader's. Rabbit even seems to have a kind of physical memory that perpetuates his unspoken love for Thelma: "All the afternoons when their bodies intertwined and exchanged fluids are not gone but safe inside him, his cells remembering" (307). Updike cites Rimbaud on this unitive experience, "Your *self* . . . is other people, all the people you're tied to, and it's only a thread" (SC 218).

Like Irving's Rip Van Winkle, Rabbit's assumes the function of linking the past and the present. Because he remembers so well, he registers every nuance of change in his hometown (and in America). He eventually takes his part in the local and national life by dressing as Uncle Sam and leading Brewer's Fourth of July parade—a parade he had watched as a child. And it is appropriately Rabbit, who recalls the whole history of Springer Motors, who receives Mr. Shimada's humiliating rebuke on the decline of American discipline (i.e., the excesses of freedom).

In some ways Rabbit progresses toward union with the other found in nature and in the women in his life. For the most part, he continues to connect his wife's body with the material world and with death, so that he is often disgusted by the physical processes and the signs of corruption he observes in Janice. He is far more successful with his daughter-in-law Pru and his granddaughter Judith. Two particular incidents show him moving toward an acceptance of nature, specifically with nature as associated with women.

In one instance, Rabbit makes progress through surrender—not surrender to the other but surrender of the other. His reckless impregnation of Ruth in *Rabbit, Run* has been discussed as a manifestation of self-assertion rather than of bestowal. In *Rabbit Is Rich*, Rabbit pursues another self-gratifying impulse by renewing his contact with Ruth, in part to reassure himself of his continued hold over her but also as part of his quest for the lost child. Ruth, of course, tolerates none of his nonsense and insists that Annie is not his child. She is right to protect Annie from Rabbit, whose belated interest arises from his need to resolve problems in his own life rather than from a sincere interest in Annie's welfare. Throughout *Rabbit Is Rich*, exploitive, possessive behaviors are presented in scatological imagery, and when Rabbit visits Ruth, she immediately recognizes his selfishness and reacts powerfully: "When I think of you thinking she's your daughter it's like rubbing her all over with shit" (419). Now in *Rabbit at Rest*, Rabbit discovers that the nurse who is caring for him during his hospitalization in Brewer is Annie Byer. Rabbit fully believes that Annie is his daughter. He has the clear opportunity to reveal himself to her and to act on her offer to arrange a meeting with her mother. Instead of interfering in their lives, he abdicates his claim. His generous action recalls the surrenders practiced in the Smiths' garden where folding the seeds into the earth sets them free: "Sealed, they cease to be his. This simplicity. Getting rid of something by giving it to itself" (*Run* 128). Willing the freedom of the other is envisioned as an aspect of love just as surrendering is a leap of faith that makes flowering possible. Rabbit not only does not reveal himself to Annie, but he reassures her, "You know best how to live your own life. Tell your mother, if she asks, that maybe we'll meet some other time" (*Rest* 293). To himself he acknowledges his deep wish to meet Ruth "under the pear trees, in paradise" (293).[3]

An instance of reconciliation through union with a woman occurs when Rabbit sleeps with Pru. Although this incident is disturbing as a betrayal of Janice and Nelson and contains other ambiguous elements, at least on one level it is an affirmation, even an act of praise, for the material world. Rabbit associates Pru's physical beauty with "the blossoming pear trees" and with paradise, conveying the possibility that nature is not just an empty show but an emblem of transcendental realities. An unusual remark made by Updike regarding his personal life helps to explain Rabbit's behavior somewhat. He said in the Howard interview that "parties are somehow deadly serious.... To say no to one is to say no to life" (80). In taking Pru, Rabbit instinctively behaves according to this morality; that is, if life offers itself, especially so beautifully, it is unthinkable to refuse. Therefore, when Janice discovers the incident and claims that he has finally "done something truly unforgivable," Rabbit is at first unrepentant and offended (*Rest* 433). As in *Rabbit, Run*, he acts spontaneously according to a morality dictated by his instincts, or perhaps his inner light, and once again, these bring him into conflict with the claims of society and the morality of responsibility (see Bernard Schopen's discussion). Updike associates this natural morality with his mother, from whom he says he absorbed the belief "that our instincts and appetites are better guides, for a healthy life, than the advice of other human beings" (*SC* 257).

Rabbit is also able to reconcile with the other he fears in nature and in woman because of his love for his granddaughter. The boating scene incorporates the water imagery critics have observed throughout the tetralogy. When Rabbit first runs away in *Rabbit, Run*, he meets "mermaids," "girls with orange hair hanging like seaweed or loosely bound with gold barrettes like pirate treasure" (*Run* 36–37). He feels like an outsider and becomes angry whenever he thinks of them. On the other hand, his favorite image of Janice is that of her coming from the bath as a rosy Venus (*Run* 94; *Rest* 90). At the poolside with Ruth, Rabbit thinks that she is a water creature and he, a land animal (*Run* 134). Rabbit is both deeply attracted to and repelled by this watery other; he both desires and fears her world, which represents to him the source of life and the certainty of death. Rebecca June's death by water results, on a metaphorical level, from Rabbit's need to reject the feminine other rather than unite and reconcile with it.

Thirty years later, Rabbit still "hates the water"; "being underwater is one of his nightmares" (*Rest* 109, 54). He can hardly bear to watch his little granddaughter eating lobster because "to him, eating lobster . . . is nightmarish, a descent back into the squirmy scrabble origins of life" (81). Nevertheless, when their sailboat overturns with "coppery"-haired Judith, Rabbit overcomes "his lifelong animal distaste for putting his head underwater" to search for the lost child (132):

> He must. His bowels burn with all the acid guilt that has accumulated since creation; he again forces himself under into a kind of dirty-green clay where his bubbles are jewels. Against the slither of cloth on his back he tries to tunnel forward. In this tunnel he encounters a snake, a flexible limp limb that his touch panics so it tries to strangle him and drag him down deeper. . . . His body convulsively tries to free itself from this grave; he flounders with his eyes shut; the sail's edge eventually nuzzles past his drowning face and he has dragged along Judy into the light. (132–33)

This immersion is a burial but also a resurrection or reconciliation, and interestingly, when Rabbit looks at Judith immediately following, "To his eyes she looks in her breathless frightened pallor less like Pru than Nelson, fine boned and white around the gills" (133–34); Nelson—that rejected part of himself that he loves and hates and fears. When he descends to the other, he finds himself. A later memory confirms this association when Rabbit connects the "shocking white" of his own semen with the color of the lobster meat (83).

By saving Judith for the second time in his life, Rabbit seems to accept the material realm (i.e., nature and woman as associated with nature).[4] As discussed in relation to *Rabbit Is Rich*, Judith, who represents physical processes and the passage of time, is inevitably a nail in Rabbit's coffin, but she also represents the treasure of something resembling physical immortality.

As we have seen elsewhere, Updike's metaphors are multidimensional, and along with the positive readings of these incidents, a number of negative alternatives should be acknowledged. It is possible that Rabbit identifies Pru and Judith not with the other but with himself. Pru looks like his mother, and he recalls that his attraction for her "felt like he was seeing himself reflected, mirrored in a rangy young long-haired left-handed woman" (*Rest* 432). He thinks of Pru as carrying his "genes toward eternity" (14). He also thinks of her "as the weakest link in a conspiracy against him" (43). Whether he refers to the family conspiracy or to the conspiracy of time and nature remains unclear, but either way, Rabbit is willing to use Pru to further his own interests.

Rabbit clearly loves his unpleasant granddaughter, but he also needs her to replace the lost Rebecca and to link him with the future. He idealizes Judith, as he does Pru, to serve his own needs. He plans to "embower" her as his princess (35). He sees in Nelson's women his last chance for immortality, and he wants them badly enough to steal them from his son. The fact that Rabbit behaves like a careless father again, endangering Judith's life by lying about his sailing experience, suggests self-interested motives that undercut his eventual heroism. In addition, the behaviors of both of these female characters can be construed as betrayals. Following Rabbit's heart attack, Judith and her mother maintain that the child, an excellent swimmer, hid under the sail deliberately to frighten her grandfather; and following his sexual encounter with Pru, Rabbit remembers having felt "used, expertly" (433). Thus, the same circumstances that speak of union also hint at continued exploitation on Rabbit's part and at betrayal and possible revenge by the ascending females.

Janice, on the other hand, remains Rabbit's other, although he regrets "that they must live, he and his little dark woman, his stubborn shy mutt of a Springer, in a world of mostly missed signals" (90). Janice seems to the reader to have improved wonderfully over the years, but Rabbit has not enjoyed her emancipation. He resents her growing energy, power, and confidence: "He preferred her incompetent" (303). Like Nelson's, Janice's development seems to have pushed Rabbit aside. In the Trueheart interview, Updike elaborates:

> As he's aged certain social differences between himself and his wife have emerged that at first were hidden, and he's increasingly found himself a kind of poor boy to her rich girl. And this is galling, perhaps, and disheartening. His original credential, which was his own body and athletic prowess, has become more and more tattered—whereas her little credential, of Daddy having a car lot, has increased in value. You might even say that as a woman she's worth more in '89 than she was in '59 because ... she's imbibed in her way the feminist currents of the last decades. He probably doesn't like that either. (F4)

Despite some positive elements in their relationship—Rabbit's obvious pride in Janice's appearance and what she describes as his new respect for her—Janice remains a Springer to him. Rabbit continues to identify her body with death, and he feels himself limited by her control over their wealth. He not only rejects Janice sexually, but in this novel, it is revealed that he has kept Thelma Harrison as his mistress for ten years and now is unfaithful with Pru. Even though Janice is devalued by Rabbit in many ways, it becomes clear that it is she who consistently manifests the cosmic other in his life. It is her capacity for forgiveness that he tests. It is her call that he anxiously awaits in Florida and "her silence [that] frightens him" (*Rest* 469).

Rabbit's final reconciliation (perhaps not with nature or woman but with the cosmic other through them) is also conveyed through water imagery. This reconciliation is connected to a series of previous incidents focusing on water and thirst. Following his first sexual encounter with Ruth in *Rabbit, Run*, Rabbit, having failed their union, remains unsatisfied and asks Ruth for a glass of water. When she returns, water in hand, Rabbit has fallen asleep. The reader knows that Updike has affirmed Ruth's capacity to provide, even in the face Rabbit's devaluations and his inability to receive.

In the Old Testament, Abraham sends a servant to find a wife for his son Isaac from among his own people. The servant miraculously identifies the right woman, named Rebecca, because she offers him water to drink. After their marriage, Isaac has Rebecca pose as his sister. By naming Rabbit's daughter Rebecca, after Bessie Springer, Updike suggests Rabbit's need to find an other who is both a stranger and yet incorporates something of the self. This combination of self-other is what fascinates Rabbit in his own sister, Mim, who seems like "himself, with the combination jiggled" and in Annie Byer, himself "turned into cunt" (*Redux* 361; *Rich* 30). The lost child, Rebecca Springer-Angstrom, would also have effected the necessary resolution. But Rebecca's death, a consequence of Rabbit's rejection of other, has not only left Rabbit guilty, "with all the acid guilt that has accumulated since creation" (*Rest* 133), it has also apparently left him thirsty. References to his now insatiable thirst occur throughout *Rabbit at Rest*, where "a kind of drought has settled over the world" (56). He says, "It felt like the Gobi Desert out there," and he drinks beer after beer to quell his spiritual thirst (71), until finally near death, Rabbit sees Janice above the oxygen tubes:

> He sees her, sees his wife here, little and dark-complected and stubborn in her forehead and mouth, blubbering like a waterfall and talking about forgiveness. "I forgive you," she keeps saying while he can't remember for what. He lies there floating in a wonderful element.... There is a terrible deep dryness in his throat, but he knows the sensation will pass, the doctors will do something about it. (511)

This final scene confirms Rabbit's earlier intuition that his tie with Janice "must be religious ... it made so little other sense" (204). It would seem that, as Neary suspected, that "dumb mutt" Janice Springer was to be the instrument of Rabbit's salvation all along, whether the novel is read in secular or in religious terms. Rabbit has long needed, sought, and avoided reconciliation. In *Rabbit at Rest*, reconciliation arrives in the form of the love and forgiveness that only the other can provide. Furthermore, it is provided generously as a gift to the undeserving. And it is only Janice, as other, who knows and loves Rabbit sufficiently to affirm his specialness in one of Updike's most moving passages:

> When she sees her Harry lying in one of the [hospital beds]... an emotion so big she fears for a second she might vomit hits her from behind, a crashing wave of sorrow and terrified awareness of utter loss like nothing ever in her life except the time she accidentally drowned her own dear baby. She had never meant never to forgive him, she had been intending one of these days to call, but the days slipped by; holding her silence had become a kind of addiction. How could she have hardened her heart so against this man who for better or worse had placed his life beside hers at the altar? ... He saw something in her that would hold him fast for a while. She wants him back, back from this element he is sinking in, she wants it so much she might vomit, his desertions and Pru and Thelma and all whatever else are washed away by the grandeur of his lying there so helpless, so irretrievable. (510–11)

Withdrawal

Toward the end of the chapter "PA," Rabbit briefly meets Cindy Murkett at Thelma Harrison's funeral. Thelma, Rabbit's mistress for ten years, has died of kidney failure, and Cindy remarks that "you know, don't you?... I mean you sense when the time is near if you're sick like that" (375). Often, as though with prescience, the dying do make unconscious preparations, and throughout *Rabbit at Rest*, but especially after he returns to Pennsylvania, Rabbit engages in a process of leave-taking and disengagement as a preparation for death.

Previously, using Slethaug's analogy for the relationship between the first two novels (237), I considered Rabbit's initial fear of being overwhelmed (his fear of self-loss) and his consequently flawed perception of the relationship between self and threatening other, to be like a pebble dropped into water forming ever-widening concentric circles. Rabbit's perception affects his personal and spiritual development, shapes his relationships and, eventually, is reflected in his society. Now, as Rabbit loses his place in the larger society and detaches himself from friends and family, the expanding circles seem to contract. The suitable analogy now is of a spotlight that narrows but intensifies its focus on Rabbit and the unresolved dilemma of spirit and matter, self and other. Critic Sven Birkerts calls this "the most interior of the Rabbit books," and indeed, the spotlight finally becomes an interior light focusing on the other that is death, that Rabbit carries within his body (4). Ironically, the solipsistic young man of *Rabbit, Run* who "just lived in his skin" (139) is now "tied to" his own "carcass" (*Rest* 446). Narrative perspective, which has been modified to suit the purpose of each of the Rabbit novels, accommodates this change. *Rabbit at Rest* is written predominantly in the third-person present, but the perspective is almost exclusively Rabbit's again—so much so that in the end, when Rabbit is no longer able to communicate with the outside world, he is imprisoned within in that perspective much as Ruth and Janice were in the narrated interior monologues of *Rabbit, Run*. In *Rabbit, Run*, perspective equals power, a looking outward to control; in *Rabbit at Rest*, it progressively becomes powerlessness, a looking inward and discovering vulnerability and isolation.

Rabbit's withdrawal is also, structurally, a journey toward death, his last descent into the underworld. In 1989, Wagner's complete operatic cycle, *Der Ring des Nibelungen*, was performed in the United States for the first time in many years. In addition, the four musical dramas in the cycle appeared for the first time on PBS. As most Americans had never seen the cycle staged before, the performances were a matter of public interest. These performances may have brought the material to Updike's mind as he wrote *Rabbit at Rest*; a number of details confirm that the Norse legend is the mythological underpinning for this novel. Not only does the novel share the themes of debt, theft, obsession, incest, destiny, and death, but Updike builds the novel on a structure similar to Wagner's in which Rabbit simultaneously withdraws from friends and family and progresses toward death. The novel, like the myth, is also concerned with the paradox of the protagonist who is both a fated victim and a collaborator in his own destruction. Updike returns to the idea of the powerful victim, discussed previously, and it is in this area (of willful self-destruction) that Rabbit's stereotypical masculinity becomes most apparent.

As in the other novels, the correspondences are suggestive rather than exact. Rabbit, who is described as "a big Swede" and whose ancestors were German, now lives in semi-retirement in Valhalla Village where the sign marking the entrance features a gold ring "inlaid and epoxied-over" to discourage theft (*Rest* 58, 31). The "Mead Hall," where the Angstroms eat, is decorated with paintings of fierce Viking warriors. When Nelson, who is "no giant," arrives, he is cast as the dark, dwarfish, obsessed (addicted) thief Alberich to play against Rabbit's Wotan (37).

In the Ring cycle, Alberich steals the Rhinegold from the Rhinemaidens, forges a ring of power, and conspires to overthrow Wotan. In *Rabbit Is Rich*, Updike establishes the connection linking male power, gold, and women, which is carried over into *Rabbit at Rest*; women equal treasure, and the possession of either signifies male power and sexual dominance. In *Rabbit Is Rich*, Nelson steals the gold (power over the dealership and sexual dominance) that Rabbit would now like to reclaim.

Nelson suspects as much. He already blames his father for stealing two women, Rebecca and Jill, and now accuses Rabbit of "kidnapping" Judy at the airport (*Rest* 25). Numerous references to kidnapping and stealing appear throughout *Rabbit at Rest*. Nelson's fear is not unfounded, as Rabbit almost immediately tries to move "precious" Judith into a room adjoining his own and as he eventually does steal Nelson's wife Pru, at least for one night. Two other similarities come to mind: Wotan is betrayed by his beautiful daughter Brunhild while Rabbit is betrayed by his daughter-in-law Pru, and Siegfried inadvertently tastes blood, which, like Rabbit's parrot food, enables him to understand the language of birds.

More important than these details, however, is that *Rabbit at Rest* shares the poignant sense of leave-taking that pervades the operas. Wotan's fate is inescapable. At first, he consults with Erda (the Earth Mother) and the three wise Norns in the hope of avoiding his fate. When he learns that he is powerless and hopeless, he begins to withdraw from the world of action. After the first drama, *Das Rheingold*, Wotan yields the stage to others. He assumes the disguise of the Wanderer and eventually becomes merely an observer. The "twilight of the gods" (*Götterdämmerung*) involves a twofold process; on the one hand, Wotan seems gradually to fade as he becomes increasingly powerless. On the other hand, he is implicated in his own death; having initiated its cause, his machinations then hasten its execution.

The structural similarities between *Rabbit at Rest* and Wagner's cycle are apparent. Like Wotan, Rabbit implicitly or explicitly asks each of his friends and everyone he meets how to avoid death and, failing that, how to face it: "*Help me, guys. Tell me how you've got on top of sex and death, so they don't bother you*" (*Rest* 71). This device allows Updike to present a sampling of cultural perspectives on the nature of humankind and the problem of death while enabling him to maintain the interrogative stance of not imposing solutions. Indeed, Rabbit questions his three wise Norns, his Jewish golfing partners; his Earth Mother, Thelma; his old adviser, Charlie Stavros; and even Lyle, the dying embezzler. In the end, Rabbit is left to make his own way. He withdraws from the world of action, retreats into observation and memory, and, finally, becomes a wanderer awaiting death.

As in the earlier novels, Updike offers at least two plausible readings. In the first, Rabbit is once again the victim of a society that demands adjustments that he is ill-equipped to make. The idea that masculine self-esteem is culturally linked with being a worker-provider has been previously discussed. The consequent dilemma for the retired man in America is well known. Not only is the retired worker cut off from the source of his self-esteem, but having distanced himself from his family in order to establish his primary identity as a worker-provider, he is set adrift at retirement. In addition, he may face problems reentering the woman's world that he initially sought to escape. He may have difficulty fitting into that world; he may feel stranded if his partner, following a different life schedule, is now focusing on outside interests; and he may feel powerless in her world or in relation to her growing self-determination. In Rabbit's case, Nelson, with Janice's help, has maneuvered his father out of the Springer dealership. Rabbit feels displaced and useless, and as his doctor confirms, such "a man needs an occupation. He needs something to do" (*Rest* 476).

Rabbit also feels jealous that his son has replaced him at the "heart of the world's business, making babies," and he wants Pru to confirm that he is a better man than Nelson (101). In addition, Rabbit has not adjusted well to Janice's emancipation. Janice not only decides how to handle the family's crises but eventually prepares to sell the only house Rabbit ever loved in order to settle Nelson's debts. The problem is not now so much that Rabbit impedes Janice's or Nelson's development as that he has failed to construct a new identity, or to use Janice's phrase, "valid identity," for himself (*Redux* 104). Even before his health deteriorates drastically, Rabbit wanders the stage as an observer rather than an active participant.

As Rabbit loses his social identity, however, he begins to regain his original identity. Intensely aware of his mortality, Rabbit revisits the neighborhoods of his childhood, renews his memories, and reawakens to the wonder of life. He parks his car to walk under Brewer's flowering pear trees, whose astonishing beauty he later associates with Ruth and Pru.

According to this positive reading, Rabbit is a sympathetic victim, a basically good man who is misunderstood and mistreated and who is certainly more sinned against than sinning. At this point, shunted aside by his society and out of grace with his family, Rabbit returns to his original values and pursues the freedom he had hoped to gain in *Rabbit, Run*. He flees to Florida where he wanders through black neighborhoods and rediscovers himself. He finds a group of teenagers (one of whom wears a Muslim hat "of concentric circles" [391]) and reenacts the opening scene from *Rabbit, Run* (487, 491–92). Later, he plays basketball with a black teenager he calls Tiger, reminding readers of his attraction to Skeeter (black Jesus) and of Jill's comment in *Rabbit Redux* that "God is in the tiger as well in as the lamb" (162). Rabbit suffers a massive heart attack while making the same perfect two-handed shot he makes at the opening of *Rabbit, Run*. A golfer in *Rabbit at Rest*, Rabbit still sees infinity in games (69). And best of all, Rabbit's last game is not of the competitive variety fostered by society via Tothero but rather contains all of the freedom and play that Rabbit remembered from his "best night" in high school (*Run* 65). "He feels loose and deeply free at last" (*Rest* 504).

Rabbit finally achieves the union and transcendence expressed in the metaphor of concentric circles introduced in *Rabbit, Run*: "The hoop fills his circle of vision, it descends to kiss his lips, he can't miss" (*Rest* 506). The basketball glides through the hoop and the blood in Rabbit's veins bursts through the wall of his left ventricle simultaneously. Once again is "lovely life eclipsed by lovely death" (*Run* 260). Later at the hospital, Janice arrives in time to forgive Rabbit, although he can't remember why, and both Janice and Nelson affirm Rabbit's specialness with their love.

The alternative reading is grim; it highlights Rabbit's collusion in his own death as he continues to pursue a course of action consistent with his stereotypical masculinity. This possibility is consistent with Michiko Kakutani's sense of the novel as a "somber, elegiac book" ("Just 30 Years Later" C13) and with Updike's own comment that *Rabbit at Rest* is "a depressed book about a depressed man, written by a depressed man" ("Why Rabbit Had to Go" 24). Updike balances two possibilities in the story line. The novel can be read as the story of a doomed man who reclaims his specialness in the jaws of death, or it can be read as the story of a man who turns away from those he loves, and who love him, and willfully pursues death in a final act of self-assertion.

Rabbit, Wotan, Oedipus, and Lear share this similarity: while they are ultimately powerless against their fate, they nevertheless bring down that fate upon their own heads. Then, by their manipulations, performed in desperate efforts to reestablish control, they hasten the fulfillment of the fate they initiated but hoped to avoid. Wotan originally strikes a bargain with the giants who built Valhalla whereby he promises to exchange the goddess Freia, who confers immortality, for the castle of his dreams; trying to regain Freia puts him in contact with the cursed gold. Wotan's foolishness (like Rabbit's) involves both a greedy materialism and a betrayal of the feminine. Not only must Wotan die, but because he is tainted by the stolen Rhinegold, he "must renounce whatever he loves, betray whoever trusts him, and wait in resignation for the end" (Freeman 520). So must Rabbit.

Previous argument has focused on the idea that Rabbit betrayed the feminine in the bargain he struck with the forces of patriarchy and materialism. The issue of a bargain aside, however, Rabbit's curse arises from his original failure to reconcile the matter/spirit, body/soul dichotomy. This failure to reconcile his nature forces him into the oppositional framework where he must choose between his body and soul. In this framework, in order to affirm himself as a spiritual being, Rabbit makes a Manichean choice against his body.

Doctors, family members, and friends all tell Rabbit that if he will diet, exercise, and submit to bypass surgery, he can live. Such sensible behaviors follow from an acceptance of material limitations, but Rabbit has always understood limitation, whether natural, social, or interpersonal, as a diminishment of the self. His refusal to accept the limitations of his body at fifty-five and fifty-six translates into "treating gluttony as an athletic event, a stretching exercise" (*Rest* 84). When Bernie Drechsel reminds Rabbit, who is eating corn chips, that "that crap's loaded with sodium," Rabbit tellingly responds, "Yeah, but it's good for the soul" (70). In his framework, body and soul are in opposition, and by expressing contempt for the body, he affirms the soul. In other words, Rabbit asserts his will (albeit his destructive will), which he identifies with his spirit, over his body. Updike suggests this reading with the narrator's comment that Rabbit's response "is about as religious a remark as he dare put forth" (*Rest* 70). Rabbit's position has some appeal in a materialistic society that worships the body. Nevertheless, the fact is that Rabbit is not a pure spirit; he lives within nature as a material being, and his unwillingness to reconcile his nature leads directly to his death.

Joyce Carol Oates also suggests that by abusing his body, Rabbit acts "unconsciously (that is deliberately)" ("So Young!" 43). Rabbit's knack for unconsciously deliberate destruction has been problematic throughout the tetralogy, so it is worth considering that while his death is ultimately inevitable, the present timing of the event is not; it is also worth considering that Rabbit deliberately pursues death in an act of self-assertion, an assertion of the spirit over matter and self over other.

This idea raises again the issue of the male protagonist as powerful victim, as already discussed in relation to *Rabbit, Run*. In that discussion, Frederich von Schiller was cited in elaboration of the idea that the tragic hero is a powerful manipulator en route to discovering his powerlessness. Having advanced to the point of the discovery that death is inevitable, Schiller says that such a person may, in order to maintain a self-definition as one who wills rather than as one who is acted upon, destroy the capacity of nature to act against him or her by conforming the will to necessity (resignation) or by aggressively choosing death. Schiller wrote the following about people in Rabbit's situation:

> Cases can occur in which fate surmounts all the ramparts upon which man founds his security and nothing else remains but for him to flee into the sacred freedom of the spirit—cases in which there is no other recourse in order to placate the lust for life than to will that fate—and no other means of withstanding the power of nature than to anticipate her, and by a free renunciation of all sensuous interest to kill himself morally before some physical force does it. (208)

Rabbit wills that fate, not only killing himself morally but actually. His life has been a continual struggle to gain power over the other in all of its guises in order to avoid being overwhelmed himself. Now he faces death in the same way, seeking to assert and enhance the self by controlling the ultimate other. Rabbit bears a surprising resemblance to Hemingway's macho protagonists who seek a means (preferably a game or sport) by which to control the approach of death.[5]

Rabbit's health rapidly deteriorates as he continues to abuse his body and postpone treatment. Now Updike highlights the relationship between Rabbit's masculinity and his reluctance to take the measures necessary to prolong life. Bernie describes his own bypass surgery as a kind of death. He says, "Six hours I was on the table.... They *freeze* you, so your blood flow is down to almost nothing. I was like locked into a black coffin. No. It's like I was the coffin" (*Rest* 63). Not only has Rabbit always "been squeamish about things being put into him" (269), but as earlier, he has "no taste for the dark, tangled, visceral aspect of Christianity, the *going through* quality of it, the passage into death and suffering" (*Run* 219). He was frightened by even the "little death" involved in the intimacy of sex. Now his refusal to surrender to the little death of bypass surgery leads to his actual death.

Even more interesting is that Rabbit chooses the angioplasty because it seems a "far less deep a violation than the coronary bypass" (*Rest* 270), but he still experiences the procedure as a sexual invasion of his body with particularly revolting overtones of *feminization*. As he watches "The Rabbit Angstrom Show" on the operating room monitor (271), he sees

> the thin wire tip of the catheter, inquisitive in obedience to Dr. Raymond's finger on the trigger, noses forward and then slowly eels, in little cautious jerking stabs, diagonally down into a milky speckled passageway, a river or tentacle within him, organic and tentative in shape where the catheter is black and positive, hard-edged as a gun. Harry watches to see if his heart will gag and try to disgorge the intruder. (273)

Immediately afterward, he wonders: "How do women stand it, for nine months? Not to mention being screwed in the first place? Can they really like it? Or queers being buggered?" (273). He feels the "worm of death" within him and thinks of nauseating "boneless seacunts" (274). Contact, invasion, and surrender are paralyzing concepts to Rabbit, and he refuses the recommended bypass surgery because it threatens him with even greater powerlessness and feminization.

Not only does Rabbit demonstrate contempt for his body, a need for control, and a willingness to die rather than submit to the self-violating procedures necessary to sustain his life, but Updike also suggests that Rabbit pursues death by severing the relationships that bind him to this world. He may be nostalgic about what and whom he leaves behind, but he nevertheless arranges to terminate his closest relationships, sometimes brutally, cutting himself off from family and friends. He thinks he has "unloaded Thelma" by telling her won't see her anymore because he is afraid of contracting AIDS (238); he continues to compete with and belittle Nelson (which Janice recognizes as a "territorial thing" [227]); he takes yet a third beloved woman away from his son, "doing Nelson in" (448); he betrays his wife Janice again; and he is even "too tired for Ruth" (271). We anticipate that as a dying man Rabbit will seek reconciliation, but he frustrates our expectation over and over by perversely injuring everyone he loves, even though the full extent of his love is revealed. He knows that his very cells remember Thelma (307). He associates Ruth and Pru with the gorgeous flowering pear trees he hopes to see in paradise and in Florida, he waits desperately for Janice's arrival.

While Rabbit is not entirely the solipsistic person he was in earlier years, he is, unfortunately, still the same man who withdrew in despair at the moment of contact, fearing that the surrender essential to union was too dangerous to endure. He is still the man who would not tell his wife he loved and needed her for fear of giving her power over him. And he is still the man who believes that "the best defense is to be offensive" (*Redux* 107). Faced with the inevitable loss of those he loves, Rabbit takes control of the situation and anticipates the action of fate by severing relationships in advance of his death. By the time he reaches Florida, Rabbit has cut himself off from the world of men; the lock on the condo has been changed, no one remembers him, and the golf shop has lost his shoes. Each of the previous novels recounts a different manifestation of Rabbit's withdrawal from the other. In this novel too, although he regains his original sense of himself, he misses the opportunity for contact with his wife and son, and his withdrawal becomes irreversible.

In the preceding novels, Rabbit manipulates Janice with his power plays. This time, however, as he waits for her in Florida, he discovers that "there is a whole host of goblins, it turns out, that Janice's warm little tightly knit body . . . protected him from" (*Rest* 472). Now, "in his solitude, his heart becomes his companion" (470). When his heart talks to him, "it seems a tiny creature, a baby, pleading inside him for attention, for rescue, and at others a sinister intruder, a traitor muttering in code, an alien parasite nothing will expel. The pains, when they come, seem hostile and deliberate, the knives of a strengthening enemy" (473). Obviously, Rabbit's "pleading" baby is associated with Rebecca June. As for the other, Rabbit has always experienced the parent-child relationship as a life-and-death struggle. He has resented the rising males, athletes, and children who pushed him aside. Eventually, the strengthening enemy is incorporated into Tiger, the young black basketball player, who "begins to exploit his opponent's slowness more cruelly, more knifingly, slipping and slashing by (504). But the sinister intruder and traitor is even more like sullen, inarticulate little Roy who yanks off Rabbit's oxygen mask in the hospital in Florida and whose "fierce little crab of a hand" claws at his grandfather's face when he senses Rabbit's interest in Pru (179, 265).

Faced with his own mortality, Rabbit increasingly internalizes the death-bearing other he has projected onto women for so long. The last three novels focus increasingly on relations between men. This shift in focus in *Rabbit at Rest* may reflect a sense that adult male life involves more transactions with men than with women; it reflects Rabbit's waning sexual interest, and it suggests that he achieves some peace with women in *Rabbit Is Rich* and *Rabbit at Rest*. The male relationships are important because they reveal Rabbit's negative feelings about himself. Confronted with death and unable to reconcile his nature, Rabbit now directs his antagonism against the enemy within, and his self-hatred is revealed not only in his abuse of his own body but also in his intense hostility toward Nelson and Roy.

Fear of and hatred for the self seems to be a part of Rabbit's masculine legacy via Marty Tothero. By the end of *Rabbit, Run*, Tothero becomes a "smirking gnome," and it is he who first applies the word "monster" to Rabbit in that novel (*Run* 257, 46). He is now remembered as looking like "a dying rhinoceros" (*Rest* 473). In *Rabbit, Run*, Rabbit manifests his unconscious fear of becoming like Tothero when he thinks that his child Rebecca will be born a monster. Essentially, Tothero's ideology (materialism and patriarchy) misdirects Rabbit's natural appetites and spiritual longings and then justifies Rabbit's objectification and exploitation of others to fill his needs. Rabbit's behavior not only leaves him unsatisfied and leads him to become "Mr. Death" for others, but it apparently produces a monstrous guilt (*Run* 279).

In *Rabbit Is Rich*, the same legacy of self-hatred is manifested in Nelson's belief that his child will be a "pink-eyed baby rhinoceros" (337). Now, near the opening of *Rabbit at Rest*, Rabbit sees a "two-headed monster," Nelson carrying Roy, approaching (24), and later, Nelson describes having felt that a monster had taken over his body when he attacked Pru during cocaine withdrawal (261).

Fear of their uncontrolled appetites and fear and guilt regarding their destructive capacities haunt Rabbit and Nelson. In *Rabbit Is Rich*, Rabbit begins to understand Tothero's insatiable appetite, and he remembers again in this novel his old coach saying, "You eat and eat and it's never the right food" (*Run* 50). Rabbit is now spiritually starving in a materialistic society, and as his vitality declines, he gorges himself on salt and sugar in an effort to experience more life. Rabbit seems close to catching his mistake when he thinks that sex with Thelma has been "soul food" or that salt is "good for the soul" (197, 70). In the earlier novels, Jill and Melanie have tried to teach Rabbit to distinguish between spiritual and material needs; they have also provided a model for "doing without." Now Mr. Shimada, a businessman rather than a spiritual guide, deplores the lack of discipline he sees in America and speaks of a "hope to strike proper barance between needs of outer world and needs of inner being" (392).

A fear of their sexual nature may also be involved in Rabbit's and Nelson's self-hatred. Tothero was involved in a mutually degrading relationship with Margaret. Rabbit once associated the possibility of a monstrous offspring with the "perverted entry" he forced on Ruth (*Run* 183). He felt guilty about using Jill's still childlike body in *Rabbit Redux*. Now Rabbit becomes involved in quasi-incest with his daughter-in-law and continually wonders whether Nelson is "queer" (*Rest 51*).

In the Trueheart interview, Updike himself comments on the growing interest in homosexuality in *Rabbit at Rest*. Some preliminary clarification may be in order, as Updike gives homosexuality particularly offensive connotations in *Rabbit Is Rich* and *Rabbit at Rest*. He is, I believe, not exploring or commenting on male homosexuality as a sexual preference, which even conservative Rabbit understands as difference rather than depravity. Rabbit thinks, "So he and Pru did fuck, once. What are we put here in the first place for? These women complain about men seeing nothing but tits and ass when they look at them but what are we supposed to see? We've been programmed to tits and ass. Except guys like Slim and Lyle, the tits got left out of their program" (*Rest* 471). Sexual preference may be programming, but at the same time, Updike also uses a very lurid version of homosexuality to signify the objectification of other, especially under the influence of materialism. In this case, the connection between homosexuality and corruption in *Rabbit Is Rich* (the gaudiness of Slim's apartment, the bathroom book of Nazi boys, and Lyle's association with Fiscal Alternatives) is expanded in *Rabbit at Rest* to include associations with sickness and death by AIDS, Lyle's self-interested exploitation of Slim, the embezzlement of funds, and Lyle's abject terror in the face of death. This version of homosexuality operates exactly as pornography does in the novels' heterosexual relations. When authentic union fails and the other is objectified, distortions occur. Thus, Webb Murkett, the materialist and hedonist introduced in *Rabbit Is Rich*, transforms his marital relations with Cindy into pornography. Similarly, Lyle's version of homosexuality is consistent with the portrait of a materialistic, exploitive, spiritually exhausted society.

Updike uses this version of homosexuality in a second way. It is set beside a number of other distortions to signify the strange, violent, unhappy things that happen when men are unable to form loving relationships with one another. As discussed before, a homosocial society encourages men to engage in close, intense contact with other males and, at the same time, maintains taboos against homosexuality. In such a society, according to Sedgwick, "intense male homosocial desire [is] . . . at once the most compulsory and the most prohibited of social bonds" ("Beast in the Closet" 247). This arrangement is designed to manipulate male behavior, and it creates more anxiety, "homosexual panic," overcompensation, and self-hatred in heterosexual men than in others. The prohibition against loving, affectionate relationships between adult males is augmented by the demands of "masculine reserve," which involves not only an unwillingness to express emotion but, as Peter Schwenger suggests, an unwillingness to accept the vulnerability that comes with emotion (*Phallic Critiques* 30–50). The prohibition is further strengthened by the cultural emphasis on performance and competition among males who may have no other model of relationship.

When homosocial desire has no outlet, it may surface in a number of unhappy, violent ways. Skeeter and Rabbit bond and then share in the destruction of Jill. Skeeter recalls interracial male bonding as a positive aspect of the Vietnam War. Rabbit and Ronnie Harrison spend a lifetime playing games and hurling vicious insults at one another. Nelson smashes cars in order to get through to his father. And Rabbit takes his son's wife. In her study of homosocial desire, Sedgwick recalls René Girard's suggestion in *Deceit, Desire and the Novel* that conflict functions as a medium of relationship. She says:

> What is most interesting for our purposes in his study is its insistence that, in any erotic rivalry, the bond that links the two rivals is as intense and potent as the bond that links either of the rivals to the beloved: that the bonds of "rivalry" and "love" are equally powerful and in many senses equivalent. For instance, Girard finds many examples in which the choice of the beloved is determined in the first place, not by the qualities of the beloved but by the beloved's already being the choice of the person who has been chosen as a rival. (*Between Men* 21)

In view of these observations, it is significant that Rabbit shares Ruth and Thelma with Ronnie, Janice with Stavros, Jill with Skeeter, and Pru and Jill (and Janice) with Nelson.

In addition to the social prohibition against male intimacy, Rabbit's thoughts about Ronnie Harrison in *Rabbit at Rest* suggest another reason why such indirect forms of relationship between men are preferred. Men, finally, are even more of a danger to the self than women. Whereas women, for Rabbit, represent the threatening other out in the world, men represent the other that is unreconciled and hidden within. Initially teammates and athletic rivals, Rabbit and Ronnie have become sexual rivals. They socialize and play golf, but Ronnie Harrison is "just about his [Rabbit's] least favorite person in the world" (304); that is, until in Florida, Rabbit suspects that "maybe we're all queer, and all of his life he's been in love with Ronnie Harrison" (448). As it turns out, Ronnie is something of a double or mirror for Rabbit. Rabbit thinks: "Funny, all his life Harrison has been shadowing Harry with a fleshly mockery, a reminder of everything sweaty and effortful Rabbit hoped squeamishly to glide over and avoid" (305). And later: "Ronnie has always been with him, a presence he couldn't avoid, an aspect of himself he didn't want to face but now does. That clublike cock, those slimy jokes, the blue eyes looking up his ass, what the hell, we're all just human bodies with brains at one end and the rest just plumbing" (410). Unreconciled Rabbit, who affirms himself as spirit, sees in the other man the absolute confirmation of his materiality, the absolute confirmation of his limitations, the absolute confirmation of his mortality. These unpleasant realities, of course, are also what he sees in Nelson (the Knell-son), which is partly why in *Rabbit Is Rich*, he is able to reconcile with his granddaughter but never with his son.

One of bleakest aspects of the ending of *Rabbit at Rest*, in relation to the problem of masculinity, is that Rabbit leaves behind him two more generations of needy men who have inherited the legacy of self-hatred, a sense of grievance, and a conflicted inner sense of masculinity. Nelson's inability to breach the distance between himself and his father suggests that the son is also unreconciled, and as his vaguely sinister relations with Slim and Lyle suggest, Nelson will be unable to relate to other men except in the most distorted ways. On the flip side, Nelson continues to have trouble relating to women; he blames his wife for entrapment and, on one occasion in this novel, beats her. Little Roy—sullen and unlikable—is especially troubling because, as Janice and Rabbit notice, he already associates expressing love with inflicting pain. Updike links the boy's desire to hurt what he loves not only with Nelson, who hurts his family, but also with the grandfather, who dislikes the boy and who, on two occasions, recognizes his own "sadistic" impulses toward the grandchildren (97, 139). Rabbit's death may reflect the declining power of a certain version of masculinity, but the prospects for better relations in the future are negligible as a loss of masculine power without inner transformation is likely to lead to different, not better, manifestations.

To return to the subject of Rabbit's final withdrawal, in the moving scene at the hospital, Janice and Nelson affirm their love for Rabbit, who is now unable to speak so as to be heard. Nelson begs Rabbit not to die. No doubt the powerless young man feels that his father is abandoning him once again and with all of their conflicts unresolved. Rabbit tries to give his son two pieces of information that are exactly what Nelson needs to resolve the masculine dilemma: "*You have a sister*" (the feminine is not wholly lost or other), and "It isn't so bad" (death is not so terrible that the fear of it need rule one's life) (512). Nelson, of course, cannot hear him. Ironically, Rabbit, who has passed on all of the problems of masculine gender identity is unable to pass on the solutions. The novel folds back to *Rabbit, Run*, but this time Rabbit's withdrawal is irreversible, and it is he who is locked in a prison of silence.

One of the television shows that Rabbit's family watches in *Rabbit at Rest* is called *Unsolved Mysteries*. Ironically, the name of the show draws attention to the fact that many of the mysteries surrounding Rabbit's life remain unsolved. Although Updike once again invites readers to consider a range of cultural perspectives, he does not impose solutions. What he does is affirm the value of life and the possibility of hope in the presence of unyielding uncertainty. Rabbit meets death in a manner entirely consistent with his character. He remains limited to the end and dies only as well as he can. Yet he also dies better than he knows. Updike, and through him, Janice and the reader stand at Archimedean points beyond the self wherefrom understanding and forgiveness are possible. Updike celebrates the specialness, the specificity, the richness, and the mystery of Rabbit's life, and he offers encouragement in the hope of reconciliation with a cosmic other who remains generous and surprising.

Conclusion

Rabbit Angstrom represents a universal condition in that he cannot achieve his aspirations and that the cause of his failure resides within himself, but the *manner* of his failing derives from the defensive attitudes and behaviors that are part of his cultural inheritance as a male. In *Rabbit at Rest*, Updike directly confronts Rabbit with the universal problem of cognizance and powerlessness before death, and I suggest again that even in this extremity, or perhaps especially in this extremity, Rabbit's gender identity shapes his response. Updike addresses a similar issue in regard to Rabbit's national identity when he says, "We are all creatures of history.... I was trying to write about the human predicament, but naturally being an American you write with an American accent, as it were" (Trueheart F4). If, as a representative American man, Rabbit faces the world from the perspective of a particular cluster of national ideas, beliefs, and attitudes, even more so, he faces the world from a masculine perspective.

As a result of developments in the fields of gender theory and feminist criticism, we are now better able to see gender in this light, not as a preexisting reality, but as a culturally transmitted cluster of ideas, beliefs, values, attitudes, and behaviors as susceptible to scrutiny as any others. And as I have said, one reason why a gendered approach to the Rabbit series has proven fruitful is that it keys into and unlocks the symbiotic relationship between the cultural preoccupation with gender division and the philosophical and religious paradigms that have shaped American society. Another reason is that by his use of an interrogative form, the author himself opens the floor to questions, and each novel yields generously to a resisting and skeptical reader.

From the outset, Rabbit envisions a world in conflict. He dreads the possibility that his individual, spiritual spark of consciousness will be overwhelmed by materiality and that the desirable other, the nonself that offers transcendence, also threatens destruction. Instead of helping Rabbit to resolve this dilemma, the learned attitudes, values, and behaviors of socially constructed masculinity exacerbate his fears and intensify his need for control.

The Rabbit tetralogy provides a comprehensive portrait of the dominant version of masculinity in American society and places John Updike among the precursors of the contemporary movement among men to reexamine their cultural inheritance as males.

Notes
Bibliography
Index

Notes

Preface

1. "Indeed, Updike's people do not go around killing themselves or (with one poignant exception) each other. They go back to work, Updike says, 'That's the real way that people die.'" See Jane Howard 74. Also see Updike's response to Charles Thomas Samuels's question "Why is there so little [violence] in your pages?" in *Picked-Up Pieces* (482). In contrast, see Strandberg 180. Also, since this book was submitted for publication, two feminist critics have focused attention on Rabbit's abusive behavior; see Gordon and Olster.

2. Catherine Belsey defines an interrogative text as one that contains multiple, contradictory possibilities rather than the "unified perspective" of the "classic realist text." "The interrogative text . . . disrupts the unity of the reader by discouraging identification with a unified subject of enunciation. The position of the 'author' inscribed in the text, if it can be located at all, is seen as questioning or as literally contradictory" (92). See also Bernard Schopen 195–206 and Suzanne Uphaus 22; these critics are among those who also react positively to Updike's avoidance of absolute answers.

3. I owe a debt to more scholars than I can name. However, germinal works include the following: Josephine Hendin's thought-provoking essay "Updike as Matchmaker: *Marry Me*," which observes that "Updike puts life together as a sophisticated Oedipal knot in which a man is tied at both ends. His men fear being in control, in charge, but are equally afraid of being suffocated and controlled" (102); see Mary Allen's essay "John Updike's Love of 'Dull Bovine Beauty,'" which focuses on the first two novels' misogynistic representations of women (and in which Allen identifies Updike with his protagonist); and see Judie Newman's book *John Updike*, which provides invaluable

insight, especially into *Rabbit Redux* and *Rabbit Is Rich*, and which I have reconsidered in the light of gender. On dualism, see Hunt, *Updike* and Wood.

1. Introduction

1. The overview of gender theory presented here draws primarily on the following works, which are recommended to readers seeking a fuller understanding of the subject: Toril Moi, *Sexual/Textual Politics*; Showalter, "Introduction," in *Speaking of Gender* 1–13; and Garner, Kahane, and Sprengnether, "Introduction," *The (M)other Tongue: Essays in Feminist Psychoanalytical Interpretation* 15–29.

2. Gerry Brenner discusses the connection between Rabbit's uncircumcised condition and his role as a "natural" man in the essay "*Rabbit, Run*: John Updike's Criticism of the 'Return to Nature.'"

3. Peter Schwenger observes that "few people realize that where sexual definition is concerned cultures differ from one another; and, as time passes, these cultures differ from their earlier selves. An example of such a shift within a culture is the English proscription against men crying. In the eighteenth century it was downright fashionable to be a 'Man of Feeling' and to cry publicly at any suitable provocation. But the nineteenth century saw major changes in the idea of masculinity, and among them the rise of the 'stiff upper lip'" (*Phallic Critiques* 3).

4. Rosemary Reuther clarifies: "It has been axiomatic in biblical theology that the relation of God to creation must be defined as that of transcendence and separation of natures. Genesis language that sounds as though the world *flowed* from or was *born* out of God is condemned as 'pantheistic.' The proper stance of God to creation is one of a Spirit Ego who 'makes' the world as an object over against and other than 'himself.' In other words, the language for genesis is instrumental, rather than the language of gestation. The world is to be seen as something outside of, beneath and other than God. It exists as an inferior and dependent artifact which 'He' makes from nothing" (409–10).

2. *Rabbit, Run*

1. According to Updike, *Rabbit, Run* was occasioned by "a sense of horror that beneath this skin of bright and exquisitely sculpted phenomena, death waits" ("View from the Catacombs" 74). See Victor Strandberg's excellent article "John Updike and the Changing of the Gods," which discusses the fear of extinction in Updike's work. I have relied on his analysis of the role of dualism and agape and on his observations regarding George Caldwell's redemptive sacrifice. See Wood; Plagman; and Hunt, *Updike*.

2. In *Rabbit at Rest*, Updike suggests that Rabbit's dichotomous view of the world may have been a construct. Rabbit, who feels nostalgic for the "clarifying" framework of a divided world, says, "The cold war. It gave you a reason to get up in the morning" (*Rest* 353).

3. See Elizabeth Tallent, who interprets Updike's references to the solstice and equinox in relation to the ceremonial lives of primitive peoples (75–90).

4. Robert Detweiler writes about the imagery of falling in *Rabbit Is Rich* (*John Updike* 175); Michiko Kakutani also mentions this imagery in his review of *Rabbit at Rest*, "Just 30 Years Later." The images of falling in *Rabbit at Rest* also incorporate explosions, as in the references to the explosion of the Pan Am flight over Lockerbie, Scotland. Near the end of the novel, Rabbit's heart bursts, and he stumbles and falls. Images of balance, imbalance and falling, and of withdrawal and return are consistent with the metaphor of the earth's revolution.

5. On George Caldwell in *The Centaur*, see Kathleen Verduin 254–66; Strandberg 175–94; and Mellard 217–30.

6. Derek Wright asks whether "within the context of Updike's fiction, the whole theory of love as an oppositional, anti-entropic force has always begged the question of whether female characters are ever allowed sufficiently well defined and distinct identities to resist being merged into and annihilated by the wills of their dominant males" (36).

7. See Larry Taylor who translates *Schussel* as a "fidgety, hasty, careless person" (141).

8. Numerous critics discuss the Smiths' garden. See Vargo, who observes that "by the communion with nature that he [Rabbit] experiences in the garden of Mrs. Smith, he comes closest to the type of religious celebration for which he searches" (65). Uphaus suggests that the garden is not a redemptive symbol because "Updike stresses traditional religious connotations, only to show that they are no longer applicable (28–29). Alice and Kenneth Hamilton see the Smiths' garden as one of merely "brainless flowers" where "Rabbit's mind runs along the pagan path of Horace's *carpe diem*" (*The Elements* 151). And Joyce Markle says Rabbit's gardening activities "provide him with a contrast to "society's belief in ultimate human responsibility"; God is responsible for the seed Rabbit sows, while "Rabbit is returned to the larger cosmos and is temporarily freed from the smaller human cosmos" (50).

9. Strandberg's essay brought this poem to my attention (178).

10. The epigraph to *Rabbit, Run* is taken from Pascal's *Pensées* and reads in full: "The motions of Grace, the hardness of the heart; external circumstances."

3. Gender Formation

1. John Neary, in his work *Something and Nothingness*, explores a number of connections between *The Collector* and *Rabbit, Run* (7–84).

2. For another interpretation see Hendin 102; her essay suggests the possibilities in this nightmare. See also Cox 40.

3. Detweiler considers Rabbit's oedipal relationship with Mary (*John Updike* 53–57); see also Ancona and Nickens.

4. Rabbit not only remembers Tothero's words in *Rabbit Is Rich* and

Rabbit at Rest, but he manifests the same insatiable appetites himself. In those novels, his appetite reflects universal human "wants" (Trueheart F1) as well as the fact that Rabbit is spiritually starving in a materialistic society. However, such appetites are also part of Rabbit's masculine legacy from Tothero, and Rabbit's son, Nelson, in his turn, develops an addiction.

5. Belsey presents the different critical perspectives on this subject. Archetypes can be understood, as they are by Northrop Frye, as recurring "because human nature is constant, not just in its physical needs but in its desire for the forms of civilization, its rage for order in the face of chaos. Literature is the autonomous embodiment of this order" (24). On the other hand, Jacques Lacan, Louis Althusser, and Jacques Derrida and their followers "have all from various positions questioned the humanist assumption that subjectivity, the individual mind or inner being, is the source of meaning and of action" (Belsey 3).

4. The Power of Naming

1. After Rabbit abandons her, Ruth's narrated interior monologue reveals that her weight has been the focus of lifelong feelings of helplessness and self-loathing. She thinks: "It's like when she was fourteen and the whole world trees sun and stars would have swung into place if she could lose twenty pounds just twenty pounds what difference would it make to God Who guided every flower in the fields into shape" (*Run* 179). See Clinton Burhans on Rabbit's compulsion to manipulate and dominate Janice.

2. See Detweiler's discussion of Don Juanism in "Updike's *Couples*: Eros Demythologized." Also see Strandberg's comments on sex, de Rougemont, and Don Juan in "John Updike and the Changing of the Gods." Updike's review of de Rougemont's *Love Declared* (1963) appears in Updike, *Assorted Prose* 283–300.

3. Among the critics who discuss the roles of religion and of the two ministers are Hamilton and Hamilton in *The Elements* 145–54 and George Hunt in *Updike* 13–48. See also Brenner 92; Henry Petter 106; Burhans 157–60; Vargo 71–72; and Markle 51–55.

4. Also in "Why Write?" Updike says, "The writer's strength is not his own; he is a conduit who so positions himself that the world at his back flows through to the readers on the other side of the page. To keep this conduit scoured is his laborious task" (*PUP* 54).

5. Rabbit Redux

1. According to Dinnerstein the burial of joy, the denial of loss, and the refusal to face death are the basis for our contaminated, adult involvement in the "malignant aspect of enterprise" and our unresolved mixed feelings for the flesh (123)

2. Markle uses this phrase in reference to the "wasteland-limbo-Hades

of Eccles's community which seeks to recapture Rabbit" in *Rabbit, Run* (40–41). Conditions have worsened in the intervening years.

3. Detweiler examines the space tropes as well as imagery of water (especially of drowning, which becomes crucial in *Rabbit at Rest*), ghosts, and black-and-white imagery (*John Updike* 128–31). All of these have been carried over from *Rabbit, Run*, and like the overlapping metaphors there, also "function not only individually to provide imagistic continuity throughout the novel; they also merge, blending in and out of each other, to produce a sense of interconnectedness that gives the book its integrity and vast allusiveness" (Detweiler, *John Updike* 130). See also Markle's observations on the use of whiteness and frozenness (9–10; 150–55); and see Wayne Falke's comments on light (68).

4. In her useful discussion of the decline of paternal figures in Updike's work, Verduin notes Hook's remark in *The Poorhouse Fair* that "women are the heroes of dead lands" (258). Also see Schopen's speculation on this reversal (203–4).

5. This reading is partially consistent with Linda Plagman's sense of the continuity in Rabbit's behavior. Plagman offers a religious and philosophical interpretation with reference to Karl Barth's *Church Dogmatics* and Denis de Rougemont's *Love in the Western World*. She essentially says that Rabbit's concern with protecting and enhancing the self distorts his relationships with God and man. Plagman, however, does not see the problem of self expressed in Rabbit's masculinity. On the contrary, she finds Updike in comfortable agreement with Barth's traditional conception of male and female roles in a divinely ordained hierarchy (12–13).

6. See Newman's excellent discussion of technology in *Redux* (43–61). I have reinterpreted several of Newman's findings in the light of Rabbit's masculinity.

7. Allen notes that "Angela Hanema of *Couples* half jokingly claims that her husband sleeps with women when he is really trying to kill his mother" (71).

8. Over the years, Stavros's perspective unfolds. In *Rabbit at Rest*, his view that "you're just a soft machine" contrasts with Rabbit's hope for immortality (237). However, Stavros accepts death and does not manifest the Manichean contempt for the body that keeps Rabbit from preserving his own.

9. This interpretation is also consistent with Rabbit's sexual attraction to Skeeter, noted by a number of critics. Rabbit does not seem particularly threatened by this attraction until Skeeter's behavior puts Rabbit in the feminine or powerless position. Then he bolts.

10. Ironically, Nelson gets the same kind of relief from smashing cars in *Rabbit Is Rich*.

6. Life in Furnace Township

1. Oxidation figures in *The Centaur* as well; George Caldwell teaches that $C_6H_{12}O_6 + 6O_2 = 6CO_2 + 6H_2O + E$, and says, "That's the way the world goes round.... Round and round, and where it stops, nobody knows" (143).

The glint of light also reflects off the policeman's badge during the fire (*Redux* 323).

2. Detweiler mentions Dante's *Inferno* in his analysis of *Rabbit, Run* in *John Updike* 44. George Slethaug comments that, in *Rabbit Redux*, Rabbit's "residence becomes a prison of conflict and despair, strongly suggestive of Dante's *Inferno*, where Rabbit will be trapped or pass to new understanding of himself" (248); see Slethaug's "*Rabbit Redux*: 'Freedom is Made of Brambles'" 237–53.

3. Donald Greiner notes the adjustment Updike makes for Janice. He says, "Updike knows that many readers already familiar with Harry Angstrom from the earlier novel will naturally sympathize with Rabbit in the standoff with Janice, so he develops her point of view in *Redux* in order to maintain a balance of sympathy" (*John Updike's Novels* 73). See *John Updike's Novels* for further discussion.

4. "A restricted code will arise where the form of the social relation is based upon closely shared identifications, upon an extensive range of shared expectation, upon a range of common assumptions. . . . The use of a restricted code creates social solidarity" (Bernstein 476).

5. Updike acknowledges a similarity between himself and Rabbit in regard to the written word: "Even the way Rabbit sits in front of his Linotype machine day after day reminded me of myself, of the way I sit in front of the typewriter" (qtd. in Vaughan 72). This similarity is interesting in view of the analogy drawn here earlier regarding Janice's and Updike's speech difficulties.

6. Newman says that the death of Rebecca June in *Rabbit, Run* is the "horrible price of social cohesion" (39), and while I differ somewhat with her interpretation of that novel, Jill's death now is clearly a purchase price.

7. Revolution and Chaos

1. Vargo sees the fire as the "ritual cleansing," "a burning clean of accumulated waste, of deterioration, of impure ways of *doing* rather than of *seeing*" (167). In *Self-Consciousness*, Updike says, "Peace is . . . an illusory respite we earn. On both the personal and national level, islands of truce created by balances of terror and potential violence are the best we can hope for" (131).

8. Is Rabbit Rich?

1. The first epigraph reads: "At night he lights up a good cigar, and climbs into the little old 'bus, and maybe cusses the carburetor, and shoots out home. He mows the lawn, or sneaks in some practice putting, and then he's ready for dinner" (George Babbitt, of the Ideal Citizen). The second, from Wallace Stevens's "A Rabbit as King of the Ghosts," reads: "The difficulty

to think at the end of day, / When the shapeless shadow covers the sun / And nothing is left except light on your fur. . . . " See Greiner's comments on the relevance of the epigraphs, especially on the Rabbit-Babbitt connection; *John Updike's Novels* 84–100. See Campbell on the Stevens reference.

2. Cindy Murkett is referred to as Webb's "treasure to barter" and Rabbit's granddaughter, of course, is "fortune's hostage" (*Rich* 381, 437).

3. Newman also discusses Updike's emphasis on the role of media advertising and "the need to create consumer wants" in this novel (61–62).

4. Unfortunately, this association works to the detriment of both; for example, Gerda Lerner observes, "Since every culture devalues nature as it strives to rise above it through mastery, women have become symbolic of an inferior, intermediate order of being" (25). Dorothy Dinnerstein, on the other hand, suggests that nature suffers from its association with women: "Inextricable from the notion that nature is our semi-sentient early mother is the notion that she is inherently inexhaustible, that if she does not provide everything we would like to have it is because she does not want to, that her treasure is infinite and can if necessary be taken with force. . . . The murderous infantilism of our relation to nature follows inexorably from the murderous infantilism of our sexual arrangements" (109–10).

5. See Ancona on Rabbit's Oedipus and Laius conflicts and Gullette on his midlife passage. These critics find the Rabbit "resolves his Oedipal identity crisis in *Rabbit Is Rich* (Ancona 84).

6. The pattern of overlapping images in *Rabbit, Run* is discussed in chapter 2, and the "orchestration of tropes" in *Rabbit Redux* is discussed in Detweiler, *John Updike* 125–37. On the interlocking imagery in *Rabbit, Run*, see also Uphaus and Newman; on this imagery in *Rabbit Redux*, see Daniel Vanderwerken 73–77; and in *Rabbit Is Rich*, see Newman.

7. Newman provides a useful, quick review of the psychoanalytic theories derived from Freud's *Three Essays on the Theory of Sexuality*: "Essentially, the crux of psychoanalytic theories of the anal character of money lies in the idea that faeces are the child's first autonomous product and first material possession, exposing the child also to the power of parents and providing the first opportunity to exercise power over his surroundings. By being taught to be clean the child recognizes the power of his environment and realizes that it is necessary to subordinate self to others. Rewards are obtainable from parents for prompt discharge, and defecation in itself offers auto-erotic pleasure. Alternatively the child may discover that faeces retention provides an opportunity to challenge parents and that such retention may intensify pleasure. . . . the adult who has become arrested in the anal stage. . . . conform[s] to three basic types. Firstly, unmodified anal eroticism may express itself through coprophilia, homosexuality, or the desire for rectal coitus. Alternatively the instinct may be sublimated, creating an acquisitive, thrifty, miserly character for whom savings replace faeces. Lastly, in reaction, the anal instinct may express itself in an obsessive concern with order and cleanliness, as opposed to dirt, creating an over-conscientious, rigid character type" (62–63).

8. An interesting manifestation of Rabbit's inability to surrender oc-

curs in his pursuit of Annie Byer, which is discussed chapter 10. In *Rabbit is Rich*, Ruth recognizes that Rabbit's desire to maintain a claim on Annie is motivated by a self-interest that she associates with feces: "When I think of you thinking she's your daughter it's like rubbing her all over with shit" (419).

9. Newman notes Updike's allusion to the house hunting episode in Thoreau's *Walden*, which symbolizes a "withdrawal from a materialist world to a simplified existence at Walden Pond" (77). Rabbit's "gardener's cottage," by the way, also has a little cement pool in the yard. I would add that Updike's allusion further suggests that Rabbit reclaims some of his lost freedom and independence.

9. Laius and Oedipus

1. Samuel Osherson repeatedly observes the striking disparity between the perceptions that fathers and sons have of one another. In *Rabbit at Rest*, Rabbit is astonished when Janice attributes Nelson's defensiveness to having "grown up in the shadow of a dominating father." He responds, "I am *not* dominating. I'm a pushover if you ask me" (189).

2. Not everyone sees Nelson's character and the developing father-son conflict as focal issues in Rabbit's later years. Donald Greiner remarks that Updike "tells the reader more about him [Nelson] than he wants to know" (94) and also suggests that the "persistent contrast" between father and son only "stresses the uniqueness of Rabbit's lifelong run" (*John Updike's Novels* 94). Greiner draws support from Thomas Edwards, who says, "Nelson seems to me to be the one failure in *Rabbit Is Rich*, an irate caricature of the 'Me Generation' where there might better be a difficult, confused vulnerable human presence" (101); and Eliot Freemont-Smith also supports Greiner's argument: "Rabbit's son Nelson is too much of a nerd; he seems more programmed by Updike's loyalty to Rabbit than by Rabbit's genes or will" (55).

3. Detweiler interprets "Nelson's destructiveness with Rabbit's cars as displaced sexual aggression against his father" (*John Updike* 174).

10. Rabbit at Rest

1. Rabbit's aggressive, insensitive remark to his grandson here is strikingly like his response to Janice's plea for understanding in *Rabbit Run*: "I can but I don't want to, it's not the thing, the thing is how *I* feel" (230). Both responses invalidate the other's reality by decentering him or her. Rabbit desperately wants to have his own importance affirmed by God and others, but his words demonstrate his continued willingness to maintain his specialness at the expense of, or in competition with, others. Such a remark, made in this garden, associates Rabbit's attitude with a godless and loveless world.

2. Schopen provides a general discussion of the alternative moral

frameworks in Updike's work. See Schopen's "Faith, Morality, and Novels of John Updike."

3. Updike hints that the slight heart attack that Rabbit has in the hospital occurs as a result of recognizing Annie. If this is the case, then this lost daughter is, like Judith, another nail in his coffin (*Rest* 276).

4. In *Rabbit Is Rich*, Janice represents the choice of returning home from vacation or not as a choice between life and death. Rabbit doesn't understand the rush home when "Nobody's died." Janice says, "Not yet... Is that what you need?" (398).

5. Updike's mention of a "bullring" during Rabbit's last game recalls Hemingway's *The Sun Also Rises* (1926): "The clouds have gathered in an agitated silvery arena around the blinding sun, a blue bullring" (*Rest* 504). This reference also recalls Rabbit's dream of overlapping circles in *Rabbit, Run*.

Bibliography

Aldridge, John W. "The Private Vice of John Updike." Bloom 9–13.
Allen, Mary. "John Updike's Love of 'Dull Bovine Beauty.'" Bloom 69–95.
Alter, Robert. "Updike, Malamud and the Fire This Time." Thorburn and Eiland 39–49.
Ancona, Francesco Aristide. *Writing the Absence of the Father: Undoing Oedipal Structures in the Contemporary American Novel.* Lanham, MD: UP of America, 1986.
Astrachan, Anthony. *How Men Feel: Their Response to Women's Demands for Equality and Power.* New York: Doubleday, 1986.
Beauvoir, Simone de. *The Second Sex.* Trans. H. M. Parshley. 1949. New York: Vintage, 1989.
Belsey, Catherine. *Critical Practice.* London: Methuen, 1980.
Bernstein, Basil. "A Sociolinguistic Approach to Socialization; with Some Reference to Educability." Gumperz and Hymes 465–97.
Berryman, Charles. "The Education of Harry Angstrom: Rabbit and the Moon." *Literary Review* 27 (Fall 1983): 117–26.
Bersani, Leo. *A Future for Astyanax.* Boston: Little, 1976.
Birkerts, Sven. "The Inner Rabbit." Rev. of *Rabbit at Rest*, by John Updike. *Chicago Tribune* 30 Sept. 1990, sec. 14: 1, 4.
Bloom, Harold, ed. *Modern Critical Views: John Updike.* New York: Chelsea, 1987.
Bly, Robert. *Iron John: A Book about Men.* New York: Addison-Wesley, 1990.
Braudy, Susan. "A Day in the Life of Joan Didion." *Ms.* Feb. 1977: 109.
Brenner, Gerry. "*Rabbit, Run*: John Updike's Criticism of the 'Return to Nature.'" Macnaughton 91–104.

Brod, Harry. *A Mensch among Men: Explorations in Jewish Masculinity.* Freedom, CA.: Crossing, 1988.
Burchard, Rachael C. *John Updike: Yea Sayings.* Carbondale: Southern Illinois UP, 1971.
Burhans, Clinton S., Jr. "Things Falling Apart: Structure and Theme in *Rabbit, Run.*" Macnaughton 148–63.
Campbell, Jeff H. "Light on Your Fur: Regeneration in Updike's *Rabbit Is Rich.*" *Lamar Journal of the Humanities* 10 (Spring 1984): 7–13.
Cath, Stanley H., Alan R. Gurwitt, and John Munder Ross, eds. *Father and Child: Developmental and Clinical Perspectives.* Boston: Little, 1982.
Chodorow, Nancy. "Being and Doing: A Cross-Cultural Examination of the Socialization of Males and Females." Gornick and Moran 259–91.
Cixous, Hélène, and Catherine Clément. *The Newly Born Woman.* Trans. Betsy Wing. Minneapolis: U of Minnesota P, 1991.
"Consumerism and Women." Gornick and Moran 658–64.
Cox, David. *An Examination of Thematic and Structural Connectedness Between John Updike's Rabbit Novels.* Diss. Ohio U, 1978. Ann Arbor, MI.: UMI, 1979. 7904828.
Daly, Mary. *Beyond God the Father: Toward a Philosophy of Women's Liberation.* Boston: Beacon, 1973.
Davis, Angela Y. *Women, Race and Class.* New York: Random, 1981.
De Bellis, Jack. "The 'Extra Dimension': Character Names in Updike's 'Rabbit' Trilogy." *Names* 36 (1988): 29–38.
Deen, Carol. *Women in the Novels of John Updike.* Diss. Texas A&M U, 1980. Ann Arbor, MI.: UMI, 1980. 8023021.
de Rougemont, Denis. *Love in the Western World.* Princeton, NJ: Princeton UP, 1983.
Derrida, Jacques. "Difference." *Speech and Phenomena and Other Essays on Hursserl's Theory of Signs.* Trans. David B. Allison. Evanston, IL.: Northwestern UP, 1973. 129–60.
———. *Of Grammatology.* Trans. Gayatri Chakrovorty Spivak. Baltimore: Johns Hopkins UP, 1976.
Detweiler, Robert. *John Updike.* Rev. ed. New York: Twayne, 1984.
———. "Updike's *Couples*: Eros Demythologized." Macnaughton 120–39.
Dinnerstein, Dorothy. *The Mermaid and the Minotaur: Sexual Arrangements and Human Malaise.* New York: Harper, 1976.
Donner, Dean. "Rabbit Angstrom's Unseen World." *New World Writing* 20 (1962): 58–75.
Doyle, Paul A. "Updike's Fiction: Motifs and Techniques." *Catholic World* Sept. 1964: 356–62.
Dworkin, Andrea. *Our Blood: Prophecies and Discourses on Sexual Politics.* New York: Harper, 1976.
———. *Pornography: Men Possessing Women.* London: Women's, 1981.
Edwards, Thomas R. "Updike's Rabbit Trilogy." *Atlantic Monthly* Oct. 1981: 94, 96, 100–10.

Ellmann, Mary. *Thinking about Women*. New York: Harcourt, 1968.
Epstein, Joseph. "John Updike: Promises, Promises." *Commentary* 75.1 (1983): 55.
Erikson, Erik. *Childhood and Society*. New York: Norton, 1963.
Esman, Aaron H. *Father and Child: Developmental and Clinical Perspectives*. Boston: Little, 1982.
Falke, Wayne. "*Rabbit Redux*: Time/Order/God." *Modern Fiction Studies* 20 (Spring 1974): 59–75.
Farrell, Michael P., and Stanley Rosenberg. *Men at Midlife*. Boston: Auburn, 1981.
Fetterley, Judith. *The Resisting Reader: A Feminist Approach to American Fiction*. Bloomington: Indiana UP, 1978.
Fiedler, Leslie A. *Love and Death in the American Novel*. New York: Dell, 1966.
Fitzgerald, F. Scott. *The Great Gatsby*. 1925. New York: Scribner's, 1953.
Fowles, John. "Hardy and the Hag." *Thomas Hardy after Fifty Years*. Ed. L. St. John Butler. London: Macmillan, 1977. 28–42.
Freeman, John W. *Stories of the Great Operas*. New York: Norton, 1984.
Freemont-Smith, Eliot. "Rabbit Ruts." *Village Voice* 6 Oct. 1981: 35, 55.
French, Marilyn. *Beyond Power: On Women, Men and Morals*. New York: Simon, 1985.
Frye, Northrop. *The Secular Scripture: A Study of the Structure of Romance*. Cambridge: Harvard UP, 1986.
Gado, Frank. *First Person: Conversations on Writers and Writing*. Schenectady, NY: Union College P, 1973.
Galloway, David. "The Absurd Man as Saint: The Novels of John Updike." *Modern Fiction Studies* 11 (Summer 1964): 111–27.
Garner, Shirley Nelson, Claire Kahane, and Madelon Sprengnether, eds. *The (M)other Tongue: Essays in Feminist Psychoanalytical Interpretation*. Ithaca, NY: Cornell UP, 1985.
Gilbert, Sandra M., and Susan Gubar. *The Madwoman in the Attic: The Woman Writer and the Nineteenth-Century Literary Imagination*. New Haven: Yale UP, 1979.
Girard, René. *Deceit, Desire and the Novel: Self and Other in Literary Structure*. Baltimore: Johns Hopkins UP, 1966.
———. *Violence and the Sacred*. Baltimore: Johns Hopkins UP, 1977.
Gordon, Mary. "Good Boys and Dead Girls." *Good Boys and Dead Girls and Other Essays*. New York: Viking, 1991. 3–23.
Gornick, Vivian, and Barbara K. Moran, eds. *Woman in Sexist Society: Studies in Power and Powerlessness*. New York: NAL, 1972.
Greiner, Donald J. *Adultery in the American Novel: Updike, James and Hawthorne*. Columbia: U of South Carolina P, 1985.
———. *John Updike's Novels*. Athens: Ohio UP, 1984.
———. *The Other John Updike: Poems/Short Stories/Prose/Play*. Athens: Ohio UP, 1981.

Gullette, Margaret Morganroth. *Safe at Last in the Middle Years*. Berkeley: U of California P, 1988.
Gumperz, John J., and Dell Hymes, eds. *Directions in Sociolinguistics: The Ethnography of Communication*. New York: Holt, 1972.
Guttman, David. "Individual Adaptation in the Midlife Years: Developmental Issues in the Masculine Mid-Life Crisis." *Journal of Geriatric Psychiatry* 9 (1976): 41–59.
Hamilton, Alice. "Between Innocence and Experience: From Joyce to Updike." *Dalhousie Review* 49 (1969): 102–9.
Hamilton, Alice, and Kenneth Hamilton. *The Elements of John Updike*. Grand Rapids, MI.: Eerdmans, 1970.
———. "The Validation of Religious Faith." *Studies in Religion/Sciences Religieuses* 5 (1975–76): 280–85.
Hamilton, Edith. *Mythology*. New York: NAL, 1969.
Harper, Howard M., Jr. *Desperate Faith: A Study of Bellow, Salinger, Mailer, Baldwin & Updike*. Chapel Hill: U of North Carolina P, 1967.
Harrison, Fraser. *The Dark Angel: Aspects of Victorian Sexuality*. London: Fontana, 1979.
Hartmann, Heidi. "The Unhappy Marriage of Marxism and Feminism: Towards a More Progressive Union." *Feminist Frameworks: Alternative Theoretical Accounts of the Relations Between Women and Men*. Ed. Alison M. Jaggar and Paula S. Rothenberg. New York: McGraw, 1984. 172–89.
Hendin, Josephine. "Updike as Matchmaker: Marry Me." Thorburn and Eiland 99–106.
Horton, Andrew S. "Ken Kesey, John Updike and the Lone Ranger." *Journal of Popular Culture* 8 (Winter 1974): 570–78.
Howard, Jane. "Can a Nice Novelist Finish First?" *Life* 4 Nov. 1966: 74–82.
Hunt, George W. *John Updike and the Three Great Secret Things: Sex, Religion and Art*. Grand Rapids, MI: Eerdmans, 1980.
———. "Reality, Imagination, and Art: The Significance of Updike's 'Best' Story." Macnaughton 207–16.
Jackson, Edward M. "Rabbit Is Racist." *College Language Association Journal* 28 (1985): 444–51.
Jaggar, Alison M., and Paula S. Rothenberg, eds. *Feminist Frameworks: Alternative Theoretical Accounts of the Relations Between Women and Men*. New York: McGraw, 1984.
Jardine, Alice A., and Paul Smith, eds. *Men in Feminism*. New York: Methuen, 1987.
Jones, Ernest. *The Life and Work of Sigmund Freud*. Vol. 1. New York: Basic, 1953–57. 3 vols.
Kakutani, Michiko. "Just 30 Years Later, Updike Has a Quartet." Rev. of *Rabbit at Rest*, by John Updike. *New York Times* 25 Sept. 1990: C13+.
———. "Turning Sex and Guilt into an American Epic." Interview. *Saturday Review* Oct. 1981: 14–22.

Kaplan, Cora. *Sea Changes: Culture and Feminism.* London: Verso, 1986.
Kolbenschlag, Madonna. *Kiss Sleeping Beauty Good-bye: Breaking the Spell of Feminine Myths and Models.* New York: Bantam, 1981.
Komisar, Lucy. "The Image of Woman in Advertising." Gornick and Moran 304–17.
Lacan, Jacques. *Ecrits.* Paris: Seuil, 1966.
Le Pellec, Yves. "Rabbit Underground." *Les Americanistes: New French Criticism on Modern American Fiction.* Ed. Ira D. and Christiane Johnson. Port Washington, NY: Kennikat, 1978. 94–99.
Lerner, Gerda. *The Creation of Patriarchy.* New York: Oxford UP, 1986.
Levinson, Daniel, et al. *The Seasons of a Man's Life.* New York: Knopf, 1978.
Lévi-Strauss, Claude. *The Elementary Structures of Kinship.* Boston: Beacon, 1969.
Lyons, Eugene. "John Updike: The Beginning and the End." *Critique* 14 (1972): 44–59.
Macnaughton, William R., ed. *Critical Essays on John Updike.* Boston: Hall, 1982.
Markle, Joyce B. *Fighters and Lovers: Theme in the Novels of John Updike.* New York: New York UP, 1973.
Mead, Margaret. *Male and Female.* New York: Morrow, 1949.
Mellard, James M. "The Novel as Lyric Elegy: The Mode of Updike's *The Centaur.*" Macnaughton 217–30.
Miller, Roger. "Updike says this year's will be the last Rabbit tale—but no promises." *Milwaukee Journal* 1 July 1990: E6.
Millett, Kate. *Sexual Politics.* Garden City, NY: Doubleday, 1970.
Moi, Toril. *Sexual/Textual Politics.* London: Methuen, 1985.
Moyers: A Gathering of Men. Prod. Betsy McCarthy. Dir. Wayne Ewing. With Robert Bly. Exec prod. Judith Davidson Moyers and Bill Moyers. PBS, New York. 10 Jan. 1990.
Muradian, Thaddeus. "The World of Updike." *English Journal* 54 (Oct. 1965): 577–84.
Neary, John. *Something and Nothingness.* Carbondale: Southern Illinois UP, 1992.
Newman, Judie. *John Updike* New York: St. Martin's, 1988.
Nickens, Susan Jean. *A Right Relation: John Updike's Norm of Marital Commitment.* Diss. U of Maryland, 1981. Ann Arbor, MI: UMI, 1982. 8214392.
Oates, Joyce Carol. "So Young!" Rev. of *Rabbit at Rest*, by John Updike. *New York Times Book Review* 30 Sept. 1990: F1,43.
———. "Updike's American Comedies." Bloom 57–68.
Olster Stacey. " 'Unadorned Woman, Beauty's Home Image': Updike's *Rabbit, Run.*" *New Essays on* Rabbit, Run. Ed. Stanley Trachtenberg. New York: Cambridge UP, 1993. 95–117.
Ortner, Sherry. "Is Female to Male as Nature Is to Culture." *Women, Culture & Society.* Ed. Michelle Rosaldo and Louise Lamphere. Stanford, CA: Stanford UP, 1974. 66–88.

Osherson, Samuel. *Finding Our Fathers: The Unfinished Business of Manhood.* New York: Macmillan, 1986.
Parrington, Vernon L. "Sinclair Lewis: Our Own Diogenes." Schorer 62–70.
Petter, Henry. "John Updike's Metaphoric Novels." Macnaughton 105–14.
Plagman, Linda Marie. *The Modern Pilgrims: Marriage and the Self in the Work of John Updike.* Diss. Marquette U, 1974. Ann Arbor, MI: UMI, 1975. 7514994.
Podhoretz, Norman. "A Dissent on Updike." *Doings and Undoings: The Fifties and After.* New York: Farrar, 1964. 251–57.
Prince, Gerald. *A Dictionary of Narratology.* Lincoln, NE: U of Nebraska P, 1987.
Pritchett, V. S. "Updike." Rev. of *Rabbit Is Rich*, by John Updike. *New Yorker* 9 Nov. 1981: 201–6.
Raban, Jonathan. "Rabbit's Last Run." Rev. of *Rabbit at Rest*, by John Updike. *Washington Post Book World* 30 Sept. 1990: 1, 15.
Reich, Charles A. *The Greening of America.* New York: Random, 1970.
Reuther, Rosemary Radford. "Sexism and God-talk." *Women and Men: The Consequences of Power, Selected Papers from the Bicentennial Conference.* Ed. Dana Hiller and Robin Sheets. Proc. of the conference "Pioneers for Century III." Apr. 1976. Cincinnati: Office of Women's Studies, U of Cincinnati, 1976. 409–10.
Reynaud, Emmanuel. *Holy Virility: The Social Construction of Masculinity.* London: Pluto, 1983.
Ristoff, Dilvo I. *Updike's America: The Presence of Contemporary History in John Updike's Rabbit Trilogy.* New York: Lang, 1988.
Rowbotham, Sheila. "Imperialism and Sexuality." Jaggar and Rothenberg 423–27.
Rupp, Richard H. "John Updike: Style in Search of a Center." Bloom 15–28.
Samuels, Charles Thomas. "The Art of Fiction XLIII: John Updike." *Paris Review* 45 (1968): 85–117.
———. *John Updike.* Pamphlets on American Writers 79. Minneapolis: U of Minnesota P, 1969.
———. "Updike on the Present." Rev. of *Rabbit Redux*, by John Updike. Macnaughton 63–67.
Saussure, Ferdinand de. *Course in General Linguistics.* Trans. Wade Baskin. London: Fontana, 1974.
Schiller, Friedrich von. *Naive and Sentimental Poetry and On the Sublime.* Trans. Julius A. Elias. New York: Ungar, 1975.
Schopen, Bernard A. "Faith, Morality, and the Novels of John Updike." Macnaughton 195–206.
Schorer, Mark, ed. *Sinclair Lewis: A Collection of Critical Essays.* Englewood Cliffs, NJ: Prentice, 1962.
Schwenger, Peter. "The Masculine Mode." Showalter, *Speaking of Gender* 101–12.
———. *Phallic Critiques: Masculinity and Twentieth-Century Literature.* London: Routledge, 1984.

Searles, George J. *The Fiction of Philip Roth and John Updike*. Carbondale: Southern Illinois UP, 1985.
Sedgwick, Eve Kosofsky. "The Beast in the Closet: Henry James and the Writing of Homosexual Panic." Showalter, *Speaking of Gender* 243–68.
———. *Between Men: English Literature and Male Homosocial Desire*. New York: Columbia UP, 1985.
Showalter, Elaine. "Introduction: The Rise of Gender." Showalter, *Speaking of Gender* 1–13.
———, ed. *The New Feminist Criticism: Essays on Women, Literature, and Theory*. New York: Pantheon, 1985.
———, ed. *Speaking of Gender*. New York: Routledge, 1989.
Slethaug, George J. "*Rabbit Redux*: 'Freedom is Made of Brambles.'" Macnaughton 237–53.
Sokoloff, B. A. *John Updike: A Comprehensive Bibliography*. Norwood, PA: Norwood, 1973.
Speeth, Kathleen Riordan. *The Gurdjieff Work*. Los Angeles: Tarcher, 1989.
Stafford, William. "From 'The Curious Greased Grace' of John Updike." Macnaughton 67–71.
Strandberg, Victor. "John Updike and the Changing of the Gods." Macnaughton 175–94.
Tallent, Elizabeth. *Married Men and Magic Tricks: John Updike's Erotic Heroes*. Berkeley, CA: Creative Arts, 1982.
Tanner, Tony. "A Compromised Environment." Bloom 37–56.
Tate, M. Judith. "Of Rabbits and Centaurs." *Critic* 22 (Feb.–Mar. 1964): 44–47.
Taylor, Larry. *Pastoral and Anti-Pastoral Patterns in John Updike's Fiction*. Carbondale: Southern Illinois UP, 1971.
Theroux, Paul. Rev. of *Rabbit Redux*, by John Updike. *Washington Post Book World* 14 Nov. 1971: 3.
———. "Too Far to Go." Macnaughton 86–88.
Thorburn, David, and Howard Eiland, eds. *John Updike: A Collection of Critical Essays*. Englewood Cliffs, NJ: Prentice, 1979.
Tiger, Lionel. *Men in Groups*. New York: Random, 1984.
Todd, Janet. *Gender and Literary Voice*. New York: Holmes and Meier, 1976.
Tolson, Andrew. *The Limits of Masculinity: Male Identity and the Liberated Woman*. London: Tavistock, 1977.
Trudgill, Eric. *Madonnas and Magdalens*. New York: Holmes, 1976.
Trueheart, Charles. "Sex, God and John Updike." Rev. of *Rabbit at Rest*, by John Updike. *Washington Post* 28 Oct. 1990: F1, 4.
Updike, John. *Assorted Prose*. New York: Knopf, 1965.
———. *Bech: A Book*. New York: Knopf, 1970.
———. *Bech Is Back*. New York: Knopf, 1982.
———. *The Centaur*. Greenwich, CT: Fawcett, 1963.
———. *The Coup*. New York: Knopf, 1978.
———. *Couples*. New York: Knopf, 1968.
———. *Hugging the Shore: Essays and Criticism*. New York: Vintage, 1983.

———. *Marry Me.* New York: Knopf, 1976.
———. *A Month of Sundays.* New York: Knopf, 1975.
———. *Museums and Women.* New York: Knopf, 1972.
———. *The Music School.* New York: Knopf, 1966.
———. *Of the Farm.* Greenwich, CT.: Fawcett, 1965.
———. *Picked-Up Pieces.* New York: Fawcett, 1966.
———. *Pigeon Feathers.* New York: Fawcett, 1962.
———. *Problems and Other Stories.* New York: Fawcett, 1979.
———. *Rabbit at Rest.* New York: Knopf, 1990.
———. *Rabbit Is Rich.* New York: Fawcett, 1981.
———. *Rabbit Redux.* New York: Knopf, 1971.
———. *Rabbit, Run.* New York: Fawcett, 1960.
———. *Roger's Version.* New York: Knopf, 1986.
———. *S.* New York: Knopf, 1988.
———. *The Same Door.* New York: Knopf, 1962.
———. *Self-Consciousness: Memoirs.* New York: Knopf, 1989.
———. *Too Far to Go.* New York: Fawcett, 1979.
———. *Trust Me.* New York: Knopf, 1987.
———. "Updike on Updike." *New York Times Book Review* 21 Sept. 1981, sec. 7: 1, 34–35.
———. *Verse.* Greenwich, CT: Fawcett, 1965.
———. "Why Rabbit Had to Go." *New York Times Book Review* 5 Aug. 1990, sec. 7: 1, 24–25.
———. *The Witches of Eastwick.* New York: Fawcett, 1984.
Uphaus, Suzanne Henning. *John Updike.* New York: Ungar, 1980.
Vanderwerken, David L. "Rabbit 'Re-docks': Updike's Inner Odyssey." *College Literature* 2 (Winter 1975): 73–78.
Vargo, Edward P. *Rainstorms and Fire: Ritual in the Novels of John Updike.* Port Washington, NY: Kennikat, 1973.
Vaughan, Philip H. *John Updike's Images of America.* Reseda, CA: Mojave, 1981.
Veblen, Thorstein. *The Theory of the Leisure Class.* 1899. New York: Modern Library, 1934.
Verduin, Kathleen. "Fatherly Presences: John Updike's Place in the Protestant Tradition." Macnaughton 254–68.
"View from the Catacombs." Rev. of *Couples*, by John Updike. *Time.* 26 Apr. 1968: 72–84.
Waldmeir, Joseph. "It's the Going That's Important, Not the Getting There." *Modern Fiction Studies* 20 (1974): 13–27.
Waller, Gary. "Stylus Dei or the Open-Endedness of Debate: Success and Failure in *A Month of Sundays*." Macnaughton 269–80.
Ward, J. A. "John Updike's Fiction." *Critique* 5 (Spring–Summer 1962): 27–40.
Weeks, Jeffrey. *Sex, Politics and Society.* London: Longman, 1981.
Weisstein, Naomi. "Psychology Constructs the Female." Gornick and Moran 207–24.

West, Rebecca. "Babbitt." Schorer 23–26.

Whipple, T. K. "Sinclair Lewis." Schorer 71–83.

Wolcott, James. "Running on Empty: Can John Updike's Rabbit Find Happiness As a Car Dealer?" Rev. of *Rabbit Is Rich*, by John Updike. *Esquire* Oct. 1981: 20–23.

Wood, Ralph C. *The Comedy of Redemption: Christian Faith and Comic Vision in Four American Novelists.* Notre Dame, IN: U of Notre Dame P, 1988.

Woodcock, Bruce. *Male Mythologies: John Fowles and Masculinity.* Sussex, Eng.: Harvester, 1984.

Wright, Derek. "Mapless Motion: Form and Space in Updike's *Rabbit, Run*". *Modern Fiction Studies.* 37.1 (Spring 1991): 35–44.

Zylstra, S. A. "John Updike and the Parabolic Nature of the World." *Soundings* 56 (1973): 323–37.

Index

Adolescence, 37–38, 46, 47, 58, 59, 62; capitalism and, 115, 169
Allen, Mary, 38, 88, 102, 136, 150; on development, 70–71; on Janice, 109, 110; on Jill, 141, 148
Alter, Robert, 101–2, 148, 152
Althusser, Louis, 66
American Dream, 58, 59, 61, 137–38; Lone Ranger imagery and, 122; righteousness and, 138. *See also* Capitalism
Anderson, Sherwood, 37, 189
Angstrom, Earl (*Rabbit, Run*), 50–53, 80
Angstrom, Harry. *See* Angstrom, Rabbit
Angstrom, Janice (*Rabbit* tetralogy): anxiety of, 71, 82; critical dislike for, 78, 246n.3; death and, 107–8, 109; degradation of, 129; Mim and, 48–49; progress of, 221–22; self-interest of, 18; silencing of, 81–82, 87
Angstrom, Judith (*Rabbit* tetralogy), 201–3, 206, 220–21

Angstrom, Mary (*Rabbit* tetralogy), 23, 43–46, 63; death and, 104–7; language and, 76, 80–81; loyalty and, 46, 47–49; as repressed, 44, 80–81
Angstrom, Nelson (*Rabbit* tetralogy), 4, 22, 161, 192, 195, 196; betrayal of, 225; critical dislike for, 248n.2; development of, 112–13, 114; drug addiction of, 209; as father, 187; as feminine, 115–16; heredity of, 207; as immature, 186, 187, 190; innocence of, 143; materialism of, 113; obnoxiousness of, 192, 194, 196; Rabbit's resentment of, 45, 114–15, 191, 192; resentment of Rabbit, 173, 178, 179, 189; as rival, 175, 181, 183, 192, 194–95, 205, 209, 225; seasonal metaphor and, 18; self-hatred of, 232, 233; silencing of, 76; source of rage, 187
Angstrom, Pru (*Rabbit* tetralogy), 201, 204, 205, 209, 218–19, 220, 221

259

Angstrom, Rabbit (*Rabbit* tetralogy), ix–x, 8, 9, 91; abusiveness of, 38–39, 241n.1; as American, 236–37; as anal-retentive, 182–83; avoidance strategies of, 103; childhood of, 45–46; as "Chuck," 127; conformity of, 125–26; control and, 15, 40–41, 109; daughter and, 89–92, 174, 179, 183, 197, 202, 218; death and, 14, 105, 117, 126–27; dependence of, 221–22; depersonalizing behavior of, 23, 24–26; destructiveness of, 192, 196; domestic security and, 171; as Don Juan, 71, 72; dualism and, 11, 12, 13, 15–16; Earl and, 51–52; early sexual encounters, 50; fears of, 14, 22–23, 26, 164–65, 175, 192, 195; freedom and, 173, 185, 227; God and, 32, 33, 173, 176–77, 213, 214, 215, 248n.1; as Gutenberg man, 119, 130, 134, 141; identity and, 42–43, 126–27, 134, 226; inability to love, 143, 174, 198; individualism of, 19; as initiate, 156–58; insatiable appetite of, 200–201, 222, 228, 232; introspection and, 204–5; irresponsibility of, 89–90; lack of development, 13, 70–71, 114; likability of, xii, xiii; as manipulative, 42, 50, 62, 63, 65, 71–72, 78, 109–10, 129, 231; material success of, 164; misogyny of, 172, 241n.3; money and, 59, 180; mother and, 22–23, 104–5; name, significance of, 22, 42, 171; national/personal and, 123–24, 130, 147; passivity of, 100–103; perspective and, 42, 73, 131–32, 177; progress of, 201, 202; reconciliation and, 216, 217–19; repression of, 173; as resistant, 24, 34, 101, 104, 192–93, 228, 229–30; sacrifices of, 179, 221; self-destruction of, 227, 228–30, 232; self-hatred of, 212, 227, 228, 229, 232; self-interest of, 17–18, 26; sexuality and, 4, 20, 38–39, 87, 141, 213; socialization of, 35–36; society and, 96–97, 103; spirituality and, 14, 20, 24, 98, 99; technology and, 102, 104; union and, 91; verbal prowess of, 77–78; as victim, 101, 110, 129, 226; view of America, 138, 242n.2; violence of, 120–21; withdrawal of, 223–26, 230–31; women and, 26, 82, 175. *See also* Fatherhood; Father/son relationship

Angstrom, Rebecca June (Becky) (*Rabbit* tetralogy), 88–92, 174, 246n.6; death imagery and, 89–90, 91, 108; language and, 89

Archetypal patterns, 67

Astrachan, Anthony, 115

Athletic model, 113–15, 128

Author, 88, 169; ambivalence of, 148, 192; as homosocial, 154; as narrator, 76–77; third person and, 77, 203. *See also* Perspective; Updike, John

Babbitt (Lewis), 165–68, 169, 198, 200

"Beast in the Closet, The" (Sedgwick), 154

Beauvoir, Simone de, 87, 107

Bech, Henry, 173

"Being and Doing" (Chodorow), 7, 8–9

Belsey, Catherine, xiii, 66, 241n.2, 244n.5; on patriarchy, 71, 73, 74

Berger, John, 85, 86

Birkerts, Sven, xiii, 224

"Birthmark, The" (Hawthorne), 86

Brenner, Gerry, 4, 42

Burhans, Clinton S., 35

Index

Byer, Annie (*Rabbit* tetralogy), 218, 248n.8

Capitalism, 52, 55, 69, 188; garden imagery and, 213; leisure-class theory, 57; sex/money relationship and, 56–58. *See also* Materialism
Centaur, The (Updike), 21, 35, 51, 93, 179
Chaos, 126, 127, 137–63; character and, 131; vs. patriarchy, 130–34
Chodorow, Nancy, 3–4, 5, 9
Cixous, Hélène, 4–5, 7, 10–11
Collector, The (Fowles), 38
Coup, The (Updike), 73, 93
Couples (Updike), 72, 100, 161, 166
Cox, David, 132

Daly, Mary, 75
Davis, Angela, 157
Death, 103, 104, 111, 117, 128; continuity and, 19; dream imagery, 105, 106; economic metaphor and, 184; icebox symbolism and, 47; as limitation, 206; marriage and, 60–61; masculinity and, 227; novelistic structure and, 225–26; sacrifice and, 21, 90; seasonal metaphor and, 18; as self-assertion, 227, 228–29; sexuality as, 107, 108; spiritual, 32; withdrawal and, 223–26
De Bellis, Jack, 199, 201, 202
Deceit, Desire and the Novel (Girard), 234
de Rougemont, Denis, 25, 72, 86
Derrida, Jacques, 10
Detweiler, Robert, 134, 180, 245n.3; on economic metaphor, 106, 123–24, 127, 132, 140, 148, 184
Didion, Joan, 77
Dinnerstein, Dorothy, 7, 49–50, 160, 244n.1

Dualism, 10–11, 14, 61, 63; God and, 11–12; matter and spirit, 11, 13, 14
Dworkin, Andrea, 75, 87, 108

Eccles, Jack (*Rabbit, Run*), 30, 34, 79–80
Economic metaphor, 171, 180–85; money as feces, 182, 184; sexuality and, 183–84
Ellman, Mary, 10

Falke, Wayne, 111, 138, 148
Farewell to Arms, A (Hemingway), 41
Farrell, Michael, 189
Fatherhood, 20, 21–22, 143, 144, 158, 179, 183, 211; circle imagery and, 22; competition and, 175–76; economic metaphor and, 183, 184; garden imagery and, 31, 33; Nelson and, 112–13, 114; rejection and, 80; replacement and, 50–51; socialization and, 50–51. *See also* Father/son relationship
"Fatherly Presences: John Updike's Place in the Protestant Tradition" (Verduin), 21, 51, 100
Father/son relationship, 186–208; absentee father in, 167–68, 189, 190, 221; betrayal and, 187; competition in, 190, 191, 192; Laius complex and, 186, 188; mutual identity issues in, 189; Odysseus myth and, 190–91; sexual rivalry in, 186, 188, 195–96; vs. social order, 52; theories of, 51–53; "wounded father" in, 186, 188, 189–90; yearning in, 190, 191. *See also* Fatherhood
Femininity. *See* Women
Feminist criticism, 2, 38, 42
Fetterley, Judith, ix, 37–38, 41, 88, 135; on *The Great Gatsby*, 60;

Fetterley—*continued*
  on idealization, 86–87; on women, 75, 167
Fiction of Philip Roth and John Updike (Searles), 203
Fiedler, Leslie, 71
Fitzgerald, F. Scott, 58, 60, 61
Fosnacht, Peggy, 161
Fowles, John, x, 38, 86
French, Marilyn, 8
Freud, Sigmund, 5–6, 78
Frye, Northrop, 67, 127
Furnace Township, 125–36; Dante's *Inferno* and, 127–28

Garden imagery, 27–28, 31, 61, 160, 185, 212–15, 243n.8; capitalism and, 213; Christian imagery and, 34; death and, 215; dichotomy within, 212–14; father/son relationship and, 191; perspectives of, 33–34; racism and, 116; spirituality and, 34, 98, 213; women and, 175, 181
Garner, Shirley Nelson, 5, 6, 7, 52
Gender formation, 3, 4, 37–68, 237; cultural context of, 6–7; dualism in, 6, 7, 10; fear of women and, 49–50; identity, 4–5, 95; Jungian perspective, 10; materialism and, 8–9; socialization and, 8–10; studies, 1–2, 5; theories of, 6–9. *See also* Socialization
"Getting the Words Out" (Updike), 92, 93–94
Gilbert, Sandra M., 38, 44, 75, 77
Girard, Réne, 234
God, 160–63, 176, 242n.4
Great Gatsby, The (Fitzgerald), 58–60, 61
Greening of America, The (Reich), 141
Greiner, Donald J., 101
Gubar, Susan, 38, 44, 75, 77

Gurdjieff, G. I., 198, 199–200
Guttman, David, 178

Hamilton, Edith, 137, 147, 180
Harrison, Fraser, 55, 57–58, 85
Harrison, Ronnie (*Rabbit* tetralogy), 234–35
Hartmann, Heidi, 154
Hawthorne, Nathaniel, 86, 88
Hemingway, Ernest, 41
Hendin, Josephine, 102, 111, 147–48
History of Christian Thought (Tillich), 139
Holy Virility: The Social Construction of Masculinity (Reynaud), 63–64
Homosociality, 166, 232–35
Horton, Andrew S., 111, 122–23
Hugging the Shore: Essays and Criticism (Updike), 140, 144, 160
Hunt, George, 16, 35, 37, 132, 137; on Rabbit as victim, 101

Idealization, 83–86, 87–88
Identity, 23; plural, 198, 206, 207; social vs. original, 226, 227. *See also* Self
Imagery: basketball, 53–54, 113, 157, 227; Christian, 29, 30–31, 34, 222; circle, 22, 91, 118, 223, 227; icebox, 105; light, 118; Lone Ranger, 121–23; madness, 127, 130, 148–49; mirror, 152; monster, 62–63, 108, 232, 233; resurrection, 28; of sacrifice, 126, 127, 149–50; salesman, 59; space exploration, 99, 119, 127, 131, 134; Venus, 84, 86; visual, 83–86, 98–99; water and, 219–20, 222; weightlessness, 127, 129, 130–31; whiteness, 193, 220; white vs. black, 102. *See also* Garden imagery
Imagination, xii, 73, 203

Inferno (Dante), 127–28
Interrogative text, xi, xii–xiii, 226, 237; definition, 241n.2; distancing and, 66–67
Irigaray, Luce, 10
"I Want to Know Why" (Anderson), 37, 189

John Updike (Detweiler), 106
John Updike (Newman), 55, 119
"John Updike's Love" (Allen), 150
"John Updike's Metaphoric Novels" (Petter), 15
John Updike's Novels (Greiner), 101

Kahane, Claire, 5, 6, 7, 52
Kakutani, Michiko, 227
Kaplan, Cora, 9
"Ken Kesey, John Updike, and the Lone Ranger" (Horton), 122
King Lear, 129, 130, 183, 228
Kohler, Dale, 161
Kolbenschlag, Madonna, 11–12
Kruppenbach (*Rabbit, Run*), 34, 80

Lacan, Jacques, 6, 52, 74–75
Language, 7, 76; differentiation and, 73–74; Law of the Father and, 52; manipulation and, 79, 83–85; patriarchal ideology and, 73–75, 80–81; perspective and, 87; silencing and, 79, 81–83, 85, 87, 89, 90–91; structure and, 76–77, 88; Symbolic Order and, 6, 52; transparency and, 77, 78; uncertainty of, 133–34; visual images and, 83–85; women and, 80–81. See also Perspective
Law of the Father, 52, 153
"Leaves" (Updike), 16
Leighton, Frederick, 85
Le Pellec, Yves, 101
Lerner, Gerda, 130, 154, 159, 161, 247n.4
Levinson, Daniel, 178–79

Lévi-Strauss, Claude, 153–54
Lewis, Sinclair, 165–68
Literature, 73, 75; romance, 90; self-magnification and, 92–94
Lord of the Flies, The (Golding), 162
Lyons, Eugene, 138

Madness, 127, 130
Madwoman in the Attic, The (Gilbert and Gubar), 38, 44, 75
Male Mythologies: John Fowles and Masculinity (Woodcock), x, 92
Markle, Joyce, 20–21, 27, 78, 126, 243n.8; imagery, view of, 98; on Rabbit as microcosm, 124; on Rabbit's passivity, 100
"Masculine Mode, The" (Schwenger), 204
Masculinity, 2–3, 12; ambivalence and, 38, 39, 66, 67, 186, 188–89; athletics and, 113–15, 128; authorial ambivalence and, 38, 39; corruptness of, 61–62; culturally-approved, 52–53; generational descent and, 193–94; hierarchy and, 63–64, 153; imperialism and, 55; male bonding, 155–56, 158, 160; marriage and, 56–58, 56–60; midlife crisis and, 177–78; money-making and, 166, 181; powerlessness and, 40–42; power struggle and, 63–64, 192; schematization of, 69, 71, 73; self-image and, 65, 194; shifting nature of, 5, 8, 9, 69–70; social problems and, 95–96; structure of opposition and, 54–55; subversion of, ix, x; versions of, 40; view of women, 53, 56–60; visual idealization and, 83–86. See also Patriarchal ideology
Materialism, 162, 165–68, 174, 232; body and, 228; contempt to-

Materialism—*continued*
ward, 199; language and, 78; Lone Ranger imagery and, 123; seasonal metaphor and, 180; selling out and, 171–72; status and, 113; as weakness, 195. *See also* Capitalism

McLuhan, Marshall, 119
Mead, Margaret, 100
Melanie (*Rabbit Is Rich*), 197, 198–99, 200, 201
Melville, Herman, 37–38
Miller, Roger, 211
Millet, Kate, 7
Miriam (Mim) (*Rabbit, Run*), 46–47, 155, 162; as manipulative, 110–11; Rabbit's betrayal of, 48
Mitchell, Juliet, 6
Moi, Toril, 5, 6, 7, 10, 11
Myth: Iphigenia, 90, 127, 137, 144, 147, 160; Laius, 186–208; Odysseus/Telemachus, 190–91; Oedipus, 186–208, 228

Naming, 69–94; language and, 73–88; lost feminine and, 88–92; perspective and, 73, 77, 87; theory and form, 92–94; vulnerability, 71–72
National/personal metaphors, 95, 123–24, 130, 147
Neary, John, 36, 206, 210, 223
Newman, Judie, 50–51, 118, 119, 149, 180, 205, 247n.7; on economic metaphor, 182, 183; on freedom, 174; on God, 172; on imagination, 73; on materialism, 195; on perception, 204; on technology, 102; on television images, 167; on work, 55

Oates, Joyce Carol, 84, 86, 211, 228–29
Of the Farm (Updike), 35, 129
"On Not Being a Dove" (Updike), 139
"On One's Own Oeuvre" (Updike), 68
"On the Sublime" (Schiller), 43
Ortner, Sherry, 175
Osherson, Samuel, 52, 167, 178, 186; on Oedipus myth, 187, 188, 189, 190, 191
Otherness, 152–53; race and, 116, 151; reconciliation and, 222–23; self and, 220; of Springer family, 114, 116; water metaphor and, 219–20, 222; withdrawal from, 231

Parrington, Vernon L., 67
Passivity, 99–103
Pastoral and Anti-Pastoral Patterns in John Updike's Fiction (Taylor), 29
Patriarchal ideology, xiii–xiv, 9–11, 156, 232, 245n.4; absence and, 171, 181; accommodation to, 178–79; adaptability of, 69–70; avoidance and, 103; vs. chaos, 130; female repression and, 146–47, 159–60; female sacrifice and, 159–60; gender formation and, 6–8; God and, 161; hierarchical order in, 153, 158; homosociality and, 154; internalized, 171, 181; language and, 73–75; Law of the Father and, 52; male bonding and, 153–58; midlife crisis and, 177–79; other's place in, 99, 103; on personal level, 71; perspective and, 73–74; phallocentricity, 6–7, 10–11; power and, 40–42, 103, 224; racial issues and, 152; representation and, 83; resistance of, 202–3; signifying practices and, 75–76; social determinism and, 66; sports and, 113–15; Victorian era, 56–58, 70; women

and, 70, 81, 149–50. See also
   Masculinity
Pendleton, Jill (*Rabbit* tetralogy),
   95, 99, 108, 144, 160; destruction of, 147–50; God and, 161;
   transformative power of, 116–17; vulnerability of, 141, 142, 143–44
Perspective, 42, 77, 224; feminine, xii, 90–91, 177; masculine, xi, 87, 203, 204; Rabbit's control of, xi, 69; third-person, 224. *See also* Author; Language; Reader; Updike, John
Petter, Henry, 15
Picked-up Pieces (Updike), 133, 135, 138, 140
Plagman, Linda, 245n.5
Politics, xii, 137, 148–49
Pornography (Dworkin), 75, 108

Rabbit at Rest (Updike), 209–37; betrayal in, 225; closure in, 211; freedom vs. responsibility in, 211; heredity in, 235; homosexual theme in, 233–34; as introspective, 224; kidnapping references in, 225; leave-taking in, 225; seasonal metaphor in, 18; structure of, 225; Wagnerian motif in, 224–226, 227–28. *See also individual characters*
Rabbit Is Rich (Updike), 164–85; *Babbit* and, 165–68; daughter symbolism in, 91; economic metaphor in, 180–85; equinox and solstice in, 184–85; falling imagery in, 243n.4; father/son relationship in, 186–208; freedom in, 172; garden imagery in, 185; monster imagery in, 62–63; nature in, 174–75; racial issues in, 182; seasonal metaphor in, 18; wealth as poverty in, 168. *See also individual characters*

Rabbit Redux (Updike), 95–124; character in, 131; class issues in, 49; Earl's role in, 51; family relationships in, 95; language in, 81; national/personal aspects in, 147; perspective in, 131–34; political aspects of, 137–63; ritual ceremonies in, 158, 159; seasonal metaphor in, 18; "Special Message," 90; structure of, 131–34; themes in, 97–98; as thesis novel, 137–38. *See also individual characters*
Rabbit, Run (Updike), 13–36; abuse of women in, 38–39; Christian imagery in, 29, 30–31, 34; class issues in, 49; cleanliness in, 32, 33; converging circles in, 15, 17, 19–27; dichotomy in, 29, 30; distancing in, 42, 49; dreams in, 18–20, 23, 24; equinox and solstice in, 16–19; fatherhood in, 20, 21–22; garden imagery in, 27–36; as interrogative text, 66–68; narrative technique in, 42; opposing realms in, 15–16; perspective in, 42; plurality of, 65–67; reconciliation in, 16–19, 20, 31, 63; structure of, 131–34; symbolism in, 16; third person form in, 42; union in, 16–19, 23–24, 29, 30. *See also individual characters*
Rabbit tetralogy: biblical imagery in, 222; Dalai Lama figure in, 214; dust jacket designs for, 19; heredity in, 207–8, 220, 235; homosexuality in, 80; limitations in, 206–7; metaphors in, 220; narrative perspective in, 203–8; repetition in, 205–7, 210, 211; significance of names in, 202; structure of, 205–6; union in, 215–23; water imagery in, 219–20. *See also individual characters; individual novels*

Racial issues, 116, 169, 182, 227; Lone Ranger imagery and, 122; male bonding and, 157; perspective and, 133–34; union and, 150–52

Rainstorms and Fire (Vargo), 20

Reader: and author's position, xii–xiii; bond with Rabbit, xiii, 88; Janice and, 221; perspective of, 204; resisting, ix, xi, 37–38, 41, 135; self-negation and, ix. *See also* Perspective

Reich, Charles A., 141

Resisting Reader, The (Fetterley), ix, 41

Reuther, Rosemary, 242n.4

Revolution, 137–63; American Dream and, 137–38; fallen nature, 139; male bonding and, 153–63; motivation and, 147–50; parable of, 140–47; psychodrama, 148–49; union and, 150–53

Reynaud, Emmanuel, 63–64

Ristoff, Dilvo I., 169

Roger's Version (Kohler), 161

Rosenberg, Stanley, 189

Rowbotham, Sheila, 138

Ruth (*Rabbit, Run*): anxiety of, 71, 72, 244n.1; circle imagery and, 20; as depersonalized, 32–33; as observer, 42, 54, 55, 72; reader response to, 82; as repressed, 83; sexual vastness of, 24; silencing of, 82–83, 87

Samuels, Charles, 102, 147

Saussure, Ferdinand de, 73–74

Schiller, Friedrich von, 43, 229

Schopen, Bernard, xiii, 27

Schwenger, Peter, 204, 234, 242n.3

Searles, George, 101, 203

Seasonal metaphor, 131, 178–79; death and, 210; nativity and, 184–85; repetitive elements and, 205

Second Sex, The (Beauvoir), 107

Secular Scripture, The (Frye), 67, 127

Sedgwick, Eve Kosofsky, 154, 234

Self, 14, 63, 96, 128; fear of loss of, 175; fixed, 128–29; God and, 161; hierarchy and, 65; influences on, 215–16; language and, 74; materialism and, 174; as prisoner, 200; relationships and, 128–29; specificity of, 216; in transition, 129; union and, 150–51. *See also* Identity

Self-Consciousness: Memoirs (Updike), 139, 141, 161, 172; on God, 176; on popular movements, 39–40; on printing trade, 80; self-portrait in, 215, 216

"Seven Stanzas at Easter" (Updike), 29

Sexuality: death and, 107, 108; economic metaphor and, 183–84; money and, 56–58, 170; weightlessness and, 127, 129

Sexual Politics (Millet), 7

Showalter, Elaine, 1–2

Silencing, 109, 177; of Janice, 81–82, 87; language and, 79, 81–83, 85, 87, 89, 90–91; of Nelson, 76; of Rabbit, 236; of Ruth, 82–83, 87

Siskind, A., 189

Skeeter (*Rabbit* tetralogy), 95, 99, 110, 245n.10; inability to love, 146; as manipulator, 152, 153; as revolutionary, 140, 145–46; as sinister, 148, 152; on social relationships, 129; violence against, 120–21

Slethaug, George J., 125, 223

Smith, Horace (*Rabbit, Run*), 30, 31

Socialization, 50–53; fathers and, 50–51; institutions of, 52–53. *See also* Gender formation

Social order, 95–96, 103
Speeth, Kathleen Riordan, 199, 200
Spirituality: garden and, 34, 98, 213; Janice as redemptive, 222–23; Rabbit's, 14, 20, 24, 98, 99; self-will and, 228
Sprengnether, Madelon, 5, 6, 7, 52
Springer, Fred (*Rabbit, Run*), 71, 80
Springer, Rebecca (Bessie) (*Rabbit, Run*), 80–81
Stavros, Charlie (*Rabbit Redux*), 81–82, 111–12, 197–98, 245n.8; Rabbit's interview with, 109, 110
Strandberg, Victor, 22

Tallent, Elizabeth, 18, 25, 38, 111
Taylor, Larry, 29, 30, 42
Technology, 104, 117–20
Thelma (*Rabbit* tetralogy), 197, 198
Theroux, Paul, 100
"Things Falling Apart" (Burhans), 35
Tiger, Lionel, 3, 137, 155–56, 159
Tillich, Paul, 139
Tolson, Andrew, 45, 51, 52, 64, 81, 203
Tothero, Marty (*Rabbit, Run*), 53–59, 60–63, 64–65; corruptness of, 61–62; ideology of, 54–56; as manipulator, 54–56; silencing of, 76; view of women, 54–56; wants of, 244n.4
Trueheart, Charles, 210, 221

Union, 215–23; attention and, 216, 217; circle imagery and, 91; earth's rotation and, 16–19; garden imagery and, 28–32; memory and, 216, 217–18; resistance to, 17–18; revolution and, 150–53
Updike, John, ix, x, xiii, 3, 7, 244n.14; ambivalence of, 2, 3, 66, 67; America and, 9, 237; on characterization, 133; distancing techniques, 61; fatherhood and, 39–40, 90; fear of death, 13–14, 242n.1; on God, 161, 176; on homosexuality, 233; on idealization, 86; on identity, x, 126, 135; on inarticulateness, 92–93; on irreconcilability, 16, 35; on life, 172; on masculinity, 38, 100, 177; on materialism, 171–72; on moral function, xi; as narrator, 77; on pacifism, 141, 142, 246n.1; personal realm and, 71, 73, 219; perspective and, 26, 27, 61, 77; on *Rabbit at Rest*, 227; on *Rabbit Redux*, 138; on Rabbit's daughter, 174; on racial issues, 151; relationship to Rabbit, xii, xiii, 246n.5; religion and, 32, 79–80; revolution and, 137; on self, 90, 174, 215, 216, 217; skepticism of, 139–40; social observation of, 38; on violence, 241n.1; as visually oriented, 17. *See also* Author
Uphaus, Suzanne, 20, 102, 145, 146, 158, 243n.8

Vargo, Edward P., xii, 20, 100, 121, 144, 148, 151, 158; on garden imagery, 243n.6
Vaughan, Philip, 101, 133
Veblen, Thorstein, 57, 167
Verduin, Kathleen, 21, 51, 72, 100, 245n.4
Victorianism, 56–58, 70, 166
Vietnam War, 108, 119, 120, 121; Lone Ranger imagery and, 123
Violence, 120–21

Wagner's ring cycle, 224–26, 227–28
Waller, Gary, 39
Weeks, Jeffrey, 52
Weisstein, Naomi, 3
West, Rebecca, 165, 166
Whipple, T. K., 166

Whitman, Walt, 91, 97
"Whitman's Egotheism" (Updike), 35
Witches of Eastwick, The (Updike), 73, 203
Wolfsheim, Meyer (*The Great Gatsby*), 58, 59
Women: death and, 218, 231; femininity and, 88–92, 114–15, 173, 174, 228; identity and, 243n.6; literature and, 44, 45, 75; as money, 167, 170–71, 225, 247n.2; as murderous, 202; nature and, 181, 247n.4; as resource, 56, 57–58, 60, 75, 154–55, 170, 180, 247n.4; silencing of, 177. *See also individual characters*
Wood, Ralph, 198
Woodcock, Bruce, x, xi, xiv, 14, 69; on ambivalence, 38, 39; on feminism, 70; on idealization, 86; on male myths, 92; on patriarchy, 1, 7–8; on sexuality, 212

Zim family (*Rabbit, Run*), 46

Mary O'Connell received a B.A. from Nazareth College of Rochester, an M.A. in English Literature from Georgetown University, and a Ph.D. in American Literature from George Washington University. She now lives in Virginia and teaches at George Washington University.

DATE DUE

Demco, Inc. 38-293